MY BOY WILL DIE OF SORROW

MY BOY WILL DIE OF SORROW

A MEMOIR OF IMMIGRATION FROM THE FRONT LINES

Efrén C. Olivares

BOOKS

New York

Hachette Books
Hachette Book Group
1290 Avenue of the Americas
New York, NY 10104
HachetteBooks.com
Twitter.com/HachetteBooks
Instagram.com/HachetteBooks

First Edition: July 2022

Published by Hachette Books, an imprint of Perseus Books, LLC, a subsidiary of Hachette Book Group, Inc. The Hachette Books name and logo is a trademark of the Hachette Book Group.

The Hachette Speakers Bureau provides a wide range of authors for speaking events. To find out more, go to www.hachettespeakersbureau.com or call (866) 376-6591.

The publisher is not responsible for websites (or their content) that are not owned by the publisher.

Library of Congress Cataloging-in-Publication Data

Names: Olivares, Efrén C., author.
Title: My boy will die of sorrow : a memoir of immigration from the front lines / Efrén C. Olivares.
Description: First edition. | New York, NY : Hachette Books, [2022] |
Identifiers: LCCN 2021059948 | ISBN 9780306847288 (hardcover) |
ISBN 9780306847271 (ebook)
Subjects: LCSH: Immigrants—Family relationships—United States.
Classification: LCC HQ536 .O38 2022 | DDC 305.9/06912073—dc23/eng/20220217
LC record available at https://lccn.loc.gov/2021059948

ISBNs: 978-0-306-84728-8 (hardcover), 978-0-306-84727-1 (ebook)

Printed in the United States of America

LSC-C

Printing 1, 2022

To my family. And to the millions of families around the world who have dared to move across the earth in search of safety and opportunity.

Contents

CONTENTS

And the yelp
Of the coyote morphing
Into an infant's cry, filled
With such longing, I wondered
What country I'd stepped into.

From the poem "Owl,"
by José Antonio Rodríguez

Prologue

Borders separate. Borders divide and alienate. Borders make some feel secure, others trapped. Borders rise up and dissolve. Borders appear, disappear, reappear, and shift, sometimes slowly over decades and centuries, sometimes overnight. The Rio Grande River, which demarcates part of the boundary between the United States and Mexico, shifted its course time and again—taking the border with it—until the 1970s, when the two countries agreed to fix the line for good with coordinates in a treaty. The river that served as a natural boundary turned out to be a poor marker to achieve the political purpose of a border: to separate. The U.S.-Mexico border, wrote Gloria Anzaldúa in the opening chapter of *Borderlands/La Frontera*, is an open wound, *"una herida abierta* where the Third World grates against the first and bleeds. And before a scab forms it hemorrhages again."

This book explores this "bleeding" from a deeply personal perspective, a bleeding that sometimes gushes out violently, as it did in 2018, and other times slows down to a trickle. But it never stops.

In the summer of 2018, I found myself representing hundreds of immigrant families separated at the Texas-Mexico border under the Trump Administration's Zero Tolerance policy. That policy called for the mandatory prosecution of every person who crossed the border without authorization, charging them with the misdemeanor crime of illegal entry, or, if they had been deported before, the felony of illegal reentry. Zero Tolerance led to thousands of children being separated from their parents at the U.S. southern border, and I interviewed dozens of these parents and heard first-hand how Border Patrol agents took their children from them through deceit, subterfuge, and sometimes outright violence.

Twenty-five years earlier, I had been separated from my father when he migrated to the United States to look for work. He emigrated first, and the rest of us stayed behind, seeing him only when he was able to visit, but without him in the day-to-day of our lives in Mexico. For four years, we saw my father only occasionally, until we were finally able to join him. In 2018, it took me months to fully appreciate the extent to which the separation I lived when I was just a boy has informed the work I did, and continue to do, for immigrant families.

Although being without my father was not easy, my experience pales in comparison to those I have heard from my clients over the years. Like millions before us, we migrated out of economic necessity, in search of work and a better future. We were not fleeing violence, death threats, or persecution. To the extent migrating to the United States was a choice, it could be said that my family chose to be separated. The circumstances pushed us to migrate, and the law forced us to be separated, but if it was a choice at all, we had the "privilege" of choosing to be apart. By contrast, the hundreds of immigrant families I encountered in federal court in McAllen, Texas, had no say in the separation whatsoever: our government forced the separations upon them. What my family and I lived in four years of an episodic and voluntary separation, these families experienced in an intense, compelled, and violent rupture. And they were powerless to prevent it.

In the pages that follow, I strive to tell their stories as accurately as they shared them with me, and as faithfully as I lived through those weeks and months. In telling their stories, I also share part of my own, and reflect on what borders do to families. Whether over many years or in a flash, the effects borders have on those they separate are long-lasting. Sometimes it is the physical, geographical border, sometimes it is the legal and psychological, the indeterminable border between identities, cultures, and statuses that Anzaldúa so powerfully explored, "at the edge where earth touches ocean / where the two overlap / a gentle coming together / at other times and places a violent clash."

This book is about the suffering and resilience of those who find themselves separated by a border. My hope is that it will stir us to question the foundation of our immigration laws, and push us to reimagine our understanding of political borders and those who cross them into one that is more humane for individuals, for families, and for communities on both sides.

CHAPTER 1

Zero Tolerance

(May 24, 2018)

Georgina and I walked into the courtroom and found Azalea as she shuffled through the day's docket looking for her handwritten notes, which she had made on the right margin in blue ink. Azalea was an assistant federal public defender in McAllen, Texas, and this morning she wore a spotless pastel suit that contrasted with the disarray happening in the courtroom. "We only have five today," she said, referring to the separated parents of the day. A couple of moms, both from Guatemala, one of them with three children, ages seven, eight, and eleven. And three dads, each of them traveling with a son. "This one is from El Salvador," and she continued flipping the pages hurriedly.

I had to interrupt before she kept going. "Where can we talk to them?"

"Here."

I don't know where I was thinking we would interview them. It seemed somehow wrong to discuss something as significant as the whereabouts of their children and how they had been separated in the middle of this crowded chaos. I looked around and spotted a corner next to the witness stand. "Ok," I told Georgina. "Let's go over there."

We would talk to them and figure it out as we went. The immigrants were confused enough as it was. Most of them thought that this was an immigration court, that they would have to speak to the judge, and he would rule on their immigration case and decide whether they would be allowed to stay. Many did not understand that this was a federal criminal court. Georgina and I would have to explain to them that we were not their immigration lawyers, and we were not their criminal defense lawyers. We were here only to talk to them about the separation, about their children, and to try to find them.

"Try to get as much detail as you can for the narrative," I told Georgina. "Because these will become our affidavits."

I had done plenty of intakes, in English and Spanish, and interviewed a fair share of victims of human rights violations in the Mexican state of Chiapas and further south in Guatemala. My first summer in law school, I interned at an indigenous rights nonprofit and was a human rights observer in the highlands of Chiapas, near Acteal, the site of a 1997 massacre in which a paramilitary group with alleged ties to the Mexican military murdered forty-five indigenous men, women, and children while they prayed. And after law school, I was part of a delegation to Guatemala while I worked at the Inter-American Commission on Human Rights. In both of those situations, the interviews were for purposes of documenting an abuse or violation, and there was always the opportunity to meet a second or even a third time, a chance to clarify a detail, double-check a date, correct a misspelling. Those interviews were usually conducted in a quiet, private setting, at a house or in an office. Today was different. We were creating handwritten declarations, in no more than ten minutes, and there was no margin for error. If something was incorrect, the declarations could be tossed out on a technicality, and we were going to have to live with it.

I started with Dagoberto, the first father who stood up when we asked the "defendants," as the criminal justice system calls them, if anyone had been traveling with a child. He was tall and had a commanding demeanor that contrasted sharply with the worry on his face. Holding the stack of intake forms in my left hand, I jotted down his A-Number. While Dagoberto was a "defendant" in the eyes of the criminal justice system, in the eyes of the immigration system he was an "alien." On the first day of detention, the system assigns each immigrant a unique nine-digit Alien Registration Number, or "A-Number." In immigration court, each time the immigration judge calls a case, he—and it is almost always a he—reads out the last three digits of the A-Number, instead of the immigrant's name. Stripping them of their name is one of the earliest, most visible ways in which immigrants are denied their personhood when they arrive in this country. The person becomes a registered alien, and the alien becomes a number.

I explained to Dagoberto that I was a human rights lawyer there to talk to him about his son so I could try to find him. I made sure to tell him that I was not his immigration lawyer, and he nodded, disappointed, but said he understood. I understood his disappointment too.

"When did you cross?"

"When were you arrested?"

"Is this the first time you have come to the United States?"

"You were traveling with your . . . ?"

At least I stuck to good lawyering practice. Never feed information to your interviewee.

I had barely gotten the name and date of birth of Dagoberto's son when I heard someone sobbing right behind me. The sobbing came in rapid, short-breath bursts as the woman tried mightily to contain it. But she couldn't. It was the type of sobbing that was loud and quiet at the same time, the type of sobbing that when she tried to speak, she couldn't. She tried to raise her hands to wipe her tears, but the handcuffs made it impossible.

"She's telling me that her husband was murdered," Georgina said, looking at me, puzzled, and asking me, with her look, what to do. I stared back as if to say that I had not the slightest clue. "In February," she added, as if it might be useful to know that particular detail. Georgina had joined our office as a paralegal six months earlier, and this morning in court she was way out of her depth. And so was I.

Weeks later we would learn the gruesome details of the murder: how Viviana's husband was brutally beaten to death in a field, how the murderers were now after Viviana and her son, and how she had fled to save him. But now, in the middle of the intake and with less than thirty minutes to go, there was no opportunity to be sad, no time to pause and embrace her.

"Ok, *a ver*, let me see, hold on...Sir, a moment please?" I told Dagoberto and didn't wait for him to answer. Georgina and I tried to calm Viviana down, her round face flushed red from all the crying. We needed to get her affidavit drafted and signed. The hearing was going to start at 9 a.m. sharp, whether Viviana was still crying or not, whether we had her affidavit or not.

Georgina managed to calm Viviana down and handwrite the rest of her affidavit. Viviana was a month away from her thirtieth birthday, and this was the first time she had been apart from her eleven-year-old son Sandro since her husband's murder. When she finally reached the U.S., the place where she believed her son could be safe, agents in green uniforms had taken him. She did not know where he was and hadn't seen him in two days.

NARRATIVA/NARRATIVE *Cuando los detuvieron les preguntaron para donde iban. Vilma les dijo a los agentes que salieron del país por la razon de que asesinaron a su esposo (el 12 de febrero 2018) Esposo nombre: Remigio Coc Choc. Salieron del pais para salir adelante. Tambien su esposo antes de morir lo amenazaron y lo golpiaron y murio en consecuencia de la golpiza que le dieron. Vilma le dijo al agente de estos datos. El agente le dijo que dejaba estos datos. Le dijieron que su hijo estava en el mismo lugar que Vilma pero no lo podia ver. No le dijieron si su hijo va a regresar con ella a su pais.*

This declaration is made pursuant to 28 U.S.C. §1746. I hereby declare under penalty of perjury under the laws of the United States that the foregoing is true and correct. / Esta declaración se realiza de conformidad con 28 U.S.C. §1746. Por la presente declaro bajo pena de perjurio bajo las leyes de los Estados Unidos que lo anterior es verdadero y correcto.

FIRMA/SIGNATURE: _(mother)_

When they were detained, they were asked where they were going. Viviana told the agents that they left the country because her husband was murdered (on February 12, 2018). Name of husband: Remigio Coc Choc. They left the country to improve. Her husband, before he was murdered, was threatened and beaten and he died as a result of the beating. Viviana told the agent this information. The agent told her that he would write down this information. They told her that her son was in the same place as Viviana but she couldn't see him. They did not tell her if her son would return with her to her country. (Actual Declaration of Viviana Martínez Juc. English translation by the author.)

Although Azalea had told me about the separations, hearing it directly from Viviana still caught me unprepared. Listening to her describe, as she fought back tears, how her husband's face was so badly beaten that she could not recognize him, made me take a deep breath, and I lost my concentration. Hearing her tell us that Border Patrol agents told her that if she was deported, they were not sure that Sandro would go with her made me fear the worst: that she might not see him again. Hearing it all in Viviana's voice made me feel the despair she was feeling herself.

Once we finished Viviana's interview, I returned to Dagoberto and completed his affidavit. Not nearly as tragic as Viviana's, but a similar overwhelming desire to save his son. Thirty-nine-years-old, he had fled El Salvador to save his teenage son Jorge from the country's notorious gangs, and they were headed to Los Angeles, where Dagoberto's brother-in-law lived. I paraphrased some of his answers, and then read the full narrative back to him to confirm that everything was accurate. He shuffled with his handcuffs and signed at the bottom.

I asked him if he had a phone number for his brother-in-law. Instead of answering, he rolled up the left sleeve of his denim shirt and showed me the underside of his forearm. There, written in blue pen, was the 626–area code number. I wrote it down, he thanked me, and struggling to walk with the shackles around his ankles, only able to take one tiny step at a time, he slowly made his way to his seat. As he stumbled along, his laceless shoes flapped and dragged along the floor. It was probably the first time in his life walking with shackles, probably the first with handcuffs too. Maybe it was even the first time he had seen the inside of a courtroom.

After Dagoberto, I made eye contact with the next father, and motioned for him to come forward. Antonio Bol Paau had been traveling with his twelve-year-old son, Rivaldo, from Quiché, in Guatemala. With more than sixteen million people, Guatemala is the most populous country in Central America, and depending on which statistic one believes, somewhere between 40 and 60 percent of its population is indigenous; more than twenty distinct indigenous peoples—of Mayan, Garifuna, and Xinca origins—have lived inside the territory that is Guatemala today. At least twenty-three different Mayan languages are spoken, and some of them, such as Mam, have multiple regional variations and dialects. The peoples with the largest populations include the K'iche', Kaqchikel, Mam, Q'eqchi', Achí, and Ixil, although the latter were heavily decimated in the early 1980s during the Ixil Genocide, when the U.S.-backed Guatemalan military killed as many as 200,000 indigenous Guatemalans, according to the historical commission established after the genocide.

There is some controversy around the question, but the country's name appears to have derived from the Nahuatl word *Cuauhtēmallān*, place of many trees. In the mid-1980s, as part of an anti-colonization movement to reclaim the country's indigenous origins and identity, indigenous peoples moved away from the "Spanishized" version, Guatemala, and agreed on another indigenous word to refer to their country: *Iximulew*, meaning "land of corn" or "land of maize" in K'iche' and several other Mayan languages. Today, it is not uncommon for indigenous peoples and human rights defenders to refer to the country only as Iximulew.

When Antonio told me he was from Guatemala, I smiled and said, "Iximulew." He smiled too, a little surprised to hear me say it, and gave me a silent look of mutual understanding.

"Who separated you from your son?" I asked Antonio.

"Were they wearing a green uniform, or blue?"

"Did they tell you why you were being separated?"

"Did they tell you where they were taking your son?"

"Did they tell you when you will see him again?"

Antonio had been separated from his son for two days. Agents wearing green had placed him in a cell, and his son had remained outside. When Antonio came out of the cell, Rivaldo was gone. The agents did not tell him that they would be separated, did not give him a chance to say goodbye, but there was no time to dwell on these routine cruelties. Like Viviana, he had no family in the United States. "The agents told me that I would see my son tomorrow, but that was two days ago and I have not seen him."

NARRATIVA/NARRATIVE *Los agentes de la Patrulla Fronteriza que me detuvieron me separaron de mi hijo. No me dijeron por qué me separaron de él. Me metieron a una celda, y cuando salí, mi hijo ya no estaba. Ni me pude despedir de él. Desde que me separaron no he vuelto a ver a mi hijo. Yo lo único que quiero es reunirme con mi hijo. No sé por qué me separaron de él. Si a mí me deportan, mi hijo se quedaría solo acá en EE.UU., porque no tenemos a nadie aquí en este país. Los agentes me dijeron que "mañana" voy a ver a mi hijo, pero eso fue hace dos días y no lo he visto. No sé cuándo lo volveré a ver.*

This declaration is made pursuant to 28 U.S.C. §1746. I hereby declare under penalty of perjury under the laws of the United States that the foregoing is true and correct. / Esta declaración se realiza de conformidad con 28 U.S.C. §1746. Por la presente declaro bajo pena de perjurio bajo las leyes de los Estados Unidos que lo anterior es verdadero y correcto.

FIRMA/SIGNATURE: *[signature]*

The Border Patrol agents who detained me separated me from my son. They did not tell me why they separated me from him. They put me inside a cell, and when I came out, my son was no longer there. I was not even able to say goodbye to him. Since I was separated from him I have not seen my son. The only thing I want is to be reunited with my son. I don't know why I was separated from him. If I am deported, my son would stay by himself here in the United States, because we don't have anybody here in this country. The agents told me that I would see my son "tomorrow," but that was two days ago and I have not seen him. I don't know when I will see him again. (Actual Declaration of Antonio Bol Paau. English translation by the author.)

At that point, I began the first of what would become among the most difficult conversations I have ever had as a lawyer. When Antonio told me that he would see his son the next day, I told him what I would end up telling dozens of other parents over the next month. "I hope that your son is still at the processing station when you go back later this afternoon, and that you see him tomorrow." I paused. "But there's a chance he may not be there." In truth, I was all but certain that his son wouldn't be there. It was one of those moments when the gears inside your head can't quite turn. I knew his son wouldn't be there, but I didn't want to say that, and I also didn't want to lie. I looked at Antonio. The rattling of the shackles as he shifted around reminded me that time was short.

"There's a chance that you won't see him today, or tomorrow, that he'll be at a shelter, with other children." I purposely did not use the Spanish word for shelter. Instead, I said, *en una casa hogar*. "*Casa hogar*" sounded so much better, more comforting. The two words translate literally as "house home," *casa hogar*, and in my mind at least, they evoke a homey feeling, a warm place, someone taking care of you, maybe even cooking for you, somewhere you want to be. Shelter, on the other hand, is what you seek in a moment of crisis, when a hurricane is approaching, when you have nowhere else to go. It is somewhere you do not want to be.

When I told each parent that their child might not be at the place where they last saw them, and that they might not see them that afternoon, they did not flinch. Invariably, their next question was, Ok, if not today, then when will I see him again?

That was an impossible question to answer. When Antonio asked, I don't think I kept my poker face. I know I stuttered. The truthful answer was that I had no idea. It could be months. This was late May; news coverage of the separations had been scant. I didn't know when the children were going to see their parents again. I didn't even know *whether* they were going to see them again ever, but I tried to suppress that thought. I simply could not bring myself to contemplate the possibility that these children were going to be lost, forever trapped in a bureaucratic maze of immigration agencies, social workers, and foster care.

I got better at this conversation over time. But not this very first time. I must have said something like, "Well, we're doing everything we can, everything in our power to make sure that you get to see your son...that you get to see him as soon as possible." I got a confused look in response. I blundered on: "It may be a few days...

or several days...It, it may be...a few, a few weeks...or, or...or several weeks...It may be, it may be a month, or...." That's when Antonio, and almost every other parent after him, broke down crying.

I had countless conversations like this over the following days and weeks. It dawned on me that the agents had led virtually all the parents to believe that they had been separated because their children couldn't come to court, and that once their court appearance was over, they would be reunited later that day, or, as in the case of Antonio, the next day. But this was at best a half truth; at worst, a full-on lie.

Although I had had some warning, I wasn't fully prepared for what I found in court that morning. The day before in the afternoon, as I was pulling into the Costco parking lot, I had picked up a call on my cell phone. Azalea and I had been playing phone tag for days, but this Wednesday afternoon, with my fifteen-month-old son Julián yapping away behind me in his car seat, I answered.

What Azalea explained was hard to believe. Fathers and mothers who had been detained crossing the border illegally were being separated from their children, of all ages, and parents and children had no idea where their other family members were or when they might see each other again.

My mind swirled. It simply couldn't be that the prosecutors didn't *really* know where the children were. Or that the parents weren't given *any* information about where the children had been taken, who was caring for them, or when they might see them again. "Is there anything your office can do about this?" she asked. "Your office" was a reference to me, the sole attorney; Georgina, our paralegal; and Roberto, our part-time community outreach coordinator. It seemed like a ludicrous overstatement given the task at hand. But Azalea didn't know that.

My lawyer brain immediately clicked into overdrive. I asked her to write a sworn statement incorporating all the details she was giving me. We could then use her statement as evidence in a lawsuit to try to stop the separations. "Let me check and I'll call you back," Azalea said.

Less than ten minutes later, I was standing inside Costco with the phone to my ear, listening to her say that she couldn't do it. Something involving the attorney-client privilege. But, she added, her boss—the head of the McAllen Federal Public Defender's office— said that I could go to court and interview the parents myself for a few minutes before their criminal hearings began.

"What time should we be there?" I asked.

As soon as we hung up, I dialed Georgina's cell phone number. I adjusted my headphones as I pushed the shopping cart into the frozen food aisle and past a display of what seemed like seventeen different varieties of Kirkland Signature coffee. As I waited impatiently for her to answer, Julián tugged on the dangling headphone cord and scarfed down his third serving of veggie dumpling samples.

"Are you still at the office?" Of course she was. "We need to create an intake form. Can you make one really fast?"

I began to think what we might need on the form. In the background I could hear the click of the keystrokes as Georgina typed while I spoke. I started with the interview's date, the person's name, date of birth, country of birth, city of birth.

"What else?" she asked.

I told her we needed all of the same information for the child. Name. Date of birth. Country of origin. Little did I know that this trio of ordinary details would become our guiding star that summer.

City of birth too, I thought that might be useful for some reason. We also needed blank lines so that we could handwrite the answers to each question. Then, at the bottom of the page, we needed to include as many blank lines as we could fit, to write down a narrative about how the separation had happened. Who took the child away? Did they say why? Did they say where they were taking them? Did they say for how long?

"We're going to interview separated parents tomorrow, at the federal courthouse in McAllen. I'll see you there at 7:30 a.m." I was eager to get to court, although uncertain about what I would find— and what I might be able to do about it. That night, my sleep was fitful, I drifted in and out of consciousness. The South Texas humidity didn't help, even with air-conditioning. Every time I woke during the night, I felt the warm humid sheet underneath.

The next morning, before 7:40 a.m., Georgina and I stepped out of the elevator on the eighth floor of the Bentsen Tower, where the McAllen federal courthouse is located. A black, all-glass, eleven-floor low-rise built in 1985, the "tower" sits on the corner of Bicentennial Boulevard and Business Highway 83. "Business 83" used to be the main thoroughfare connecting the dozens of cities and towns that dot the border along the Rio Grande Valley (RGV), until Expressway 83 was built, and Business 83 became "Old 83." The courtrooms occupy the eighth, ninth, and tenth floors, with unique views of McAllen's downtown, if only the blinds were ever opened.

After exiting the elevator, we made an immediate right and entered the courtroom. The scene was exactly as Azalea had described. Defendants were being shuffled into the room, even when it appeared that no more could fit. The criminal hearing was set to start at nine. There were more than one hundred people already, and more were still crowding their way in.

I had never been in this particular courtroom before, one of three magistrate courts on the floor. The dark blue carpet gave the room an old-fashioned feel and contrasted with its light cream walls. Everything else was made of wood. The two legal counsel's tables, the benches for public seating, the judge's bench, and even the window blinds were all wood, the same amber color, shiny and clean.

The room had a seating capacity of about ninety—fifteen people could fit comfortably on each of the six wooden benches, without invading each other's personal space. Today, though, there were more than twenty packed in each row. Every defendant was restrained by what are called five-point handcuffs: shackles around their ankles, handcuffs around their wrists, and the fifth "point," a chain that ties the handcuffs to a "belly chain," wrapped around their skinny and grimy waists. Looking tired and uncomfortable, they sat quietly in their assigned spots. The only sound was the clanking of the handcuffs and chains as they shifted in their seats.

It wasn't clear to me why all the defendants were handcuffed and shackled. None of them seemed to pose a danger to anybody. Being restrained in this way made it much harder to walk. Each person had to shuffle sideways to enter his or her row, stumbling as they passed. Removing the shackles would have made everyone's life much easier.

In addition to the immigrants, there were also two Border Patrol agents. Both in their midthirties, they were a little heavier than I would have expected for officers whose job requires them to chase after swiftly moving crossers in the Rio Grande Valley's 100-degree heat. There was also one man in a suit—a U.S. Marshal, proudly wearing his marshal's pin on the left lapel of his charcoal-gray blazer, just an inch or two above his tie clip—and four GEO Group private security guards, displaying oversized company patches on each of their shoulders. GEO Group owned the buses that transported the immigrants to and from court. At the time, the company also administered—for the government—dozens of detention centers around the country where thousands of immigrants and other "detainees" were held.

MY BOY WILL DIE OF SORROW

GEO is the second-largest for-profit prison operator in the U.S. by number of facilities, only behind CoreCivic (formerly Corrections Corporation of America, CCA). The guards spoke Spanish to the immigrants and English among themselves. All the guards were Latino, probably Mexican or Mexican American—one can never tell for sure in the Rio Grande Valley. One of them was certainly northern Mexican; I heard his Spanish accent and recognized my own. Swap their gray uniforms for dirty civilian clothes, and they would have been indistinguishable from the immigrant defendants.

The assistant federal public defenders and investigators had taken all the available seats at both legal counsel's tables. Arrayed among them were dozens of folders, each containing one person's file. They were preparing to interview the defendants. Along the north wall, two interpreters were setting up their equipment, testing the headphones and receivers that had been neatly organized on a roller cart. The judge's case manager and other court staff had not yet arrived. Theirs were the only empty seats in the room.

The immigrants were about to be prosecuted under a law that makes it a crime to cross the border illegally. In my ten years as a lawyer, including five at the Texas Civil Rights Project (TCRP), I had never dealt directly with this formerly obscure law, which many refer to only as "Section 1325," or "13-25," as in "a thirteen-twenty-five case." For years, I had argued forcefully with immigration hard-liners that crossing the border without authorization was a civil, not criminal, violation. Now I was learning that I had been mistaken all along. This law made it a federal misdemeanor to swim across the Rio Grande.

Tracing its origins back to 1929, Section 1325 makes it unlawful to enter the United States "at any time or place other than as designated by immigration officers," which in Texas means one of the twenty-nine international bridges. In California, Arizona, and New

Mexico, the border is a line on the ground, but in Texas the entire border is a river. It starts as a trickle in El Paso, and grows into a deep, treacherous delta that empties into the Gulf of Mexico. And if you're not crossing it at one of the bridges, you're either swimming, floating, or rafting across. The law sets the punishment for crossing the river without authorization at up to six months in a federal prison and a fine of up to $250. Immigrants who plead guilty are typically sentenced to "time served," meaning their criminal cases are automatically completed upon being sentenced, that same day, that same morning.

Earlier that month, Jeff Sessions, then the Attorney General of the United States, had held a press conference in San Diego to announce a policy change: prosecutors along the U.S.-Mexico border would now charge every single person caught making an illegal crossing under Section 1325. "One hundred percent of illegal southwest border crossings" would be prosecuted, he said. If you cross the border with a child, he added, "that child will be separated from you, probably, as required by law. If you don't want your child to be separated, then don't bring him across the border illegally." Zero Tolerance, he called it.

After Antonio, our next interview was another mother. María had been separated from her children the day before. Her husband had emigrated from Guatemala a year earlier, and she had been traveling with her three children to join him in Missouri. Upon being detained, Border Patrol had taken her two daughters and her son. She was short and stocky, calm, and methodical in how she recounted the details of the separation to Georgina. Yes, she traveled by land with her children from Guatemala all the way to Texas. No, the agents did not tell her where her children were going. Yes, her daughters were eleven and seven, and her son was eight, two weeks away from his ninth birthday. No, the agents did not tell her when she would see them again.

María's husband was now in Missouri by himself, she was in this courtroom in McAllen by herself, and neither of them knew where the children were, or even whether the three of them were together. I thought her suffering would be threefold that of parents who had lost one child. But María did not cry. As she realized what had happened—or what we thought had happened—to her children, she stood there quietly. Her reaction was one of resignation, of quiet sufferance; her face remained expressionless; her eyes stared into a void. Her short hair was disheveled, and she seemed not to be bothered by the handcuffs anymore. She seemed to have lost sense of where she was and what was happening around her. Georgina interrupted her paralysis to ask if she could sign her affidavit.

I was speaking to Leonel, who was also from Guatemala. He was less than a year younger than me, and wore a plaid short-sleeve shirt, white with dark and light blue lines, and cowboy-style buttons, the kind you snap together. He must have been no taller than five feet, seven inches. In broken Spanish, he explained that he had come with his eleven-year-old son, Daniel. Like Viviana and Sandro, they were traveling alone, and they were inseparable. He and Daniel were both first-time crossers and had no family in the United States. They were hoping to apply for asylum due to the persecution they had faced in their indigenous village.

I got all the critical information from Leonel, but I still couldn't believe that the agents had not given him any information about his son, where he was being taken, or who would take care of him. Surely the agents must have told him something about the process and about what to expect, I thought.

"What do you think would happen," I asked Leonel, "if you are deported and your son doesn't go with you, if he stays here?"

The agent asked her if she was traveling alone, and then asked for her children's information. He then took them all to a very cold room. There they interviewed her, and then separated them. He told her that she would be taken to court, and then she would get her children back. The separation was on Wednesday. María left her country with her children to join her husband and also because they were being extorted. Also so that her children may have a better life. Her husband is in Missouri. At no time did the agent ask her why she left her country. (Actual Declaration of María del Villar. English translation by the author.)

He looked down, as if thinking about it, and when he looked up, he shook his head. His look was one of resignation.

"No, pues, mi niño se muere de tristeza." My boy will die of sorrow.

For a second, my eyes didn't leave his. I struggled to write down what he was telling me. I pursed my lips and looked down, swallowed hard, and couldn't find words to respond.

I read the narrative back to Leonel, and when he agreed it was accurate, he signed his name, using his left hand to push the shiny silver handcuffs higher on his skinny wrist to be able to sign.

I hadn't been specific enough with Georgina regarding the narratives, so when I saw the two declarations that she had prepared,

NARRATIVA/NARRATIVE Los agentes que me detuvieron me separaron de mi hijo. Me dijeron que no podíamos pasar. Les pregunté a donde iban a llevar a mi hijo y no me dijeron. Y, lo único que quiero es reunirme con él, porque si me deportan a mi, mi hijo se va a morir de tristeza. Desde que me detuvieron casi no he comido, y me preocupa mucho que mi hijo tampoco haya comido. Sólo lo quiero ver, saber que está bien, y poder estar junto a él como familia. El no tiene a nadie más que a mi y a mi esposa, su mamá, en Guatemala.

This declaration is made pursuant to 28 U.S.C. §1746. I hereby declare under penalty of perjury under the laws of the United States that the foregoing is true and correct. / Esta declaración se realiza de conformidad con 28 U.S.C. §1746. Por la presente declaro bajo pena de perjurio bajo las leyes de los Estados Unidos que lo anterior es verdadero y correcto.

FIRMA/SIGNATURE:

The agents who detained me separated me from my son. They told me that we couldn't go through. I asked them where they were taking my son and they didn't tell me. The only thing I want is to be reunited with him, because if I am deported, my son will die of sorrow. Since I was detained I almost have not eaten, and I am very worried that my son may not be eating either. I just want to see him, know that he is ok, and be able to be with him like a family. He does not have anybody other than me and my wife, his mom, in Guatemala. (Actual Declaration of Leonel Chub Cucul. English translation by the author.)

for Viviana and María, I realized she had written them in the third person. I had done my three in the first. No way to change it now. We were going to have to live with that too.

Our time was already up, and Georgina and I quickly said goodbye and thank you to Azalea, and walked out of the courtroom. We took the five narratives with us, but the rest of those stories stayed unspoken in that courtroom. We walked into the same elevator, leaving behind the clanking sound of the handcuffs as soon as the doors closed. I felt uncertain. Had we missed anything? Did we forget to ask something critical?

As we rode down the elevator, part of me wished I knew more about these parents' lives. Did Viviana have plans for enrolling

Sandro in school once they reached the United States? What grade was he in? Did Leonel have other children? Did they stay behind with their mother in Guatemala? What were María's three children like? They were each two years apart—did they fight a lot, like my brother and I did when we were that age? Did Antonio name his son Rivaldo after the famous Brazilian soccer player? Did he even like soccer? Dagoberto's son Jorge was sixteen years old—was he a good kid, or a rebellious teenager?

But there was no time to ask any of that. That morning, Georgina and I had had less than ten minutes with each of them, barely enough to draft and sign the affidavits. We needed to document names, dates of birth, and countries of origin, not hopes or dreams. We had gotten what we came for, but I had no idea what we had missed. I couldn't help but think that by rushing them through this process, the Zero Tolerance machine—and Georgina and I as cogs within it—had denied them part of their dignity.

Exiting the Bentsen Tower, I also thought about the children of these five parents. Each had probably awoken that morning and wondered whether this would be the day when they would see their father or mother again. But I knew that today was not that day. And worse, on that humid morning, I did not know when that day might come, or whether it would come at all.

McAllen was home to only one of more than a dozen federal courts scattered along the southwest border—how many more separated parents were there along that line?

Georgina and I walked across 17th Street to the parking lot. I got in my car, and my body fell heavily into the seat. The heat was worse inside the car, the morning sun glaring through the windshield directly into my face, the steering wheel hot to the touch. I loosened my tie, but that did not relieve the feeling of frustration. I felt powerless that I could not reunite these five parents with their children that same day, and frustrated that I knew there would be more the next day, and more the day after that.

The plan for a human rights lawsuit began to float in my head, taking shape as I turned the car on. I put it in reverse and backed out of the parking spot. I needed to get to the office and get to work. It wasn't even 9:15 a.m. on the Thursday before Memorial Day. I was emotionally exhausted and completely unaware of what was yet to come.

Over the next several weeks, thousands of immigrant families—hundreds of them in McAllen—would find themselves at the center of a national immigration crisis, and I would find myself as their lawyer. As a lawyer, on that first day in court, I felt far from them, my life so different from theirs. Over time, as we interviewed more and more separated parents, dozens and then hundreds, I came to realize that, at its core, my story was not so different from theirs. My family and I had migrated in a different time, under different laws, but we had all moved across a border in search of a better life.

For all its cruelty, the crisis that unfolded that summer led me to insights and realizations about how the United States treats those who come knocking at its door, whether escaping violence and oppression or seeking opportunity. Time and again, immigrants have been forcibly kept out, and those who manage to make it in, especially those who are not white, have been blamed for the country's problems, from unemployment to upticks in crime. The data does not bear out those accusations, but brown immigrants have been the constant scapegoat nonetheless.

CHAPTER 2

—·—·—·—

Fridays

(1993)

This was the third time I had asked for the same favor, and there was no telling how many more times I would have to request it. I tried my best to draw up the courage again: "Can I bring back the signed progress report next week?"

The signed progress report was due on Friday morning, but my dad was not coming home until that night, and my mom wanted him to see that I had, once again, gotten almost all 10s. My dad would make the three-hour drive from McAllen, Texas, taking the old and bumpy toll-free road even after the smooth two-lane toll road was built. I never asked why he didn't take the much nicer toll road, where he would be able to pass slow 18-wheelers without having to invade the oncoming traffic lane. At my elementary-school age, I did not yet understand that paying a ten-dollar toll meant ten fewer dollars for groceries.

Ever since he had left us the year before, my father would return home on the weekends when he could. He would leave McAllen on Friday after work, and after stopping by the grocery store, he wouldn't arrive to our house until after ten in the evening. But my little brother and I stayed up, no matter how late it got, if we knew he was coming. When he came to see us, he might bring with him a bag of chicken leg quarters, or maybe a gallon of milk, and a loaf of bread tucked in the trunk of his car.

Some Fridays he didn't come at all, and some Fridays, like this Friday, the trunk was mostly empty. My mother, waiting for us in the kitchen, had stayed by the stove, knowing she did not need to come out and help us unload. This Friday was not payday.

Of course, *la Maestra* Aurora had replied that morning, "you can bring back the signed progress report on Monday." Miss Aurora was one of two fifth grade teachers at *Veteranos de la Revolución* Elementary, Veterans of the Revolution, the oldest elementary school in the town of Allende, in the northern Mexican state of Nuevo León. The school was founded in 1948, more than thirty years after the Mexican Revolution had triumphed, but the revolutionary spirit was still very much alive in our education. We learned about Emiliano Zapata and Pancho Villa and Venustiano Carranza, all icons of twentieth-century Mexican history. At our school, the Revolution was considered our proudest national moment.

Every year on November 20th, the town's students put on our winter sports uniform—warm, navy-blue sweatpants and an even warmer zip-up sweatshirt—for the parade to commemorate the Anniversary of the Revolution, even when the temperature hovered above twenty-six degrees Celsius (some eighty Fahrenheit) in this warm part of Mexico. All the schools participated, most of the stores in town were closed for the holiday, and there were hardly any cars. Shoe shiners prepared for a busy day, cleaning their stands and arranging newspapers for the day's customers. The cheering spectators lined the route, waving their handheld Mexican flags.

We marched down to the *Presidencia Municipal*, our city hall, back around the other side of the main square, past the *Parroquia de*

San Pedro Apóstol, our town's main church, and back to the school. The spectators made sure to stand on both sides of the street. We marched past the diminutive *Casa de la Cultura*, our only museum, and *La Michoacana*, the go-to ice cream shop, its shuttered windows displaying large images of strawberry and mango ice cream cones, tempting every passerby.

The parade was a sweaty affair. As we approached the intersection, everyone in my row looked to the right and left to make eye contact with one another. We nodded when our eyes met. The PE teacher blew his whistle. Five of the boys rushed to their predesignated spot, lined up side by side, and got down on all fours, their shoulders touching. They were the sturdiest and strongest. Quickly, the next group of four, myself included, got on all fours on top of the first five, putting our left arm and left leg on the back of one student, and our right arm and right leg on top of another student, until all four of us were crouched on top of the first five.

Then it was the turn of the group of three to get on top of the four of us. Theirs was a more complicated sequence. They first had to step on the backs of the bottom row, and carefully balance themselves to climb on top of us. They also had to be careful to put their left arm and leg on one student, and their right arm and leg on the other.

And then came the group of two. By now we were all shaking. I was trying to balance myself on the backs of the two boys below me, with a pair of bony knees above piercing my back, and now someone was trying to climb up still higher above me. Everything felt unstable. The smell of freshly baked bread and pastries reminded me we were at the corner where Allende's oldest bakery is located. I concentrated on the scent as the last two boys made it to their spots.

Then came the grand finale. The shortest, lightest, tiniest boy in our class climbed up four rows of unstable, shaky fifth graders.

By now I was sweating profusely, trying to remain stable so that our human pyramid wouldn't come crashing down. My hands were slippery with sweat. Out of the corner of my eye, I saw people exiting the bakery carrying brown paper bags, surely full of fresh warm bread; otherwise I couldn't see a thing. But when I heard the roar and applause from the crowd of spectators, I knew he had made it to the top, stood up straight, and lifted both arms and fists high above his head in a sign of revolutionary triumph.

Then, in a split second, the pyramid dissolved. We filed back into our rows and continued marching.

Allende sits at the foot of the Sierra Madre Mountains, the continuation of the Rockies as they rise from the earth to create a backbone in Mexico's topography. Located some fifty kilometers southeast of Monterrey, the state's capital, the town takes its name from Ignacio Allende, a storied General of the War of Independence. Heavy clouds often end their journey in Allende, where they run into the towering mountains and hover over town as if incapable of surmounting the ridge. As a result, the town receives a significant amount of rain every year, which makes the mountains in the background, and the few parks around town, always a lush, vibrant green. The Ramos River, which divides Allende from neighboring Montemorelos, flows down from the mountains lined by imposing swamp cypresses that seem impossibly tall and mysteriously ancient. Every weekend in the summer, the river and its banks are crowded with families from Monterrey and elsewhere, cooking on their portable grills, bathing in the cool water, finding refuge from the scorching heat. Unlike the summer visitors, the town's thirty thousand or so residents enjoy their river and their mountains all year long.

The Revolution Day parade was not my favorite part of school. It was a chore, our duty and responsibility, as Miss Aurora said. She would go on to become the first female mayor of Allende, after the sitting mayor stepped down following a scandal. Years later, she would become the first woman elected state representative from our district to the Nuevo León legislature. She was blond, with expressive green eyes, and I remember her as being very articulate, which to a ten-year-old like me made her highly educated. She was also our neighbor. She lived in the house on the corner, down the street from ours, across from the neighborhood store. Her house was typical of the houses on our block, built of cinderblock, with two or three bedrooms, and fitted with an air-conditioning unit in the window. When she became mayor and launched her career in politics, she remodeled her house. It became the finest home on the block.

Like Miss Aurora's, our house was also on a corner, at the opposite end of De las Rosas Street. It was fitting that our house sat on a street named "of the roses." Our house was famous in the neighborhood because of my mom's roses and geraniums. There were dozens of flowers in our front yard: white, yellow, and burgundy roses; pink, orange, and red velvet geraniums. My mom tended to them religiously, a habit she had inherited from her own mother. Whenever neighbors stopped by or a guest visited our house, they commented on her beautiful flowers.

My mother would nod and thank them and reply yes to everything they said. "You're so lucky," the visitor would say. "All the rain must make it really easy to have such a beautiful garden." It rained the same on every house on the block, but no other house had a front yard filled with blooming roses and geraniums. My mom never pointed that out.

Less than a year after my father left to find work in McAllen, the state teachers' union went on a large-scale strike. I didn't understand what a *paro* was, and I couldn't grasp why not going to work was a good way to demand better conditions at work. Most of the schools in town and around the state were shut for months, due to a lack of teachers, giving those lucky students an extended vacation. But sadly, not us. Miss Aurora and the rest of the teachers at Veterans of the Revolution crossed the picket line and refused to join the strike, so students from other schools transferred to ours. Students from *El Colegio*, the one private Catholic school, and from Ignacio Zaragoza Elementary, the other public school, arrived in my classroom that year.

My father traveled home to see us because we couldn't go to him. My mother, my younger brother Héctor, and I did not have a visa to cross to "the other side." My dad had his visa because his father, Güelito Julián, was born in Sebastian, Texas, a tiny place not too far from McAllen, at the turn of the twentieth century. Güelito Julián's parents were farmworkers, and during the harvest season, they worked in the fields in the United States. Back then, it was much easier for the family to cross back and forth and stay together. There was no Border Patrol, no Immigration and Nationality Act, and certainly no Zero Tolerance policy. If there was work and you wanted to work, you just went to the United States. So, when there was work for them, Güelito Julián's parents went. They happened to be working in the fields in early 1902, and that February, when they must have been picking cabbage or lettuce in the fields of Sebastian, on the twenty-sixth of the month, Güelito Julián was born on the American side of the border.

Because of that, Güelito was a U.S. citizen. *Jus soli*, the lawyers call it. The right to the soil. And while my father was born in Mexico, he had what in law school I learned is called "acquired citizenship" because he was the son of a U.S. citizen. Under the immigration laws of the United States, a child born to a U.S. citizen can also be a citizen regardless of his or her place of birth. *Jus sanguinis* is, instead, the right to the blood. The citizen parent has to meet certain conditions, such as residing in the United States a number of years, and the child must either be physically present or be lawfully allowed to enter the United States. My father met all the requirements, so he acquired U.S. citizenship from my grandfather.

He had to file the paperwork to get the document to prove it, and he didn't get around to doing that until 1987, five years after I was born, and three years after my brother arrived. Because of that, Héctor and I did not acquire citizenship. We did not have the "right to the blood," and we could not visit him in McAllen now.

This was not considered an important factor when my father decided to look for work in Texas. I was still a child, but I'm sure the decision-making must have gone something like this: The money he and his brother, Tío Óscar, had received from selling their trucking business was running out. They had started driving trucks to southern Mexico in their teens, even before they could get licenses. The job paid well in the 1960s, and they built a business, later owning a small fleet of green and orange "straight trucks," the kind with only two or three axles and the tractor permanently attached to the trailer, which had mostly wooden siding. These little straight trucks were not to be confused with the much more common big trailer trucks or "18-wheelers." To this day, truck driving is one of the primary industries in Allende. In fact, the truck drivers from Allende have given all of the natives the nickname *tejones*, badgers, because, like badgers, the Allende drivers are known for always traveling as a group, one behind the other and close together to watch out for each another.

Although their business had been successful, my father and my uncle Óscar grew tired of the stress and decided to sell their business the year my younger brother was born, convinced they could make a living a different way. They purchased a handful of properties in and around Allende with the proceeds and then sold those one by one. But the profits from those sales had run out too. They launched a *Norteño* band—literally translated as "northerner," a folksy music genre popular in northern Mexico—and recorded two albums, neither of which sold well. I would listen to them sing *El canto del bracero* and the words still resonate with me. "The Ballad of the Bracero" speaks to the hardships that Mexicans endured during the Bracero Program that brought millions of guest workers to United States fields in the 1940s and '50s. Recounting the ordeal of a worker who sneaked across the border without a passport or ID, leaving family, friends, and loved ones behind, the lyrics are a timeless reminder of the disappointment, discrimination, and despair that thousands of immigrants faced. The bracero experience was such that the ballad ends by asking would-be immigrants to reconsider: *"Si tú piensas ir, detente, o si estás allá, regresa / donde está tu familia y está tu gente, y el rinconcito aquel que te vio nacer / donde está un amor que puedes perder."* "If you're thinking of going, stop, or if you're there, come back / to where your family and your people are, and to that little place where you were born / where there is a love that you stand to lose."

Their band played at weddings and quinceañeras every few weeks, but that was not enough. There was simply no money. On more than one occasion, my mom had to ask her own father to loan her money to buy groceries. My brother and I were growing; money was only going to get tighter. My half-siblings—my father's three older children from a different mother—also lived with us in the house on and off, and they had all left school. The eldest, my half brother Leoba, had already moved to the States to look for work. For my father, going to the other side seemed the only sensible option, a choice made easier by the fact that five of his ten siblings already lived there. He would simply tilt the balance in favor of those who had emigrated over those who hadn't. The hardest part of his decision was leaving us and my Tío Óscar behind.

The day my father left, it did not feel like he was leaving for long. He left on a Sunday, and told us he'd see us in two weeks. No hug, no dramatic farewell. Simply a goodbye kiss, and I'll see you in two Fridays. My mother helped him pack his clothes into an old small ivory suitcase, just enough for two weeks, and he was ready. He made sure to take the makeshift rubber insole he always wore in his left shoe to accommodate his left leg being a quarter of an inch shorter than his right. It was almost as if he were going on another overnight trip with his band, except this trip was a little longer, and a little farther. When he drove off in the fading sunlight, my mom returned to watering her geraniums.

Most of his clothes stayed in his closet, neatly organized. His shoes stayed on his side of the bed. One pair of his pants still hung on the clothesline to dry. His guitar was in its black leather case where he always kept it. His shovel, pickax, and hoe, used to tend to the orange trees in our backyard, were all still there, the hoe had dirt on it from the last time he had used it. It was as if he didn't really leave. All his things were around for me to see, but he was gone.

That he was indeed gone was most noticeable in the evenings when my mother tried to bolster our spirits by making what she pronounced was our favorite dinner dish: ¡parecitos de manteca! Little pairs of beef tallow. These pairs were a simple yet delicious concoction: Take two tortillas, rub some beef tallow on each of them—maybe get lucky and include a few tiny crumbs of beef that sank to the bottom when the broth was separated from the tallow—pair them together, and then warm them up in the comal, a thin griddle used to cook and warm tortillas. Be sure not to leave them on for too long, because the tortillas might get toasted, becoming hard and crispy, and no one wants that. They are meant to be rolled into a long and tight *taquito*, evenly distributing the grease. The tallow should be fully melted and the tortillas piping hot, but still soft enough to be able to roll them. Sometimes the tallow would fall out of the tortilla into the *comal*, releasing a hiss of steam and a wonderful smell that tempted my brother and me as we waited, shirtless, seated at the round kitchen table. We dined on these little pieces of heaven a couple of times a week, and some weeks more often, when my dad hadn't come home for a while. On the rare weekends when he returned, bringing chicken and bread and bologna for sandwiches, my mom did not need to get as creative in the kitchen.

When he arrived in McAllen, my father applied for every job he could. He was about to turn fifty, hardly the ideal age to move to a new country, learn a new language, and start over. Luckily, he didn't have to learn a new skill. He was already a very skilled driver.

His truck-driving experience came in handy when he interviewed for a position as a bus driver at a school south of McAllen. He passed the driving test on the first try. He had mastered how to drive dilapidated trucks with manual transmissions over all kinds of roads in southern Mexico, driving them from cities like Poza Rica, Villahermosa, and Tapachula to Monterrey in the north, and then back south again. Now he had to show that he could drive a brand-new school bus from the 1990s, with automatic transmission and air-conditioning, around a couple of neighborhoods on wide, paved streets. Piece of cake.

The hard part was going to be the physical exam. He needed to pass a resistance test, have an acceptable blood pressure, healthy glucose levels, and of course a drug-free urine sample. The worry was his heart. He had undergone mitral valve surgery at age twenty-six. The mitral valve is made up of two tiny flaps of tissue that regulate the flow of blood from the left atrium to the left ventricle of the heart. When the valve malfunctions, the blood flow in the heart becomes irregular, and the condition, called mitral prolapse, can be life-threatening if left untreated. Open-heart surgery to repair a mitral valve in 1968 in Monterrey was something very different from what it is today. My father told me once that he remembered, like a lucid dream, starting to wake up before the surgery was completed. The doctors were still suturing his chest when the anesthetic started to fade, and he remembered hearing the voices of nurses and doctors, panicking as they realized their patient was coming to. They must have urgently reapplied the anesthetic, and dad drifted back to sleep. Twenty-five years later, he still took Lanoxin every day, prescribed to prevent cardiac failure.

The day he received the results of the physical, he called my mother. I could only hear her side of the conversation in our living room, but I will never forget it.

"Oh how wonderful, thank God!" *"¡Jesús, María y José!"* Jesus, Mary, and Joseph, my mother exclaimed, with both relief and elation. But her excitement quickly turned to worry.

"¿Pero por qué lloras?" But why are you crying?

At ten years old, I had never before been aware of my father crying. I was as confused as my mother. Why would he be crying if this was good news? This was great news! This was the news we had all been waiting and praying for. Then my mom's eyes started to fill up too. I was kneeling on a chair next to her, while she stood, holding the receiver up to her left ear as the gray coiled cord rubbed against her chest. She wiped her eyes clean with her free hand, as if telling herself don't cry, don't cry.

"Did you not pass?"

"So why are you crying then?" Her voice broke.

Then silence. When she put down the phone and walked away, I asked her what had happened. Nothing, she said. My dad had gotten the job. He was going to drive a school bus. He was going to see other people's children every day, he would greet them in the mornings and wave goodbye to them in the afternoons. But he would not see his own.

One summer afternoon after my father left, I walked out of the weekly Bible study class my mom insisted that I attend and headed home. I was surprised to see our front door closed. We typically kept the screen door shut, but the wooden door behind it was always open, especially on hot summer days. We had no air-conditioning, so we kept both the front and rear doors open to let any slight breeze flow through the screens. But today, the front wooden door was shut.

I walked to our back porch. The back door was shut too. Hesitant, I walked to the corner of the porch and reached my hand into the potted fern where we sometimes left extra house keys. I felt the dry dirt with my fingers as I dug around for the key. Nothing.

If Héctor and my mother had gone somewhere while I was at Bible study, she would have left a spare key in that fern. I searched again but found nothing. This was the first time that I had come home to an empty house with no idea where my mother was. I became concerned, but more than anything I felt confused, disoriented, and unsure of what to do next.

I walked across the street to my aunt's house, thinking my mom and Héctor might be there, or my aunt might know where they were. As I was about to ring the doorbell, one of our neighbors suddenly appeared.

"*¡Efrén! ¿Ya hablaste con tu mamá?*" Did you talk to your mom yet? she asked, agitated.

Where were they?

"*Tus tíos los llevaron.*" My aunt and uncle had given them a ride.

Where were they?

"Héctor se cayó, se pegó fuerte." Héctor had had a fall. A bad one. Where were they?

"Se fueron al seguro." They had gone to the public hospital.

My brother had been born exactly one week before I turned two years old. Our birthdays always fall on the same day of the week in June, a week apart, so the few times we had a birthday party growing up, it was one small affair for the two of us. I never minded. We were glad we *had* a party. We were always together anyway.

Héctor was nine. He had been playing with neighborhood friends and, like many other summer afternoons before, they had been climbing onto the roof of a neighbor's house. To get to the roof, he had to step onto a chest-high concrete wall first. And to get to that wall, he had stepped on an old empty pot sitting on the floor. The pot must have been about ten inches tall. As he stepped on it, the pot broke, and Héctor fell back. The fall should not have been anything, but as he fell, a rusty piece of iron rod sticking out of the wall punctured his neck and throat. Blood gushed out immediately. A lot of blood.

When my mother saw Héctor walk slowly toward the house, sobbing, pressing a friend's bunched-up T-shirt against the left underside of his chin, his neck and shirt soaked in blood, she rushed toward him.

"¡Madre santa!" My goodness!

She tried to remove the dripping T-shirt to see the wound, but there was so much blood pouring out that she stopped. It was better to keep pressing on my brother's throat to try to combat the bleeding.

If my father had been around, he would have driven them to the doctor, while my mom kept on pressing the T-shirt against Héctor's throat. My father would have helped her decide whether they should put ice on the wound, or rush straight to the hospital. He would have helped her decide whether it was better to take Héctor to the public hospital—*el seguro*, the national public health institute—or to the one private clinic in town. He would have helped her decide if this was serious enough that they should bypass Allende entirely and go to Montemorelos, where there was a bigger public hospital with surgery capabilities. But none of that was an option. My mother had to decide, and quickly.

A high school teacher in her younger years, my mother stopped working outside the home when she married my father, at the age of thirty-six. I was born nine months after they married, and she had been a stay-at-home mom ever since. After my father left for the United States, she started selling Coca-Colas to help make ends meet. More than once she told me to grab a handful of coins from the dark wooden tray where she kept the change from the sales to go buy tortillas at the corner store. Neighborhood kids would tease Héctor and me that the Cokes my mom sold were never as cold as those sold at the corner store. *"Parecen caldos,"* they would say, mockingly, exaggerating. They're like hot soup. I never bothered to explain that we kept them in the only small fridge we owned, and since we would open it frequently throughout the day, the Cokes never had a chance to get very cold.

My mother's only other experience with a medical emergency was when I fell as a toddler. She was bathing me in the sink next to the washing machine, and, slippery with water and soap, I slid through her hands and landed head-first on a tin bucket. She still gets emotional when she remembers the time she "dropped" me. I cracked my head—a small but bloody cut. My father was at work in Monterrey. Rather than take me to the local clinic, my mother decided she would take care of the wound herself, because she did not want doctors and nurses to shave my head in order to suture the wound. Carefully, she cleaned the wound with *agua oxigenada,* hydrogen peroxide, and applied copious amounts of *polvito de sulfa-tiazol*, a basic first aid antibiotic powder, and cuddled me to sleep. To this day, my mother is still proud that she took care of the emergency herself. But there was no way she was going to stop Héctor's bleeding with hydrogen peroxide and antibiotic powder.

Desperate, she took Héctor to my aunt's house across the street. Luckily, my aunt and my uncle rushed them to the bigger hospital in Montemorelos.

My mom sat alone in the waiting room desperate for news from the doctors. After the surgery, the doctor told my mother that the rod had punctured Héctor's throat in between his vocal cords and a major artery, stopping about two millimeters short of coming out the other side, which was the inside of his mouth. If the rod had grazed his vocal cords, the doctor said, it could have damaged his speech permanently. If it had ruptured that artery, he could have bled to death. If it had come out through his mouth, they would have had to send him to a specialized hospital in Monterrey. It was a miracle that none of those things happened, the surgeon said.

Héctor had a large piece of gauze covering the wound and the stitches, and he kept his left hand pressed against the gauze, where the bunched-up T-shirt had been, as if by instinct. Today, all that is left is an X-shaped scar where the rod entered.

At the time, I had no idea how close I had come to losing my brother or never hearing his voice again. Late that night, after Héctor was discharged and we were all finally home, my mother called my father in McAllen.

"Héctor fell from a roof," she exclaimed, with alarm in her voice. "We just got back from the hospital in Montemorelos," she added, as if to convey that everything had turned out okay.

"*¿De un segundo piso, de perdido?*" was my father's curt response. Was it at least from a second-story roof? That dry, dark humor, even

in these circumstances, was not surprising coming from my emotionally reticent father.

"*Si supieras*," was the only thing my mother could say, through
pursed lips. If you only knew.

Even though my brother and I wished we had our father around, at
least we had each other. We played together and passed the afternoons in each other's company. My mother, by contrast, had to raise
two boys by herself every week, figuring out how to make ends
meet, hoping for my father to visit on the weekend. Not once did I
hear her complain. But more than once I saw her open the fridge to
discover it mostly empty. She would ask Héctor and me if we could
share one Coke between the two of us that day, or skip today and
wait until tomorrow. I saw her expression when she returned with
Héctor from the hospital, and when my father joked about a second
floor. Not having my father around was hard for me, but over the
years I have come to understand that it was hardest for my mother.
We speak so much of the parents, mostly men, who head north to
the U.S. to work and send money home, but so little is said about the
women and children they leave behind.

When my father left, I did not know if he would eventually
move back to Allende, or if the plan was for us to join him later, or if
he was going to keep on traveling back and forth indefinitely. What
I did know was that he was absent from our breakfast table every
school day. One of those mornings, when we were considering join-
ing him in McAllen, Héctor and I sat at the table as our mother
made breakfast. The pan with the broken handle was on the stove,
piping hot with oil to fry a pair of eggs, the *comal* not yet hot enough
for tortillas. She was also heating water to make herself a cup of
coffee. The sun was out, but my mother kept our kitchen light on.

"You know," my mother remarked as she saw me yawn and rub my sleepy eyes with both hands. "Once we get to *el otro lado*, you are going to have to be at school by this time already."

The plan that was starting to take shape was for my mother, Héctor, and me to move to the U.S. My father would file what immigration lawyers call a "family petition" so that we could join him legally. My brother and I could attend the school where my father was a bus driver. That way, he would be around as Héctor and I settled into our new school and learned English. But the school where he had gotten a job was not in McAllen, it was in another town, and the school buses from that school did not travel all the way to McAllen. So Héctor and I would have to leave home with my father every morning to get to school. He had to be at work by 6:30 a.m., before the sun was out, at least in the winter months.

Rather than being discouraged, we were thrilled. The prospect of spending all that time with our father excited us. We did not care how early we had to wake up—we were going to be with him. I imagined bright lights and shiny billboards like I had seen in the movies, large McDonald's arches and glowing Walmart signs. I did not think about flat, dry south Texas in contrast to the evergreen mountains in Allende. I did not think of the dusty, arid Texas land, rather than the abundant greenery that surrounded me growing up. I was thinking only of the glow of bright lights that I could not see in my hometown, but that I imagined existed in McAllen. I smiled to myself as my mom handed us our breakfast plates.

As I had told Miss Aurora, my father came home that Friday night, with the trunk of his car mostly empty. It was a blue-gray Chrysler Fifth Avenue, a four-door sedan with blue fabric seats. You could tell the car had been fancy, even elegant at one point, but the passage of time had covered that elegance with dust and a cracked dashboard. It still had its original radio. After helping him unload the couple of grocery bags he brought, I showed him my progress report right away. He set the grocery bag on the kitchen table and looked at the report, zooming in on the column with the grades.

"Good, but you got two 9s," he said, noting that they weren't all 10s. He would like to see all 10s the next time, he added. I was happy he was happy, but mostly I was happy he was home. And I was going to try to get all 10s next time.

CHAPTER 3

No Limits

(May 29, 2018)

The Inter-American Commission on Human Rights' Executive Secretariat building hides quietly atop a Juan Valdez Café, on the corner of 19th and F Streets, Northwest. The red brick low-rise is less than five blocks away from the White House, in the heart of Washington, DC. It is not widely known in the United States, but in Latin America, *La Comisión* has a long, storied history of lifesaving interventions in defense of human rights. Perhaps best known among these is a visit to Argentina in 1979, during one of the cruelest years of the Argentinean military dictatorship that "disappeared" some thirty thousand people. The historic visit offered the outside world a glimpse of what was happening inside Argentina, a rare peek into the atrocities of the dictatorship. In retrospect, the Commission's visit was arguably the beginning of the downfall of one of the deadliest military juntas in Latin America.

Made up of seven individual commissioners, the Commission uses various tools to monitor compliance with human rights in North, Central, South America, and the Caribbean. The type of complaint we filed with the Commission against the United States

Government is known as "a request for precautionary measures," a procedure designed to address urgent situations, when someone's life or safety is in imminent danger, and there is no time for full-blown litigation, which can take years. Whether a government agrees to adopt such protective measures is a separate question. The United States, under both Democratic and Republican administrations, has generally had a patchy history of compliance.

Still, despite this uncertainty as to their enforceability in practice, precautionary measures seemed like a tool designed to address the family separations happening in McAllen: Viviana, Leonel, and the other parents did not know where their children were or whether they were safe, the government was not providing them any information, and every day the risk grew that they could be deported without their children, potentially orphaning their children forever. Asking the Inter-American Commission to get involved would also allow us at the Texas Civil Rights Project to shed light on the family separations in the context of international human rights law. The policy of prosecuting all unauthorized crossers under Zero Tolerance seemed lawful from the criminal law perspective. Most of these immigrants had committed a crime, albeit minor and victimless. From the immigration law perspective, these families may have violated the law by crossing the border without inspection. But from the human rights perspective, at a very basic, visceral level, what the federal government was doing—taking hundreds of children away from their parents, sending them to shelters all over the United States without any formal assessment as to the best interest of the child and with no apparent plan to reunite them—was a clear violation of the parents' and the children's human rights. In my mind at least, after hearing what the parents were telling me, the human rights perspective took precedence over the other two.

Five years had passed since I had interned at the Commission. Those days felt so distant the morning Georgina and I got back to the office from the court with our five declarations in hand. I called one of my contacts at the Commission to ask if it had ever granted precautionary measures to stop systematic family separations anywhere in the Americas. It never had, my friend said, but, she added, she was not aware of separations at the level I was describing ever happening anywhere else in the Western Hemisphere. During that conversation, it occurred to me that we should include as many separated families as we could interview in our request to the Commission, and then, even after submitting the request, we should supplement it daily with the names of additional separated parents. In my mind, doing this would show the Commission the magnitude of the separations, as well as the urgency of granting our request to stop them.

But during our second visit to the courthouse, the Tuesday after Memorial Day, that plan changed. Looking at the number of parents who raised their hands, we quickly realized that the five separated families we saw on that first visit had been an anomaly. Somehow we had gotten "lucky" with only five the first day. The daily number of separated families was much higher, with morning and afternoon shifts making it even worse: fifteen to twenty per shift was closer to the norm—out of the more than a hundred that were prosecuted each day. The way separated parents and other immigrants were being processed en masse at the Bentsen Tower reminded me of the dozens of *maquiladoras* across the border in the city of Reynosa. Conveyor belts run day and night at these manufacturing plants, assembling TV sets, seatbelts, and radiators, with workers coming in and out of shifts around the clock, because the work never stops.

Back at the office in Alamo later that day, a mere 15-minute drive away from the Bentsen Tower but a lifetime away from the separated parents, Georgina and I were getting ready to create a list to keep track of separated mothers, fathers, and children. As I put down my briefcase on the floor and the stack of papers on my desk, I looked at the intake forms from that second day. Page upon page upon page of names and dates of birth and countries of origin, scribbled by hand quickly, some names crossed out to correct a misspelling, to change an "i" to a "y," or a "z" to an "s." Gonzalo, Manuel, Máxima, Petronilo, Catarina, Otoniel, Dalia, Edis, Edwin, Héctor, Imer, Jacqueline, Jessica, Jorge, Juana, León, Lucas, Manuel de Jesús, Miriam, and Yasmin. Separated from Juana, Dani, Melani, Sel, María, Lisbeth, Belén, Edith, Wizton, Cristián, Carlos, Junior, Jeremías, Hayli, Marvin, Bryan, Josefina, Andrea, Erick, and Fabiola. Each of them a family, each of them a life story. And those were the families separated that day alone, in only one courthouse. Hundreds of other nameless immigrants had already been separated from their children in courts all along the border since the Department of Justice had announced Zero Tolerance in April. I didn't know where to start. The number of separated families had grown so quickly, the tragic stories multiplied, and we still did not know if we would see any of them ever again or, for that matter, where those children were and when they might see their parents again. "Here," I told Georgina. "You take these, and I'll take these." I handed her a stack of intakes and took the rest, pulled myself up to my computer, opened Google Sheets, and started to type.

As I was typing name after name, I decided that, contrary to what I had thought earlier, it would be counterproductive to include all the families we had interviewed in our request for precautionary measures. Including so many additional families in the request would surely delay a process that was already inherently slow. The Commission would need to look at the situation of each separated family, consider whether they were at imminent risk of irreparable harm, and then decide whether to ask the government to adopt measures to protect them. The process could take months. So, rather than supplementing with dozens of additional separations, we decided to go ahead with the five Georgina and I interviewed on our first day: Viviana, Antonio, Leonel, María, Dagoberto, and their children.

We formally filed the request on the last day of May. Via email, I started typing, "Dear Members of the Inter-American Commission on Human Rights, Please find attached an Emergency Request for Precautionary Measures on behalf of five parents and their children, who have been forcibly separated at the Texas-Mexico border by the United States of America." We asked the Commission to order the U.S. Government to reunite those five parents with their children—ensuring, in the meantime, that no parent or child was deported without the other—provide them with psychological support post-reunification, and end the family separation policy at once.

The following week, when we arrived at the courthouse early in the morning, the security officer on duty was more inquisitive than his predecessors had been. A heavyset man in his fifties, he wore the same gray pants all other security officers wore, and the same black bulletproof vest under the same navy-blue blazer. What floor are you headed to? With which judge? Do you have a hearing in one of your cases? What's the name of your client? "Court doesn't start until nine. The misdemeanor hearings are full, there is no room for the public, nowhere for anybody to sit," he insisted. I know they're full, that's why we're here, I thought, as he looked at my ID and peeked into my briefcase to make sure I didn't have any sharp objects. I explained that we were working with Azalea, the public defender—he quickly recognized the name—and that we were there to interview any separated families. I showed him my bar card, proof that I was in fact an attorney. Somewhat reluctantly, he placed my briefcase, my belt, and my shoes on the metal detector conveyor belt, and waved us through.

Once inside, we walked into the courtroom as one of the federal public defenders was giving a presentation to the crowd of over seventy defendants. I was less taken aback this time by the mass of people crowding the room. But I did notice a faint yet distinguishable smell of dozens of immigrants sitting wall-to-wall, wearing the same clothes they had been wearing for days—maybe weeks, since they left their home countries—the dirt on their clothes mixing in with the sweat on their tired bodies.

Wearing a gray suit, a perfectly ironed white shirt, and a solid navy-blue tie, the thirty-something public defender explained in fluent Spanish that the United States Government was charging them with crossing the border illegally. Most of them nodded. "The maximum penalty for that crime is up to six months in prison and a fine of up to two hundred fifty dollars," and faces of concern revealed themselves in the crowd. "But you can choose to plead guilty," he continued. *"Pueden declararse culpables*, and if this is your first-time crossing, the judge will likely sentence you to time served, which means that you don't get any jail time."

He didn't say this, but I knew what the immigration consequences of a guilty plea would be: if they pled guilty, they wouldn't receive any additional jail time, but they would likely be deported within a few days. "You have the right to choose to plead not guilty," he told them. "If you choose to plead not guilty, your case will not be decided today. You will have to spend some time in jail, probably about a month, and thirty days from today, you will be back here for your trial. The government will bring two witnesses," and the public defender paused, as if to emphasize the importance of who the witnesses would be. "One witness will be the Border Patrol agent who arrested you, and he will testify that he found you near the river, and that you did not have any documents showing you are allowed to be in the United States. The second witness will be another agent, and he will testify that he looked you up on a computer system, and he did not find your name on a database of U.S. citizens. With that, the government proves its case against you." The defendants shifted in their seats nervously, realizing the near futility of choosing anything other than a guilty plea. Their eyes shifted from one another to the suited attorney making the presentation, and then back to one another, as they seemed to ponder the choice before them, if it was a choice at all.

Moving his head left to right and up and down looking at the multiple rows of defendants, the public defender explained that he and his colleagues would call each person one by one, to discuss their cases individually and how they wanted to plea. He spoke clearly and not too fast, yet his presentation felt hurried, even rehearsed, considering what was at stake. I could tell he had given this presentation many times before. I could follow his every word and understood the process the defendants were facing, but I wondered if they did. Unlike them, I hadn't been traveling for weeks from Guatemala and Honduras; I hadn't crossed Mexico by foot, by bus, and hitchhiking; and I hadn't had my son taken away two days ago and had no idea where he was. The defender seemed satisfied that he had covered all the important points, and concluded by telling the immigrants about how important it was for them not to attempt to cross illegally again. If they did, then the crime would be much more serious, *una felonía*, and they could spend years in prison. Almost as an afterthought, the public defender told them that there was another lawyer who wanted to talk to anyone who was traveling with children. He then turned to me, nodded, and gestured for me to go ahead.

I took a couple of steps away from the wall where I had been standing and toward the center of the room. *"Buenos días,"* I said, trying to project my voice, and I got a classroom-like "good morning" response from everybody. "How many of you were traveling with your son or daughter and were separated from them?" Some tried to raise their hand, yanking at the handcuffs. Others stood up. My eyes quickly jumped around from person to person, and I counted fourteen.

Patricia was one of the first parents who came forward. I stood by the windows, and called her over, watching her as she slowly made her way from the other side of the room, still trying to learn how to walk around shackled. When we spoke, she explained to me that the father of her son was not really in the picture. "He's not... he's never really been...."

I understand, I told her. She wore a worn-out blue-gray T-shirt that was at least one size too small for her, and she pulled down on its hem several times during our conversation. Her wavy shoulder-length hair was dyed blond, the darker roots of her natural hair starting to show. Patricia said she had left Honduras because she and her son were threatened by gangs in the small town of El Encanto— The Enchantment—near the border with Guatemala. The irony of the town's name was not lost on me.

I recalled that a couple of months earlier, then–U.S. Attorney General Jeff Sessions had referred to his office a case known as "Matter of A-B-." Under a quirky immigration law procedure whereby the Attorney General can unilaterally overrule decisions issued by immigration judges by "referring to his office" certain cases, Sessions wanted to make it harder for claims like Patricia's to succeed: on the one hand by taking their children away under the guise of criminal prosecutions and Zero Tolerance, on the other by curtailing their avenues to obtain asylum. "Generally," he would eventually write, claims "pertaining to domestic violence or gang violence per-petrated by nongovernmental actors will not qualify for asylum." I knew the issue was still being litigated. There was no point in shar-ing any of this with Patricia.

"Honduras" means "depths" in Spanish, in the literal, physical sense, as well as in the figurative sense, as in the depths of despair. Starting in the mid-twentieth century, Honduras was governed by a series of military leaders, until civilian rule returned in the 1980s. In 1998, Hurricane Mitch devastated much of the country, killing thousands, and destroying some 70 percent of its agricultural crops and nearly 80 percent of its transportation infrastructure, including many bridges and roads. This led to the U.S. Government issuing Temporary Protected Status, TPS, for Hondurans, a temporary visa for those affected by the humanitarian catastrophe. In 2009, when a military coup d'état removed democratically elected President José Manuel Zelaya, the Obama Administration supported the military takeover, continuing a long-running history of U.S.-backed desta-bilizations in the region in the name of protecting U.S. "business interests." Those interests have ranged from the United Fruit Com-pany in the twentieth century, to securing access to inexpensive palm oil and other natural resources in the twenty-first.

By 2014, Honduras had the highest murder rate in the world, according to the United Nations Office on Drugs and Crime. It has since been surpassed by its neighbor, El Salvador, which held that unenviable honor in 2019. Today, over one million Honduran nation-als are estimated to live in the United States, equal to more than 10 percent of that country's domestic population, which is quickly approaching ten million. For years, Honduras has been ravaged by violent gangs known as *maras* and the government's unwillingness or inability to address the problem. Experts have shown that the rise in gang-related violence can be traced back to the deportation of prison gang members from the United States to Central America in the 1990s, which contributed to the criminal organizations becoming transnational, more resourceful, and more sophisticated. Members of gangs that had never had a presence outside of the United States were exported en masse, giving those gangs unprecedented international reach. The *Mara Salvatrucha*, more commonly known simply as MS-13, is perhaps the best known among these gangs. It originated in Los Angeles in the 1980s with an aim to protect Salvadoran immigrants from the other more established gangs. After the end of the Salvadoran Civil War in 1992, the U.S. Government deported members of that gang to El Salvador, giving MS-13 its first international foothold and enabling it to expand from there to Honduras and beyond.

"If you give me your information and the information of your son," I told Patricia, "we can try to find him, and maybe even coordinate a phone call between you and him." This was the first time she ever came to the United States, she said. Her son Alessandro was not yet seven years old; she had had him at nineteen. At the suggestion of one of my colleagues, we had started asking the parents whether their children had a disability or suffered from any medical condition, so that we could request that any needed medical assistance be provided. This information could also help us identify particularly compelling cases, and it could even lead to additional legal claims under disability laws.

"Does Alessandro have any medical issues, was he sick?" I asked Patricia.

She hesitated a little. "*Él...él no está bien...*" she said, without immediately giving me any more details. He was not well. "He has been on the Telethon for several years now," she added, and I realized that he probably had medical needs. I had become familiar with the end-of-the-year *Teletón* drives for children with disabilities and medical needs, watching them on TV in Allende, on the Televisa network, during the long days off from school during Christmas break.

"*¿Qué tiene?*" What is it? I asked.

"He has something in his brain; he swallowed fluid when he was born."

I knew from my wife, Karla, an occupational therapist, that if the flow of oxygen to a baby's brain is blocked during birth, or even in utero—whether because of fluid or otherwise—it can lead to brain damage. The longer the baby's brain is deprived of oxygen, the more severe the long-term consequences.

"How affected is he?" I asked, and felt awkward even asking the question. "Can he speak? Can he walk?" My feet flexed inside my shoes and squished the soft carpet as I shifted around in my uneasiness.

"*Más o menos*," she said. "Yes, he can speak, he can walk. I take him to see a therapist," and she allowed herself a faint smile.

If government agents were willing to take a six-year-old boy with such medical needs away from his mother, then I could think of no limit to the cruelty. If this was not a case in which they would make an exception to the Zero Tolerance policy, then all bets were off. I double-checked Alessandro's date of birth, triple-checked that it was spelled with two s's and not one, and then told Patricia that we would try our best to find out what shelter he was at and that he was taken care of. I gave her my business card, and told her to call me if she was allowed a phone call or if she was released. She thanked me as she turned around and started to walk, adjusting her handcuffs and struggling to walk as she made her way back to her seat.

The next day, in the afternoon, I came back to the Bentsen Tower. Standing outside, on the corner of 17th and Austin streets, I waited as the reporter set up the camera. Renée Feltz, with *Democracy Now!*, had traveled from New York City to McAllen to cover the separations. She was the first reporter who reached out to us about the brewing crisis, and we saw this as an opportunity to break the story to a wider audience, which was not yet aware of what we were seeing and hearing in court every day. Renée adjusted her thick glasses as she handed me the mic, and continued to run through the types of questions she was going to ask me. I wore a white linen, long-sleeve shirt, and rolled up my sleeves to try to ameliorate the heat, unsuccessfully.

"Try to set the scene," Renée said. "Tell viewers where we are, what is behind you, what happens inside of that building, things like that," she said. "There, that's good, I got that white bus in the frame." The white bus was a GEO Group bus, parked right behind the Bentsen Tower. It was the bus that had driven the immigrants to court that day and was now waiting to take them back to the Border Patrol station. There, at the station that they had come to know as *la hielera*—the icebox—the separated parents would realize that their children were gone, and not waiting for them to return from court as some agents had led them to believe.

I had seen these buses around town before, not really thinking much of them. They would drive up and down Ware Road and Old 83 at various times of the day, even on weekends, probably to and from different Border Patrol stations. Whether I was trailing behind them, driving past them in opposite directions, or met them at a stop light, their pitch-black tinted windows always prevented me from discerning whether there were any passengers. I, and all the other drivers and passersby, could not really tell whether there were immigrants, fathers and mothers, brothers and sisters, riding inside. Those inside, in contrast, could surely see the outside. They could see life in McAllen unfold as they drove past it, unseen, unheard. They did not know this place, but they could see it and wonder. They could see the golf course on Ware Road, and maybe even a few people playing on grass that inevitably turns yellow-green every summer, no matter how much it is watered. They could see Brown Middle School, and be puzzled by the angry Doberman painted on a large marquee outside, the school's mascot. They could get a glimpse of West Side Park and its empty baseball fields, and the Convention Center with its busy restaurants, coffee shops, and retail stores. They probably couldn't hear the sounds of bustling life, but they could see it all. They could see the place they had hoped to get to—it was right there, right in front of them, yet so far from their reality.

Patricia's words were still fresh in my mind when the camera started rolling. "We're in downtown McAllen," I began, "about seven miles from the Mexico border, right next to the federal courthouse. This is the McAllen Division of the Southern District of Texas." For a few days at this point, news had started to trickle around that families were being separated at the border, but there had been no specific report about the magnitude of the phenomenon in McAllen.

I held the mic firmly and close to my mouth, as the reporter had instructed. Before I could say much more, a shallow rhythmic beep behind me caught my ear. I recognized what it was before I could see it, as the beeping intensified. The reporter adjusted the camera to my right, to try to catch the GEO Group bus as it backed up away from the courthouse and toward us. I thought we may have to wait for the beeping to stop and re-start the interview, but the reporter gestured to me that she was trying to catch it on camera, and that I should explain what was happening. "These are the buses in which the immigrants, many of whom are parents who have had their children taken away, are transported to and from the courthouse, probably to a Customs and Border Protection (CBP) detention facility.

The sad thing is that many of those people have children, and many of them were separated this morning, before they came to court, and were led to believe that when they return to the detention facility, their children are going to be there. But we know that the children will not be there, because the government is separating them." Even from up close, the window tint was so dark that I could not tell whether there was anyone looking out at us or not. If there was, what would they think? Why was there a camera on a tripod and a guy in a white shirt, sweating profusely, speaking into a microphone in the middle of the afternoon and gesturing at the bus?

"So, the Border Patrol agents will arrest them out in the brush near the river, say, and then they are driven to the processing station," I continued, looking straight at the reporter and not at the camera, as she had instructed. "And right there and then, they have their photograph taken and their fingerprints, and they are processed. At that point, some of them are separated, and the children are processed separately from the parents." I was trying to explain the process as simply as possible, omitting details for the sake of conveying a clear picture of how the separations were happening in practice. I omitted that these immigrants were processed under what is called "expedited removal," and that most would not get to see an immigration judge before being deported. I omitted that neither parents or children were afforded the right to an attorney in their immigration case unless they could pay for it. I omitted that the children were sent to a shelter for unaccompanied children and that they could remain there a long time, especially if they did not have relatives in the United States.

At the same time, I also wanted to convey the sentiment that parents were conveying to us every morning. I wiped the sweat off my forehead with my sleeve. "I've heard from parents directly that they were separated, and the child was in one cell, and the parent was in another cell. But the child was crying so much because they were not with their mom, that they were brought to the mom in the middle of the night for a little while, so that they would stop crying, and then separated again. That's the kind of cruelty that we're seeing from this government."

After hearing the stories of Viviana, Leonel, Antonio, Patricia, and others—and having to repeat them to reporters and colleagues—the last thing I wanted to do was bring them home to the dinner table too. But Karla could not stay isolated, unaware of what was happening, particularly as the news coverage and social media posts ramped up. "I'm going to call CPS," she told me one evening, referring to Child Protective Services. As a health-care worker, she told me, as I washed dishes and she tidied up the dinner table, she had a duty to report any child abuse she became aware of, especially since she worked in pediatrics.

It turns out she was not the only one with a legal duty to report known or suspected child abuse. The Texas Family Code requires any person who has reason to believe that a child's physical or mental health or welfare has been adversely affected by abuse or neglect to report it immediately. The law defines abuse to include "mental or emotional injury to a child that results in an observable and material impairment in the child's growth, development, or psychological functioning." It was hard to argue that what we were seeing and hearing from parents in McAllen did not meet the definition. Under the Family Code, licensed health-care and other professionals have an obligation to report the abuse within forty-eight hours of becoming aware of it, and failure to report it is a crime punishable by up to a year in jail.

"I'm calling to report child abuse," Karla said into the phone, pushing her short black hair over her ear. We had already put Julián to bed, and she stood in our living room to make the call, as far away from him as possible so as to not wake him with the upset sound of her voice. Julián slept on a small mattress on the floor in our bedroom, right next to our bed. Every night, he would sleep on it for a couple of hours, and then invariably wake up asking to be taken onto the bed, to sleep the rest of the night securely between Karla and me.

It was after business hours when Karla made the call, but the child abuse hotline is operated twenty-four hours a day. Struggling to keep her voice from breaking, she explained to the CPS representative that she did not know where the children were, or their names, or how many of them were being abused, but that they had been taken away from their parents, and given her training, she knew that they were suffering mentally and emotionally as a result, maybe physically too. The perpetrators were the Border Patrol agents and other federal employees who separated the children from their parents, but she did not know their names either. She then listened to the man on the other end of the line for a while, and I could hear her mhms, ahas, and okays, impatient and frustrated.

"Ok, bye," and she hung up, frustration in her voice.

A lot of people had been calling about this, the man told Karla. But there was simply nothing the Texas Department of Family and Protective Services could do, because the children were in the custody of the federal government.

The Family Code did not contemplate that the government could be the one committing the abuse.

CHAPTER 4

Interdiction

(1978)

My father's early start in truck driving coincided with his start in family life. In one of his many trips down to the state of Veracruz, along the coast of the Gulf of Mexico, he met the woman who would become the mother of three of his five children. They never formally married, but they had three children and lived together on and off for at least ten years, until 1978.

That year, in the middle of a humid night in early May, a grandmother awoke a nine-year-old boy and his two little sisters in the town of Poza Rica. In the 1960s and '70s, Poza Rica was a booming town in Veracruz whose economy was fueled by heavy investment in Pemex, the Mexican national oil company. The town's name translates literally as "rich well," as in an oil well. Today, the oil boom has passed, but Poza Rica still celebrates Petroleum Day every year on March 18th to commemorate the nationalization of the hydrocarbon industry by the Mexican Government in 1938.

That night in May, forty years after oil became a national patrimony, the grandmother dressed the three siblings as quietly as she could, and hurried them outside. Their mother was not home.

Outside, three men they knew well were already waiting for them in two straight trucks. The trucks' loud engines, running idly, were the only thing that may have wakened the neighbors. The men loaded the children and the grandmother onto one of the trucks, and took off. No one commented on the fact that the children did not even bring any bags with them.

Less than an hour later, the children dozed off in the truck's crammed sleeper cabin. The youngest one, only three years old, was the first one sound asleep in her grandmother's arms, peacefully unaware that this truck ride would change her life forever. By the time they woke up, they were entering the neighboring state of Tamaulipas, to the north, atop a floating ferry that took them across the Pánuco River, bringing them ever closer to their new lives. Some eleven hours after they had furtively left their home in Poza Rica, Tío Oscar drove them to their new home in Allende. After the turmoil of the events of the previous night, he forgot to wish the boy a happy birthday.

These were my father's children. At that time, my sisters were three and seven years old, and my brother was nine, only hours shy of his tenth birthday. Their maternal grandmother had offered to help my father bring them to live with him in the northern state of Nuevo León, after he and their mother separated. Over the next few days and weeks, they met their new family. They had met Tío Oscar, but there were nine other aunts and uncles to discover, a pair of paternal grandparents, and scores of cousins, second cousins, and other extended relatives. This was their new family, a family whose existence they had been unaware of their entire life, and which was thrust upon them literally overnight. Their mother and their life as they knew it had remained in Poza Rica.

That same month, a lawyer helped my father file custody papers in Nuevo León. Years later I learned that he filed what is known as an "interdiction proceeding," a process generally designed to obtain custody of incapacitated or legally incompetent adults. I never found out how my father's lawyer was able to file such a proceeding for my siblings, who were all children at the time. Interdiction proceedings can be resolved in as little as six months, if there is no opposition. Against all odds, my siblings' mother showed up to the first hearing, traveling all the way from Veracruz, and opposed the case. But when the second hearing rolled around, she did not make the trip again. Perhaps she couldn't travel the more than a thousand kilometers a second time. Perhaps she never even received notice of the hearing. She lost the case, and my father officially became a single father with full custody of his three children.

The lawyer who helped my father obtain custody of his children was at our house a few times over the years. I never knew how they met, but Orta—as my father called him, referring to him only by his last name—visited occasionally to discuss things I couldn't understand. During one of those visits before my father had moved to McAllen, they sat in the living room. Orta wore gray dressy pants, a white guayabera, and shiny moccasins, as always, and they were drinking coffee, as always. His voice was raspy and high pitched, scratchy like that of somebody who has drunk hard liquor all his life. I sat on my knees on the imitation green velvet sofa by the living room window and tried to follow their conversation. It was the same sofa I had once sleepwalked to in the middle of the night, frightening my mother when she went to check on me the next morning and I wasn't on my bed.

Orta and my father were deliberating something I couldn't follow no matter how hard I tried. I was a good student in school, but the words Orta reeled off one after the other were beyond me. Every other word was something I had never heard before and didn't know the meaning to. *Albacea*, executor, *poder notarial*, durable power of attorney, *momento procesal oportuno*, procedurally appropriate time. I wanted to understand these words and phrases, but I didn't ask. I didn't dare interrupt their conversation. That was the very first time the thought crossed my mind: I wanted to be a lawyer. I would understand all these big words, and people would call me *licenciado* too. My motivation for becoming an attorney evolved over the years, but the aspiration stayed with me ever since.

Unbeknownst to me, the first lawyer I ever met, and who seeded in me the idea of going to law school, had been instrumental in helping my father gain custody of his children, separating them from their mother in the process. A separation of another kind, from another time, but a painful life-changing separation nonetheless.

As far back as I can remember, age three or four, my older siblings were part of our family, splitting time between our house and our paternal grandparents' house, who lived ten minutes away. Leoba, short for Leobardo—being the eldest, he shared my father's first and middle names, Julio Leobardo—Silvia, and Tania were always present, if not always around. I knew they were my siblings, but at first I didn't fully understand why they would call my mother by her first name, Idalia, and not *Mami* like Héctor and I did. I don't remember anyone ever explaining to me that they had a different mother. I also did not understand why they addressed my father using *"usted,"* the formal second-person pronoun in Spanish, whereas Héctor and I used *"tú,"* the informal, more intimate alternative. Still, to my child's mind, they were and had always been part of our family, just like Héctor, and all my cousins, aunts, and uncles.

One of my earliest memories is with my sister Silvia. I must have been four years old, and she, being twelve years my senior, would have been sixteen or so. We were in the part of the house that doubled up as laundry and storage room, an attachment to the back of our house, built at an indeterminate time and never finished. The cinderblocks were still fully exposed, and the metal door had lost one of its hinges and most of its paint. If dryers existed at the time, I did not know it. Like in every other house in the neighborhood, there was a clothesline in our backyard. We did have a washer, a noisy, white Easy-brand machine, with two open bucket-like compartments, the bigger one to wash and the smaller one to rinse the clothes. There was also a washing sink, with a rigged bottom surface where my mother would scrub the dirt and grease that the washing machine did not fully remove. My father's shovel, garden pickax, and his other rusty tools lay around the room.

Silvia brought out a small chalkboard for me. It must have been two feet by two feet, green with yellow wooden trim around the edges and a wobbly tripod for legs. I remember my sister as very tall, wearing her curly, deep black hair in a small pigtail with a colorful tie holding it together. She set the chalkboard in front of me and started marking on it with a piece of chalk.

"*Te voy a escribir el abecedario,*" she told me, "*para que te lo aprendas.*"

She wrote the alphabet on the chalkboard in all caps, so that I could memorize it. She read it a few times with me, and eventually left me in the dark humid room to practice by myself. I never attended preschool and had not yet started kindergarten at this point, so this was the first time I was seeing all of these symbols laid out like this, line after line across the toy chalkboard. I noticed the L and LL, as well as the R and RR, the only letters that had single and double versions—I did not make the same association between U or V and W. The M-N-Ñ trio also created a sequence that was easy to remember. I did not question why I should memorize them, but instead tried to say every letter as best as I could as I sat in that room by myself. Every time I struggled to remember how to say one of them, I would go fetch Silvia, who had retreated to the room she shared with Leoba and Tania.

"What's after C?" I asked, stumbling upon the CH.

"That's *CHE*," she said, with a mixture of annoyance and compassion, "as in chocolate."

I could not yet roll the R, much less the double RR, and I struggled with a few others. Sitting on a flimsy wooden crate in front of the chalkboard, I would say four or five letters out loud, add another one silently in my head, and then try all of them again out loud. Even though no one was around to hear me, I would first try to imagine the sound of the letter in my head, and only once I felt comfortable that it was right would I say it out loud, as if addressing the chalkboard.

I don't know how long I was in the laundry room looking over the alphabet—it may have been hours—but I eventually went looking for Silvia again. She was in her room, writing something in a spiral bound notebook, her pop music playing on a cassette player. She seemed annoyed at yet another interruption.

"*Ya me lo aprendí*," I said, excited, with a proud smile. "*Y también al revés.*"

She looked up, her annoyance turning to surprise first and skepticism second. I had memorized the alphabet, forward and backward. I was hopeful she would be pleased.

"*A ver*," she prodded me, putting down her pencil. Let's hear it.

Slowly and hesitantly, I recited one by one all thirty letters in the Spanish alphabet she had written. Then I did it backward, struggling and pausing a few times, but I made it all the way back to the letter A. Silvia seemed impressed, and she quickly realized that she would have to figure out, again, what else to do with me.

I never knew what prompted me to memorize the alphabet this way. Over the next few weeks and months, I was asked to perform my newfound talent and recite the alphabet backward to relatives, neighbors, and anybody who would listen. It became easier every time, and I enjoyed the unexpected celebrity status in the neighborhood for a few months. With time, this anecdote has become a silly and nostalgic childhood story in my family that makes us smile every time we remember. By the time I entered kindergarten, I could read a few simple words, and I've always been grateful to my sister for giving me a head start in school.

Having always seen my older siblings as part of my family from the start, it was shocking for me to discover, many years later, as an adult and long after my father had died, that they had never met any of their paternal relatives before they were brought to Allende. My father and their maternal grandmother had arranged to have them taken under cover of night. A kidnapping of his own children, some might say. Their grandmother was not only in on it too, but she was also a key participant to make the plan work; she, like my father, must have thought it best for them.

All this pushed me to see my father in a different, more complicated light many years after his death. I saw him not so much as my father, but as a man, a father in his midthirties, struggling to decide the best future for his three children.

My older siblings have often described my father as absent from the early years of their lives, both physically and emotionally. His physical absence for days at a time must have added distance to his natural resistance to show affection. Even after they moved to Allende, they spent more time with our paternal grandmother, Güelita Laya, than with him.

Güelita Laya and Güelito Julián lived in Loma Prieta, a three-street community with a few dozen homes just outside Allende. If "one stop light" describes a small town, Loma Prieta had none. Its name translates literally as "dark hill," as the community sits on small bluff on the banks of the Ramos River, but I never understood the "dark" part of its name; I associated the place more with abundant greenery and afternoon river swims than with anything dark. A handful of the homes were made of cinderblock, but most, including my grandparents', were made of adobe, and many were simply wooden shacks with flimsy tin roofs. My father was born and raised in Loma Prieta, and as far as I knew, my grandparents had also lived there their entire lives, other than their seasonal sojourns into the United States as farmworkers.

Their house was always cool and humid, due to—I learned years later—the adobe walls and the low ceilings. My grandmother's bedroom, located next to the kitchen near the back of the house, had poor lighting and a faint but ever-present smell of rubbing alcohol and Vick's VapoRub, from her constant application of the ointment to her joints to alleviate her pain. To this day, the smell of Vick's and rubbing alcohol never fails to take me back to Loma Prieta and my grandmother. My older siblings spent most of their childhood in that house, and my grandmother, more than any other adult in their lives, was responsible for raising them. Between work and marrying my mother in 1981, my father was not as meaningfully present in their lives as they would have wished. As much as it pains me to accept it, the reality is that he wasn't always there for them, not when they needed him most.

That was not my experience with my father. He was never emotionally expressive, and words of affection were not his style, but I still felt that if I needed help, he would be there for me. In 1991, before he left for McAllen, I needed help. I was in fourth grade, and came home one afternoon with news for my mother.

"I want to change schools," I declared, without any context, sitting at our round kitchen table.

My mother stopped tending to what she had on the stove and turned to face me. *"¿Pero por qué?"*

I hadn't thought this through. I had thought that if I asked my parents to change schools, they would simply help me make that happen. I didn't think I would have to explain the reasons.

"Just because," I said, unconvincingly.

"No, tell me why," my mother insisted, concerned. "Tell me why you want to change schools. What's wrong with *Veteranos*? You don't like your teachers anymore?"

No, the teachers were fine, I said. The school was fine. The classes were fine. The problem was Jerry. He simply would not leave me alone. I had tried ignoring his taunts, his name-calling, his pushing and shoving, and he would still keep doing it. I was used to the name-calling. *"Efren-o el freno,"* he would call me in the mornings and at recess, but he was hardly original in his attempt. Other kids had called me that at different times throughout elementary school, the moniker coming from a combination of my relatively uncommon first name and its alliteration with *freno*, the Spanish word for brake. It was annoying, but it was nothing new and didn't bother me to the point of wanting to change schools. He would also call me *"güero"* or *"güerito"*—loosely translated as blondie or fair-skinned in some parts of Mexico—or *"güerinche,"* a more pejorative variation. Maybe it was my green eyes that made me his target? But Jerry was fair-skinned himself, so this name-calling did not make much sense to me.

The real problem was the pushing and the shoving. Jerry's real name was Gerardo, but he went by Jerry, naturally with a Spanish pronunciation, Yerri. He would often pull the girls' long hair, especially if it was braided. He would push me around nearly every time we were in close proximity. On the day I came home to my mom determined to change schools, his harassment had become too much for me to bear. The fourth-grade classroom was on the second floor of the school, so at the end of the day, we would all file out in two rows, boys on the right side and girls on the left, down a long hallway and then down a flight of stairs. Yerri was right behind me, and as we approached the stairs, he kept pushing me, egging me to walk faster.

As we approached the end of the hallway and made a right turn into the steps, I was afraid that if he pushed me again, I would fall down the stairs. To avoid that, I took a few quick steps to get farther out in front of him, lower down the stairs, so that he could no longer push me. And it half worked: I was out of reach for him to push me, but since I was three or four steps lower than him, my backpack was at a perfect height for him to reach it with his feet. He could no longer push me, so he started kicking my backpack instead. The girls on the row to our left started laughing and giggling as I lost balance with each kick. After a particularly hard kick, I stumbled down and one of my knees hit the concrete steps. I barely held on to the cement railing with my right hand before I fell, my heart pounding with fear at the possibility of tumbling down who knows how many steps. I knew more kicks were coming, so I kept my hand close to the railing to stabilize myself and fend off the barrage of blows. He saw me do that and started laughing. "He's afraid to fall, he's afraid to fall," he taunted and kept on kicking my backpack, the strength of the kicks increasing each time I tried to hold on to the railing.

When I finally made it to the end of the stairs and was safely on firm ground, I knew I needed to change schools. It was the only solution to my predicament. If I went to another school, Yerri wouldn't be there to bother me or kick my backpack. I saw no other way out.

"Who are his parents?" my mother asked in our kitchen.

I had no idea.

"No, no, you won't change schools. I will talk to your father, and he will sort this out," she said, worried, but trying to project confidence.

I was not privy to the conversation between my mother and my father, but a few days later, my father drove me to school. We parked across the street from the school's entrance, and I followed him out of the car. He stood by the front of the car, rested the back side of his legs against the front end of the hood, and crossed his arms.

"Tell me when you see this kid Yerri," he said calmly.

We stood there for a few minutes as more and more children exited their cars and headed into the school. I did not know what car would bring Yerri, so I looked at all of them, concerned that I might miss him. Eventually, Yerri descended from a small white car, which promptly drove away. That's him, I said, pointing at Yerri as he loitered on the sidewalk outside the school while other students walked past him and went in. He didn't seem too rushed to go in, and that gave my father time to approach him.

"I am Efrén's father," my father said, introducing himself and getting to the point. "He tells me you've been bothering him."

Yerri denied it all. He had never called me names, he had never pushed me, he had not kicked me as we walked down the stairs the week before. He denied everything right there in front of me. But my father was not swayed. He looked at me, and I shook my head, indicating that what he was saying was not true.

"I need you to stop bothering him," my father said, sternly. I stood there, uncomfortably but unthreatened since my father was there. I feared what might happen later that day, once he left. "You are going to stop bothering him. If you don't, I'm going to talk to your father."

That last sentence seemed to send a lightning bolt through Yerri's body. He stood straighter and his face hardened. He put his hands in his pockets. "No, no, don't do that," he said. "Please don't do that."

My father walked back to the car, and Yerri and I walked into the school. We had not been in such close proximity without him shoving me that entire school year.

I expected the taunting and mocking to continue, fearing that it would intensify. I held on to the stairs' railing as we walked down that day, bracing for yet meaner kicks, but they never came. It had worked. Yerri and I never became good friends, but he stopped bothering me after that morning.

Every decision I saw my father make was for the best for his family, looking out for the best interest of his children: from moving to McAllen by himself, to arranging for my mother, Héctor, and me to join him years later. At Leoba's request, he had also helped him move to the States a few years earlier, and he eventually did the same for Tania and Silvia too. From my perspective at that age, my father, despite his lack of emotional expressiveness, was there when his children asked for his help. I grew up with the romanticized idea that all parents, and fathers in particular, always do what is best for their children, always make the "right" choices for them.

But my father's decision to take my siblings from their mother— years before I was born—forced me to question that understanding. Perhaps it had to do with the fact that my father was older and more mature when Héctor and I were born. It was the same man who fathered us all, but sometimes I feel as if he was a different father to my older siblings that he was to Héctor and me. This feeling and this realization, as difficult as they were, also redefined my view of parenting in general, and of fatherhood in particular. No parent is perfect, even if they may seem so in the eyes of their children. At the same time, only the men and women making decisions for their children know what leads to those decisions, as hard as they may seem. Whether it is taking his children in the middle of the night and moving them to another state, or taking them across an international border, only that father knows what pushed him to make that decision.

After my father moved to McAllen in 1992, he was no longer part of our daily lives in the physical sense, but the idea of my father never ceased to be present. When my mother pushed Héctor and me to be good students, to do our homework, to behave, and to try our best at school, the reason she gave us was so that we would have good news to tell our father. We should have good grades to show him, she would say, so that he could be proud of us. My mother drilled that motivation into me so effectively that it became my primary driver during my last years of elementary school.

One day toward the end of sixth grade, Miss Bertha gave us a test. It was, she told us, an assessment to select the "best student" in sixth grade. Elementary school in Mexico runs through sixth grade, and this was part of a process to select the top student in the school, who would then compete against students from other schools in town, and then some would advance to a state-wide academic competition.

"*Jóvenes*," Miss Bertha said in her usual, stern voice, "*les deseo suerte.*"

I wish you luck, she said, using the collective "*jóvenes*" to refer to us, a word that translates as "youngsters" and is often used to refer to teenagers or young adults, and to children when the speaker does not want to call them "children." We were all eleven or twelve years old, most definitely still children, but she must not have wanted to call us that, perhaps attempting to signal the seriousness of the test we were about to take.

Like every other test, I took this one seriously. I sat up in my chair as Miss Bertha handed out the test, face down, so that we would all start at the same time once she had distributed the test to everyone. The assessment consisted of multiple-choice math problems, fill-in-the-blank spelling and grammar, a few natural sciences questions, and civics questions, mostly about Mexican history. I submitted the test, and forgot about it.

About a week later, Miss Bertha made a solemn announcement: *"Jóvenes, tenemos un empate."* There had been a tie.

Jesica and I had answered the same number of questions correctly, and we would need to take yet another test to break the tie. Jesica had been one of the first students to transfer into our school from *El Colegio,* the private school, when the teachers' union initially went on strike. I remember her as refined, her navy-blue uniform shirt always perfectly ironed, her white skirt equally immaculate. Her light brown hair was usually brushed and neatly tied into a short ponytail. She was almost intimidating to me, so well put together.

Miss Bertha walked Jesica and me to the principal's office to take the tie-breaking test that same day. His desk had a glass top, which made it seem expensive, and a golden lamp lit up his workspace. He was new to the school, having come from out of town to replace the previous, longtime, and popular local principal. The office's peach-colored drapes were drawn shut, which kept most of the sunlight out and, along with the faux wooden walls, gave the room a dark and cool, cave-like feeling. Unlike the school's classrooms, the principal's office was air-conditioned and always kept a few degrees too cold.

After we greeted the principal, Miss Bertha walked Jesica and me into an adjacent room and directed us to sit in each of the pupil's desks that had been set up on opposite sides of the room, and handed us the tie-breaking test.

"There are sixty questions," Miss Bertha said. We could take all the time we needed, but we had to be sure to answer every question. She sat near the end of the room and told us to start.

This test had more math problems, and they weren't multiple-choice. I could tell from the very first few that it was more difficult. I glanced up at Jesica, but she was already face down reading problems, pencil in hand, fully focused. I felt I was already falling behind.

After a long while, Jesica and I handed in our answers, and Miss Bertha told us we could go back to our classrooms. Later that day, we would be called back to the principal's office to hear the results.

"*Antes que nada*," the principal told us in a gruff baritone voice, "*los quiero felicitar a ambos*." I want to congratulate you both, he said. "You both have done an outstanding job, but we can only send one of you to the municipal competition." After some more canned pleasantries, he told us one of us had answered fifty-seven problems correctly, the other, fifty-five. Both were outstanding scores, he continued, and we should be very proud. Our parents should be proud. The difference between the two scores was really nothing, he said, and neither of us should feel bad.

The pleasantries continued for what felt like ten minutes until he finally handed us our graded tests. I looked down at mine. At the top right corner, encircled in red ink, I saw the score: 57.

I must have cracked a smile, but I don't remember saying anything.

Again, Jesica and I were told we could return to our respective classrooms. We walked out of the office, Jesica first, and I was relieved at the warm breeze outside. When we were barely out in the hallway, once the office door was shut, Jesica turned around and faced me. It felt as if she had waited for us to be outside of the adults' earshot and eyesight. I stood there for a second, not knowing what to say.

She smiled at me, and in her sweet, kind voice, simply said, *"Feli-cidades, Efrén."*

I was so surprised by her graciousness. I must have said *"gracias"* at some point before walking back to the classroom, but I did so instinctively, like an automated response. Her simple congratulations was much more sincere and authentic than the principal's belabored diatribe. Her smile seemed to say it's okay, I'm okay, I'm happy for you. I was unprepared for Jesica's kindhearted response. Ever since that moment, Jesica's kindness and selflessness have stayed with me.

A few weeks later, I finished elementary school.

In the weeks leading up to the graduation, I worried constantly about whether my father would be able to attend. I never asked, of course—I had been taught not to be so imprudent—but I wondered every day whether he would be there to see me receive my certificate. My worry was not really whether he would make a special trip to attend the graduation because I didn't allow myself that possibility. Rather, I anguished hoping the graduation would fall on a Friday when he was already scheduled to visit us. Many mornings in school I stared longingly at the calendar hanging from our classroom wall, counting the Fridays that were left before graduation, doing my best to calculate, trying to see how things were looking, but since his visits were not always regular, I couldn't be sure.

If my mother asked him to come, I never heard that conversation. If he made a special, unscheduled trip, I never found out. But to my great relief, my father traveled home the Friday of my graduation. He had missed both the school field trip the week before and the Mass earlier that afternoon, but he made it to the ceremony in the evening, and he saw me receive my certificate. And to me, that was what really mattered.

CHAPTER 5

Father's Day

(June 17, 2018)

A s incredulous as I was when I first received that phone call from Azalea in May 2018, that was not the first time that the United States had had a systemic policy of separating families. As the days passed, I wondered how the Zero Tolerance policy of the Trump Administration stacked up against the historical record. If we look at the summer of 2018 in the longer arc of the history of immigration law and policy in this country, what kind of picture emerges?

Many argue that the advent of widespread family detention during the Obama Administration set the stage to push the policy one step further into separations. But instances of inhumane treatment of immigrant families can be traced much farther back. In its early days, in 1790, Congress limited naturalization to white people: "any Alien being a free white person, who shall have resided within the limits and under the jurisdiction of the United States for the term of two years, may be admitted to become a citizen." In the decades that followed, immigration into the country was largely unregulated in a formal sense, but this provision meant that Native Americans, free

Blacks, Asian immigrants, and any other non-white person could not aspire to the rights that citizenship conferred.

When Black Americans were bought and sold as chattel, family separations were ordinary—expected, one might say. White slave owners sold thousands of Black children of slaves in their plantations to the highest bidder; "field slaves" were segregated from "house slaves" without any regard to family relationships; children saw their fathers murdered by their masters or a slave patroller, their mothers sexually exploited. Escape also resulted in family separations, and there are documented instances of freed slaves attempting to buy the freedom of their relatives. In her 1866 memoir, *The Story of Mattie J. Jackson,* Jackson tells the history of her family, from her grandfather being brought to the United States from Africa against his will, the travails of her mother after she was separated from Jackson's father, and concluding with the heart-wrenching reunification with her stepfather years later, after the Civil War. Interviewed in the 1930s, former slave Wash Ingram shared the story of his father, Charlie, who after having run away to freedom, "voluntarily" re-enslaved himself in an act of desperation so that he could be reunited with his sons in Louisiana. Black Americans, of course, were not immigrants in the conventional sense, but family separations were their commonplace reality for decades; the daily horrors of slavery were truly the precursor of the family separation policy.

Before the Civil War, when U.S. forces invaded Mexico and captured its capital at the height of the Mexican-American War, some lawmakers proposed that the entire country should be annexed. Their views were known as the "All of Mexico Movement." Those who opposed the proposal did so not only out of an anti-imperialist sentiment, but also out of blatant racist views. For instance, John C. Calhoun, a South Carolina Senator and slave owner who had a residential college named after him at Yale University until 2017, opposed full annexation because doing so would threaten the racial makeup of the United States: "We have never dreamt of incorporating into our Union any but the Caucasian race—the free white race. To incorporate Mexico, would be the first instance of the kind, of incorporating an Indian race; for more than half of the Mexicans are Indians, and the other is composed chiefly of mixed tribes. I protest against such a union as that! Ours . . . is the Government of a white race."

Throughout most of the nineteenth century, there were few legal restrictions regarding who could come to the United States, what many today might call "open borders." That changed in 1875, with the passage of the Page Act. In letter, that law prohibited the entry of "undesirable" immigrants, defined as any person from East Asia coming to engage in forced labor, and any woman from East Asia coming to engage in prostitution. In practice, the law was enforced to ban the entry of Chinese women almost entirely. This severely impacted Chinese immigrant families. For one, the law prohibited many Chinese couples from coming to the United States together. In 1882, for example, nearly forty thousand Chinese immigrants entered the United States. Only 136 of them were women.

That same year, Congress adopted the Chinese Exclusion Act in an attempt to ban Chinese migration entirely. While the ban was originally for ten years, it was extended for ten more in 1892, and made permanent in 1904. Meanwhile, the Immigration Restriction League, a group founded in 1894 by Harvard graduates, pushed for restrictions on immigration from Eastern and Southern Europe, arguing that those immigrants would lower "the mental, moral, and physical average of our people." Similarly, the Asiatic Exclusion League sought to restrict immigration from Japan, Korea, and India, advocating for segregation in schools and restricting the ability of immigrants from these countries to acquire land.

Around this time, the immigration enforcement bureaucracy was also being created. In 1881, Congress had created a superintendent of immigration within the Department of Labor, beginning the centralization of immigration enforcement within the federal government. The same year that the Chinese Exclusion Act was enacted, the Ellis Island station opened in New York, and in 1910 Angel Island opened in San Francisco. Both stations admitted some, rejected others, and detained entire families and unaccompanied children in what can only be described as cages. In *The Deportation Machine: America's Long History of Expelling Immigrants*, Professor Adam Goodman explains how, in the first decade of the 1900s, the immigration bureaucracy began relying not only on formal deportations, but also on "voluntary departures"—a euphemistic term that describes unofficial expulsions, many under duress or coercion—as a way to remove thousands of immigrants from the country, often resulting in the breakup of families.

At the turn of the twentieth century, Irish, Italian, and other Southern and Eastern European immigrants—all of whom were not considered white at the time—were coming to the United States in increasingly large numbers. At the southern border, Mexican workers crossed the border back and forth more or less freely, guided more by the farming seasons than by any immigration policy. Among them were my great-grandparents, who happened to be on the American side of the border in 1902 when Güelito Julián, my grandfather, was born. In 1907, Congress for the very first time made "entry without inspection" a violation of the law, but notably, the provision applied only to those arriving by sea; not to those crossing by land, and not to Mexicans. As Professor Aviva Chomsky explains in *Undocumented: How Immigration Became Illegal*: "Inspection was for immigrants, and immigrants were defined as people who arrived by sea, not Mexicans, who crossed the southern border to work.

Likewise, Mexicans were exempted from the literacy requirements and head tax imposed on immigrants in 1917, as long as they were coming to work in agriculture. Mexicans weren't even required to enter through an official port or inspection point until 1919."

As the Mexican Revolution ravaged that country in the 1910s, even more Mexican nationals fled across the border, especially from the northern states. When the United States entered World War I, the increased demand for labor was fulfilled in part by Mexican immigrants. This new influx, added to the thousands who had arrived at Ellis and Angel Islands in recent years, was met with an increasingly popular eugenic and nativist movement expressly intent on keeping the United States as white as possible. "Our capacity to maintain our cherished institutions," warned Washington Representative Albert Johnson, author of the National Origins Act, "stands diluted by a stream of alien blood, with all its inherited misconceptions respecting the relationships of the governing power to the governed." Senator Henry Cabot Lodge put it even more starkly: "More precious even than forms of government are the mental and moral qualities which make what we call our race . . . they are exposed to but a single danger, and that is by changing the quality of our race and citizenship through the wholesale infusion of races whose traditions and inheritances, whose thoughts and whose beliefs are wholly alien to ours, and with whom we have never assimilated or even been associated in the past."

More precious even than forms of government? Than democracy? Lodge suggested, rather explicitly, that preserving the white race from "the wholesale infusion" of other races was more important than preserving democracy itself. The white nationalist movement popularized the phrase "America First" around this time as well, seeming to equate "America" with "whiteness." Many anti-immigrant groups still use the phrase "America First" today.

In *Illegal: How America's Lawless Immigration Regime Threatens Us All*, Dr. Elizabeth F. Cohen, a professor of Political Science at Syracuse University, explains that the "patrician white nationalists" of the early twentieth century, like Johnson and Lodge, largely got their wish in the form of the National Origins Act of 1924. That law (officially the Immigration Act of 1924) barred nearly all immigration from Asian countries and severely restricted it from Southern and Eastern Europe. Using information from the 1890 census intended to mirror the United States' population at that time, the law set a total annual quota of one hundred sixty-five thousand, and over 90 percent of it was allotted to European countries.

This law was an unapologetic effort to limit the number of non-white immigrants coming to the United States—to ensure that the U.S. looked like it had looked in decades past. Some legislators had even suggested using data from the 1790 Census to set the quotas, in an effort to reflect the population makeup of colonial times. In the words of President Woodrow Wilson during the years leading up to the enactment of the National Origins Act, "the whole question is one of assimilation of diverse races. We cannot make a homogenous population out of people who do not blend with the Caucasian race." The assumption of others blending into a white majority—if it was a majority at all—was an explicit attempt to erase anyone who was not white. Critically, though, these laws did not apply to immigrants coming by land from within the Western Hemisphere; so people coming from countries in the Americas continued to come. Mexican laborers were still able to fulfill the demands for cheap labor, particularly in the Southwest.

In 1929, Congress adopted the Registry Act, making it a misdemeanor to enter the country by land other than at a port of entry, ushering in the modern era of criminalized migration. The penalties—up to a year in prison, and up to two years for those entering a second time—were meant to enforce the quotas set by the National Origins Act of 1924. The current version of "Section 1325," which Zero Tolerance purported to enforce, was enacted in 1952, and it remains largely unchanged in its substance. The Immigration and Nationality Act of 1965 (INA), which overhauled the entire immigration system and eliminated the nationality quotas, did not change Section 1325 in the least, and neither did the 1986 Immigration Reform and Control Act—so-called amnesty reform—under President Reagan. In 1996, under President Clinton, Congress added civil penalties for illegal entry, but the criminal provisions remained unchanged. In other words, the criminal penalties that Zero Tolerance sought so vehemently to enforce in 2018 had been in the books for nearly seventy years. When the Biden Administration did away with the Zero Tolerance policy in early 2021, Section 1325 survived unscathed.

During the years and decades that followed the adoption of the National Origins Act, various immigration enforcement and administration agencies were created and centralized, first within the Department of Labor and later within the Department of Justice. Throughout this process, immigration law and policy became a constant push and pull between the nativist forces intent on maintaining the dominance of the "Great Race," and the business interests that rely on the availability of inexpensive labor coming across the border to support their economic models, which in turn, help support said dominance.

The Bracero Program and the H-2 Program are two prime examples of how the system has attempted to have it both ways: exploiting the inexpensive labor of immigrant workers without offering them citizenship or any other meaningful rights. Starting in 1942, the Bracero Program brought Mexican farmworkers to the United States, while H-2 brought Caribbean workers—mostly Jamaicans at first—to sugarcane fields in Florida starting in 1943.

The word "bracero," a derivative of the Spanish "brazo," referred to the fact that these laborers worked primarily with their arms. Braceros and those in the H-2 Program were typically men who left wives and children behind to come to work in American fields. Many went back when the farming and sugarcane seasons concluded. H-2 workers often reported beatings and widespread abuses in the fields, and some employers were even charged with peonage, the crime of forced labor. When Mexican braceros tried to settle in the country more permanently with their families, the pendulum in the system swung too far, so hundreds of thousands—up to 1.3 million, according to some estimates—were rounded up in military-style raids and deported under the unsubtle Operation Wetback in the mid-1950s. Labor Secretary Lee Williams, who oversaw the winding down of the Bracero Program in the 1960s, described it as "legalized slavery," according to Professor Cohen. And even though that program ended, the system continues to try to have it both ways to this day. Temporary agricultural workers still come to the United States every year under H-2A visas, and non-agricultural, "unskilled" workers do so under H-2Bs. The system accepts immigrant workers to come detassel the country's corn fields and help us rebuild after a hurricane, but not to become our permanent neighbors.

In 1965, the year after President Lyndon B. Johnson signed the Civil Rights Act into law, the immigration system was overhauled once more. The Immigration and Nationality Act did away with the nationality-based quotas of the National Origins Act, eliminated the nation-specific bans, and created the structures and infrastructure that govern immigration and immigration law today and under which the family separation policy came to be. The new law maintained certain per-country caps, but on its face gave priority to relatives of U.S. citizens and permanent residents, professionals, individuals with specialized skills, and certain refugees. The law set an annual worldwide limit on permanent immigration to the U.S. of 675,000 persons.

Like the laws that spawned Zero Tolerance, the agencies tasked with enforcing it had also existed for decades. In 1924, Congress created the U.S. Border Patrol as part of the National Origins Act—the same law that established the nationality quotas also created the law enforcement agency to enforce them. This was the first time the federal government had an agency dedicated solely to enforcing its land borders, especially its southern border. This was no small task, given that the border had moved significantly farther south with the annexation of Texas in 1845, and after the United States took from Mexico what is the Southwest today, after the 1846–1848 Mexican-American War. All told, the border had been pushed south to enlarge the United States by an area roughly the size of Western Europe. Nearly eighty years after that expansion, the first Border Patrol agents were deployed along the Texas border, as chronicled by UCLA Professor Kelly Lytle Hernández in her 2010 book, *Migra! A History of the U.S. Border Patrol.* "[D]uring the Border Patrol's early years in the U.S.-Mexico borderlands," writes Professor Lytle Hernández, "a region where the deeply rooted divisions between Mexican migrant laborers and Anglo-American landowners dominated social organization and interactions, Border Patrol officers— often landless, working-class white men—gained unique entry into the region's principal system of social and economic relations by directing the violence of immigration law enforcement against the region's primary labor force, Mexican migrant laborers."

The Border Patrol grew steadily over the decades that followed. In 2003, the agency was brought within Customs and Border Protection, in the newly established Department of Homeland Security (DHS), which itself had been created in the wake of the September 11, 2001, attacks. Today, the Border Patrol is one of the largest federal law-enforcement agencies in the country, with a budget of nearly $4.9 billion in 2020. CBP, its parent agency, amassed a mammoth budget of more than $17.4 billion that year.

Like CBP, U.S. Immigration and Customs Enforcement (ICE) was also created in 2003, as part of the restructuring that merged the former Immigration and Naturalization Service (INS) into DHS. The rearrangement swallowed the INS whole and placed the immigration agencies alongside all other law-enforcement agencies in the country, with the consequence—intended or not—that immigration law and policy have been inextricably intertwined with law enforcement ever since. ICE's history though, especially its customs function of regulating the entry of goods into the country, can be traced back to the original Treasury Department, which was created in the early years of the Republic to administer the imposition of tariffs on imports. For a long time, the focus of the agency remained on the influx of goods, not persons. In the 1920s, during Prohibition, the U.S. Customs Service was tasked with preventing the importing of alcohol, for instance.

That focus eventually shifted to the influx of people, particularly when non-white persons began migrating to the United States in significant numbers. In his book *Migrating to Prison: America's Obsession with Locking Up Immigrants*, Ohio State University Professor César Cuauhtémoc García Hernández details the rise of immigrant detention from the times of Ellis Island to today, including the role that "crimmigration"—the commingling of criminal law and immigration law—has played in that process since the second half of the twentieth century. In the 1980s, a wave of tough-on-crime policies gave rise to tough-on-immigration views and rhetoric. For example, thousands of Cubans who arrived in Miami in the Mariel boatlift of 1980, and Haitians fleeing the U.S.-backed Duvalier dictatorial regime in the early 1980s, received sensationalized coverage in the media. A *New York Times* article, for example, reported that the Cuban authorities had described the so-called Marielitos as *"escoria"*—literally, scum—fueling the generalized characterization of these largely dark-skinned would-be refugees as undesirables. In 1982, President Reagan ordered the INS to detain all Haitians arriving without authorization. Central American émigrés—fleeing civil wars and military dictatorships backed by the United States, including the *contras* in Nicaragua—also began arriving at the southern border in greater numbers. Immigrants were first sent to federal prisons, mostly in the South, and soon were filling up newly created immigration facilities. The present-day immigration detention complex had begun.

The creation of DHS, and ICE within it in 2003, skyrocketed immigration detention to levels never seen before. According to the American Immigration Council, in 1994 the daily average number of people in immigration detention was around six thousand eight hundred nationwide. By 2019, that number had surpassed fifty-two thousand, more than a seven-fold increase. Through a combination of a network of immigration prisons administered by private, for-profit corporations, the entanglement with local law-enforcement agencies, and an ever-increasing budget, ICE has come to detain tens of thousands of men and women every single day, many of whom are first-time crossers trying to apply for asylum or other forms of protection.

The system is an astounding money-making machine. Private detention companies' revenues reach into the billions of dollars every year: GEO Group reported revenues of more than $2.4 billion in 2019 ($166 million in net income), while CoreCivic reported nearly $2 billion in revenues ($188 million in net income) that year. During the first two years of the Trump Administration, CoreCivic and GEO Group spent at least a combined $3 million in federal lobbying, while DHS granted them contracts worth approximately $800 million. Some of the contracts with ICE contain quotas of beds that ICE must fill for them—a minimum *guaranteed* number of immigrants that will be detained every day—as well as a price per bed, per night, creating a perverse incentive to detain as many immigrants as possible, for as long as possible, in order to maximize profits. Since 2009, Congress explicitly and repeatedly mandated increases in the number of "beds" available for immigration detention; the bed became a proxy for a person behind bars for having crossed the border.

Furthering the crimmigration dynamic, ICE regularly commandeers local law enforcement in order to detain immigrants. Through the so-called 287(g) Program—whose name derives from the section of the INA that created it—ICE deputizes state and local police officers to conduct immigration enforcement duties, including interrogation and detention of suspected non-citizens. Small police departments in rural areas of the country often depend on 287(g) contracts to receive much-needed federal funds. Critics of the program have argued for years that it harms community policing efforts, as undocumented immigrants are less likely to report crimes, whether as victims or witnesses, out of fear that their local police department will turn them over to ICE. Some courts have also called into question the constitutionality of local law enforcement's detention of a person solely based on the suspicion that they may be undocumented and without a judicial warrant. Programs such as "Operation Stonegarden" and "Secure Communities," which encourage law-enforcement officers to enforce civil immigration laws, have also entangled law-enforcement and immigration agencies, blurring the lines between the former's criminal law mandate and the latter's civil nature. In early 2018, ICE expanded its use of arrangements known as Basic Ordering Agreements (BOAs). Under

BOAs, ICE pays sheriff's offices and other local law-enforcement entities $50 for every immigrant they hold and turn over to ICE, putting a price tag on every person detained.

ICE's budget has also grown consistently since its inception. In 2003, ICE was founded with a budget of around $3.2 billion. By 2020, it had grown to nearly $8.4 billion. Even in years when the net number of immigrants coming to the United States has been negative, ICE's budget has continued to grow. Combined, the budgets of the immigration enforcement agencies (ICE and CBP) surpassed $25 billion in 2020, an amount greater than the gross domestic product of countries like Cyprus, Iceland, and El Salvador, among dozens of others.

This was the legal and institutional backdrop in which Zero Tolerance came to be. The legal framework originated in and was driven by a racist impetus aimed at keeping the United States as white as possible, or at least as white as lawmakers perceived it to be one hundred years ago. Over time, many children and descendants of white immigrants have come to claim sole ownership of a country. The agencies have continued to grow, and their budgets have continued to bloat even as the number of immigrants coming to this country has decreased. According to the U.S. Census Bureau, the net migration to the United States in 2018 fell to 2010 levels, and yet the enforcement agencies' budgets ballooned. When the Attorney General announced Zero Tolerance in April of that year, it was a quintessential example of a solution looking for a problem: Even though the Administration presented the policy as a response to a "crisis at the border," there was no real crisis at the time, and in fact the policy created one.

*   *   *

When we gathered outside the Border Patrol's Centralized Processing Center in south McAllen, the summer heat topped triple digits.

With the humidity and not the slightest sign of a breeze, it felt easily over 105 degrees, and it wasn't even noon yet. Often referred to
simply as "Ursula" because of the street where it's located, the Centralized Processing Center was at the time the largest Border Patrol
station in the country, with a reported capacity for 1,500 migrants.
It was inside this facility that hundreds of immigrants were first processed, photographed, and fingerprinted, and where many had to
recount to a Border Patrol agent the traumatic experience that led
them to come to the United States, often a mere few hours after
being detained. From the outside, Ursula and its metal walls are virtually indistinguishable from the dozens of other warehouses in this
part of town, until one notices the United States and Border Patrol
flags flying high near the entrance. A sprawling, retrofitted warehouse, the building was adapted into a detention facility in late 2014
to detain and process children after an increase in the number of
unaccompanied minors arriving from Central America earlier that
year. That same year, the Department of Homeland Security under
the Obama Administration started detaining children and families
throughout Texas on a large scale, and Ursula was typically their
first stop. Ursula had just become infamous when photographs of
children of all ages detained in chain-link cages inside the facility
were circulated online for the world to see, earning the facility the
nickname of *la perrera* among the Spanish-speaking population. The
dog pound.

On this Sunday, a couple hundred of us braved the heat and gathered in the parking lot across the street to protest family separations
and kids in cages. Karla and I arrived at around noon with Julián,
not yet eighteen months, to the sight of large yellow banners reading "No Human Being is Illegal" and "Stop Detaining Children,"
and activists with bullhorns and cases of bottled water at their feet.
The congressional delegation in town also drew a number of local

and out-of-town reporters to cover the demonstration, the separations, and the indignation. A few attendees were already livestreaming the event from their cell phones.

One of the first to speak was Julián Castro, a young-looking former cabinet secretary in the Obama Administration and former mayor of San Antonio. I knew of Castro and his twin brother, Joaquín, a congressman representing San Antonio, but I had not met either of them in person. As he walked into the shade under the tent, I noticed his dressy, light tan moccasins. He had rolled up the sleeves of his baby blue shirt, but doing so did not appear to relieve him much from the scalding heat. As he grabbed the mic, someone pointed out to me that he was going to run for president, but had not made an official announcement yet. *"Feliz Día del Padre,"* he said in less-than-fluent Spanish, ingratiating himself with the crowd.

"What the government is engaging in," Castro said as sweat rolled down his face, "amounts to state-sponsored child abuse. Taking children away from their parents, and neither the parent nor the child knowing when they're going to see each other again, how long that's gonna be, children not understanding what is happening to them, crying out for mommy and for daddy." The crowd fell silent, as we all imagined the cries. As he spoke, one of the white buses leaving Ursula hissed as it released its brakes, and drove away slowly right past us. With his back to the street, Castro did not seem to notice the sound of the bus. He continued and attempted to connect with the crowd on a more personal level. "How many times in your life have you heard your child or your grandchild make that same cry, and done everything that you could to make sure they were comforted?" The demonstrators inside the tent nodded and seemed to lean their bodies forward slightly, in agreement. "We have thousands of children now that are crying out for their mother and their father. And we can't comfort them." His voice was firm, decisive, very much that of a politician who has rehearsed his remarks, but at the same time his tone conveyed genuineness and authentic concern for the children's plight.

Suffering through the unrelenting heat, Castro described what he imagined were the consequences of the trauma that the separations had on children. Such a cruel policy, he added, was also "having terrible consequences for who we are as Americans. This is not who we are or who we should be."

I had heard this refrain many times before. "This is not the real America." "This is not who we are as a country." "This policy does not reflect American values." But who was it, then, I thought every time I heard a variation of this sentiment, that was separating the families we were interviewing in court every day? We interviewed them at the United States District Court. It was "United States Attorneys" who prosecuted the parents for illegal entry. It was the Attorney General of the United States who announced Zero Tolerance. It was United States Border Patrol agents who took the children away. In my mind, there was no denying it, it was the United States of America, and doing it in our name. It was too attractive, too convenient, to say this is not us. But for these parents and these children, it was us. Maybe it was a sort of collective cognitive dissonance that did not allow Castro and others to come to terms with the fact that this policy was being implemented day in and day out by a government that was supposed to be of the people, by the people, and for the people. That same government was punishing parents and children alike on behalf of the people of the United States of America.

Is there a single, true, real United States of America? Or are there multiple facets of it that rise to the forefront at different points in time? A faction, wrote James Madison famously in *Federalist Paper* No. 10, is a number of people "who are united and actuated by some common impulse of passion, or of interest, adverse to the rights of other citizens, or to the permanent and aggregate interests of the community." It was human nature to devolve into factions, Madison reasoned, so it was not possible to eradicate them completely. Rather, the best way to control the negative effects of factions, he argued, was to create a representative system of government, enshrined in a federal Constitution: "The influence of factious leaders may kindle a flame within their particular States, but will be unable to spread a general conflagration through the other States." If it was a faction of America that was behind the Zero Tolerance policy, it had certainly spread a general conflagration throughout the border, all the way to this hot summer day outside Ursula.

"The only way that we're gonna change this," Castro concluded, "is if people throughout the country rise up and push back. Thank you for doing that. Happy Father's Day." As he wrapped up, the demonstrators clapped and broke out in loud chants that reverberated in the otherwise silent midday heat. *¿Qué es lo que queremos? ¡Justicia! ¡Justicia! ¿Cuándo la queremos? ¡Ahora! ¡Ahora!* What do we want? Justice! Justice! When do we want it? Now! Now! On this day, these demonstrators were the United States of America too. They too were a faction Madison would have allowed.

About thirty minutes into the remarks, the organizer emceeing the demonstration introduced me. I took the mic as I stepped into the shade under the tent, and looked down at my shirt to discover it drenched in sweat. Even in the shade, the mid-June temperature seemed to be going up and up. Karla held on to Julián, giving him bottle after bottle of water to keep him hydrated.

"Buenas tardes a todos y a todas." I decided to speak in Spanish first. All these years later, I still felt more comfortable using it in this setting, and I wanted my words to be as authentic as possible. "I'm so glad to see so many of us here today, despite the heat. But I wish we had ten times more people, twenty times more people. That's

what we need right now. We need to raise awareness about what is happening right now, the crisis that we're seeing here in South Texas."

I told the crowd about interviewing mothers and fathers in federal court, about how the separations were taking place, about children as young as five or six years old being taken away from their parents as soon as they were arrested, about a five-year-old daughter who was taken from her mom at a Border Patrol station but had to be brought back to her in the middle of the night because she was crying so much because her mommy was gone, and how once mom was able to calm her down and put her to sleep, the agents took her away again.

"There's no other democratic country in the world," I said, "that does what this government is doing. Separating children from their parents, before any determination of criminal guilt, or deportability. The vast majority of the parents are asylum seekers, so there's nothing to punish them for. It's a basic human right to seek asylum and protection." I did not need to mention article 31 of the 1951 Refugee Convention, ratified by over 140 countries, which provides that countries shall not impose penalties on refugees and asylum seekers merely because they entered illegally or are present in the country without authorization. I did not need to mention article 1 of the Convention Against Torture, in which governments commit not to engage in acts that intentionally inflict severe physical or mental pain or suffering to punish a person for something they or another person did. I did not need to mention all the other human rights treaties we had cited in our request for precautionary measures to argue that the family separation policy violated international human rights law. The sad irony was that the United States had not only ratified most of these treaties, but actually played a leading role in *drafting* them decades earlier.

"The crisis that we're seeing here in South Texas," I continued, "is not about politics. It's not a political crisis. Let's not fall for that. This is a human rights crisis, a human rights issue, an issue of the most basic human decency: keeping five-year-old boys and girls with their parents. That's not a very high bar. If we're falling below that bar, there's not much lower to fall." And at that moment, I truly believed that things could not get worse.

When the rally ended, Karla, Julián, and I left and drove up Ware Road, the same road the buses crammed with immigrants took every day from Ursula on their way to the courthouse. We drove past the golf course with its yellowing grass, saw the marquee outside Brown Middle School with its angry Doberman, and glanced from a distance at families spending their Sunday at West Side Park. I could see the smoke coming out of the public BBQ grills set up around the park as families enjoyed their afternoon, the sight evoking the smell of fajitas and ribs sizzling on the grills. The Sunday these families were spending seemed so distant from the Sunday of the families at Ursula, just a few miles south.

I tried to disconnect from work for a while, and we stopped by my mother's house on the way home. My brother Héctor was there with his family too, for a small Father's Day lunch. My mother was always excited to see us, but she was especially excited to see Julián and my brother's two kids. Ever since she's lived alone, my mother prefers having us over at her place, rather than all of us getting together at my house or my brother's, even though my brother lives half a mile from her house, and I lived only slightly farther at the time. I was the older brother, but for years now I had felt as if our roles had reversed. When I left for college first, and law school later, Héctor stayed back home and looked after our parents. He married before I did and had kids before I did. Before I returned to McAllen, he would be the one to visit my mother every week, most weeks multiple times, while I was away. Over the years, he had come to be the older brother.

As I watched my mother play with Julián, offering him fresh grapes cut in half—which he loved and devoured one by one—I couldn't get my mind completely off work. I couldn't shake the feeling that we needed more help with the growing caseload. I was feeling the pressure in a very real sense and wasn't sure what to do with it. I was the only attorney; Natalia Cornelio, one of my colleagues and a former federal public defender, had come down from Houston for a couple of weeks to help; we had one law student intern, Alexis, with barely one year of law school; and we relocated another intern, Priscilla, from Houston to South Texas to help with the growing crisis. But it was not enough, we needed more help. The list of cases was growing every day by the dozens. Hiring someone would take weeks or longer, and it wasn't clear our organization could afford it. We needed the help now. I knew what we needed, but I did not know how to make it happen.

Julián chuckled gaily as he squashed another grape in the palm of his hand, bits of pulp squishing through his fingers as he closed them into an awkward baby fist. He looked at the pieces with curiosity and put them into his mouth.

When we got home later that evening, I found myself, inevitably, in front of my laptop checking email. There was a message from someone whose name I did not recognize, Laura Peña. When I noticed "Pro bono Immigration Atty" in the subject line, I clicked on it right away.

"I am an immigration attorney in California," her email read. "Former ICE trial attorney under Obama," and I envisioned an experienced immigration attorney. It did not immediately register in my mind that she had been deporting people in that role, much less that she may have deported families.

"I am going to take a sabbatical from my business immigration law firm," and I grew more and more interested, "to volunteer in the RGV to do pro bono removal defense and documentation of human rights violations in regard to the family separation and zero tolerance policies." Could this be the help we needed? I wondered. "I saw your speech in McAllen today (on Facebook), and I'd love to donate some of my time to the litigation work TCRP is doing." Would it matter if she wasn't licensed in Texas?

Her email felt like a Father's Day gift, and not just for me. I assumed Laura did not have a Texas law license, but it intrigued me that she was originally from Harlingen, just thirty minutes east of McAllen. She would almost certainly have the cultural competency to do this work, having grown up among immigrants and the families of immigrants. Her experience as an immigration attorney was the type of expertise we had been longing for—we couldn't get picky about which side she had worked on. And she wouldn't cost us a dime, as she was willing to volunteer. On paper—or rather, on my computer screen—it was almost too good to believe.

I hit reply and started typing a response.

"When did you cross?" I asked Arturo the following day in court at the Bentsen Tower.

"*El sábado,*" he said in a soft, friendly voice. In blue jeans and red T-shirt, he looked a little younger than me, and I confirmed that when he gave me his date of birth. He was going to turn thirty-three in less than a month, in July. I noticed a couple of long, jagged white lines around the neck of his T-shirt, the unmistakable remnants of dry sweat stains from the past few days. Like every other defendant in the courtroom, Arturo was wearing the same clothes he had on when he was taken into custody near the river. When he spoke, a whiff of his overnight breath was still perceptible. Like the others, he had likely not been given toothpaste or a toothbrush while at the Border Patrol station.

Arturo was a bit shorter than me, probably five-nine or so, with a perpetual smile on his face, a smile that revealed his large, yellowing teeth and signaled politeness every time he answered one of my questions. He smiled and nodded when he said this was his second time coming to the United States. He smiled and nodded when he said he was from outside El Progreso, in northwest Honduras. He smiled and nodded when he said that he and Miriam, his seven-year-old daughter, had come to the United States alone. He smiled and nodded when he added that Miriam's mother had left them when Miriam was three, so he had raised her by himself. And he smiled and nodded when he said they had crossed on Saturday.

By now, this had become the norm. Like Arturo and Miriam, most families had crossed two or three days before the parents came to court, and the children had been taken from them sometime between the time they were apprehended and the time I met them in court. When the federal government arrests someone and accuses them of committing a crime, criminal law generally requires the government to bring the defendant in front of a judge within seventy-two hours to be informed of the charges, and most of our interviews confirmed the government was at least adhering to this requirement. Arturo was one of twenty-seven separated parents this Monday, and most of them had crossed sometime either Friday or Saturday. He had almost certainly been inside Ursula the day before, during the Father's Day demonstration, across the street from where I spoke.

Arturo and Miriam had left Honduras because his daughter, even at that young age, had started being threatened and harassed by gangs, and the police offered no protection. They were headed to Santa Barbara, California, where Arturo's sister lived. As I filled out my intake form, he smiled and nodded and said he was separated from Miriam two nights prior, their first night after they turned themselves in to Border Patrol agents upon crossing the river. An agent in a green uniform came to his cell that evening, he said, and told him that he was going to take his daughter away. At least he told you the truth and told you in advance, I thought. He nodded and his teeth showed again.

"And what did you do?"

He smiled shyly and said, very matter-of-factly as he continued nodding, "Well, I told her that later that night, an agent was going to come and get her to take her to a summer camp." His smile still there.

"¿*A un campamento de verano?*" I asked, perplexed, not really following. He nodded gently tilting his head to his left and shrugging a little. His timid smile could no longer conceal the look of anguish on his face. I couldn't fully articulate, even in the thoughts in my head, that he had made up this story for his daughter. Our interviews were usually quick and dirty, get the critical identifying information, chop chop chop, and move on to the next one without wasting any time, so my mind wasn't ready to fully grasp the implication of what he was saying. My gaze met his as I stopped writing and looked up, and my eyes must have widened as I realized what he meant. Arturo noticed that it had finally clicked for me. "Oh, I see," I said. "And what did she do, what did she say?"

"*No pues*, she went with him, *bien contenta*." Really happy, Miriam left with the agent with a big smile on her face, he said as he nodded, seemingly pleased that his ploy to spare his daughter the trauma from the separation had succeeded. How could he have known? How was he able to concoct this alternative reality for his daughter so quickly, under so much stress and in such precarious conditions, in a crowded Border Patrol station, tired, sleep-deprived, and uncertain about his future? I swallowed hard, and nodded back at him. I reached my left arm out, holding the clipboard with the intake forms in my right hand, and grabbed his shoulder, squeezing it softly, trying to convey my solidarity with that brief squeeze.

Arturo simply smiled.

When I got back to my car and looked at my phone, I had a missed call from my wife. Unlike other federal court buildings, the Bentsen Tower has a strict policy of no cell phones, laptops, or other electronics in the building, even for attorneys. I have seen scores of out-of-town attorneys surprised, even outraged, when the court security officers ask them, politely but firmly, to please walk back to their car and leave their cell phone there.

That Monday morning, Julián had started preschool. When he was born, I had taken the allotted six weeks of paternity leave, and Karla had taken three months, unpaid. Now, sixteen months later, he was scheduled to start preschool from nine in the morning to twelve noon. When I returned Karla's call, she told me she had had to go pick him up. "They called me less than an hour after I dropped him off, and said that he wouldn't stop crying," she explained. "I had to bring him home."

When Karla arrived at the school, Julián had been crying for almost the full hour, his eyes red and puffy. She later described him as looking lost, helpless, and she considered in that moment not taking him back to preschool the next day, or ever. This happened often, the school staff told Karla, trying to calm her down, when children came to school for the first time, especially the little ones. It was an adjustment period. They simply had a hard time being away from their mother—many of them for the very first time in their lives—for a few hours.

I couldn't help but draw the connection to what parents had shared with me in court just a few minutes earlier. I imagined the daughter who sought her mom in the middle of the night to be comforted. Except there was nobody calling the parents to come pick up their kids, no way for the parents to go pick them up and bring them home.

The following morning, when I asked the group of almost eighty defendants if anybody had been separated from a child, it felt as if half the courtroom stood up. I tried to count the parents quickly, but lost count more than once. I gave up. It was already past eight on the wall clock.

There were three of us to do interviews, luckily. Georgina had not been able to come with me, but instead, Carlos and Alexis were here. Carlos Moctezuma García is an immigration attorney, McAllen native, and father of three. He was helping us out on a pro bono basis, and in addition to his commitment to social justice causes on the border, it seemed to me that he cared about helping with the family separations even more because he was a father and the son of immigrants. Alexis Bay, also from the Rio Grande Valley, is the daughter of Cuban refugees and had just completed her first year at the University of Miami Law School. She was interning with us for the summer.

Once all the separated parents stood up, we called them over three at a time—one with each interviewer. Unlike days when there were a handful of separations and we could easily spot them on their seat and call them one by one, there were so many on this Tuesday morning that we asked them to line up against the wall one row at a time. Having them standing there created some commotion, between their shackles clinking, the murmuring by the other defendants, and the reduced space for other defendants to walk past them as the public defenders called them to discuss their criminal cases. The U.S. Marshals are in charge of the defendants and of making sure the court proceedings are not disrupted, so they are always present when there are criminal defendants in court. We lucked out that the two marshal officers in court that day allowed us to access the separated parents in this way, because if they had said no, we would have had to ask the group at large every time if they had been traveling with their child, maybe causing even more disruption.

I got through the first two intake interviews as quickly as I could, but I felt as if we weren't making any progress. It was 8:20 and we were still on the first row. Trying to get to as many parents as I could, I limited the questions to the identifying information for the parent and child, and left out many details about how the separation had happened. I did not get to ask when they had been separated or who took their children away. I had no idea why they had left their home country, or whether this was the first time they came to the United States. Maybe their children had a disability, and I did not bring that up. Maybe they wanted to tell me the most important detail of their case, the reason why they fled, or the medication their child needed to take, but I didn't give them an opportunity to tell me. I only had time to get the necessary identifying information for each parent and their child, and even that was in a hurry. I am sure I missed important details, but there was simply no time—we needed to be out of there before their criminal hearing started at 9:00 a.m. I kept looking in the direction of Carlos and Alexis, hoping that they were also moving through the questions quickly. I could only hope.

The next time I looked up at the clock, it was already 8:40, and we still had the last two rows to go. We're not gonna make it, I thought. It was twenty minutes before the judge would come out of his chambers in his black robe and take the bench, and once that happened, we needed to be out of there regardless of whether we had interviewed all the parents. By the time the judge came in through the door on the corner at the front of the courtroom to start the hearing, we could no longer continue interviewing parents, as that would disrupt the hearing; the judge would not allow it. We had to be gone, no ifs, ands, or buts; we had to be out of there *sí o sí*. The Marshals would make sure of it.

In what later seemed like a desperate attempt, but at the time felt like the most logical, commonsense thing to do, I called the next two parents up and started interviewing them two at a time. There was a general introduction that we repeated for every parent at the beginning of the interview: we are with a nonprofit organization, trying to help separated families. We don't work with the government. I am not your lawyer for the criminal hearing that you're about to have. I am not your lawyer for your immigration case. But if you give me your information and your child's information, we can try to find them, and if we find them we can try to arrange a phone call between you two and help you be reunited with them. We're trying to make sure that no parent is deported without their child against their will. I told all of this to the two parents together, hoped that they understood at least half of it, and then moved on to taking their name, date of birth, and country of origin respectively. It was far from a best practice, but at the time it felt like the only solution. In the jam-packed courtroom that morning, going through the questions quickly and not giving each parent any time to tell us more about their situation did not feel wrong. It felt necessary, and there was no alternative. It was almost as if I did not make the decision to go through the questions quickly; the circumstances made the decision for me.

I looked up at the clock again expecting to see 8:45, but was dismayed to see 8:55. We still hadn't interviewed the six parents from the very last row, and if we did not get to them before 9:00, it was a real possibility that we may never see them again. I gestured and started to call the first two parents in that row, when a U.S. Marshal said, "Ok, we gotta go," and started lining up all the defendants and escorting them out of the courtroom. The illegal entry hearings all took place on the eighth floor of the Bentsen Tower, but they took place in one of two different courtrooms. One is right next to the elevators, where Georgina and I interviewed the first five, and the other is at the other end of the floor, on the west side of the building, where we were today. Some days, like today, the public defenders would interview their clients in one courtroom—and by extension, so would we—and the actual hearing would take place in the other one. So the two U.S. Marshals were escorting the defendants to the other courtroom, the one closer to the elevators, for their hearing, which was about to start in less than five minutes.

At this point, interviewing two parents at a time would have felt like a luxury. Carlos, Alexis, and I started walking with the immigrants being escorted, holding on to our clipboards and scribbling furiously while we walked along the wall toward the courtroom entrance. I did not tell any of these parents that I wasn't their criminal defense lawyer, that I wasn't their immigration lawyer, or that I wasn't working with the government. I was fixated on getting the children's information—full name and date of birth, and just a G, H, or ES to indicate country of origin, shorthand for Guatemala, Honduras, and El Salvador. For the parents, I quickly scribbled Yesica, Milton, María, Luis, Teresa. With barely legible first and middle names on our forms, we could then look at the docket sheet and get their last names.

"*Ándele, señora, vamos vamos,*" the U.S. Marshal told the last mother, who appeared to lag behind. She was walking along as she was being ordered, but struggling with the shackles. She held a folded piece of white paper in her hand and gestured toward me, stretching her hand out as if wanting to hand me the piece of paper, as if wanting to stay behind, but walking sideways in the direction she had to go.

"*Falto yo, falto yo,*" she kept saying, exasperated even in her low voice. You haven't gotten me, you haven't gotten me, she repeated as she stumbled along. She must have overheard as we interviewed the other parents, and realized that we were getting the information of separated children. She desperately wanted to make sure that we also took down her daughter's name. She probably did not know who we were, or why we were taking down the children's information, or what we would do with it. But she knew enough to realize that if it was important for us to get the name of every other child separated from a parent that day, it was also important that we get her daughter's. She was determined to make sure her daughter's name was also recorded, and her separation documented.

I grabbed the piece of paper from her hand when we were a couple of steps away from the door, looked at it quickly, and saw a name written on it. The U.S. Marshal looked at me, as if to make sure that I handed her the piece of paper back. I hurriedly clenched the clipboard, supporting it with my forearm and against my chest, and scribbled María Luisa on the form.

"What's her date of birth," I asked as I handed the piece of paper back to her, already outside the courtroom. She stepped into the hallway, struggling to follow the single file of shackled defendants. She slowly walked away and turned her head to tell me a day, a month, and a year imprinted in her memory.

"*Tiene ocho*," she said hurriedly, in a single breath, before disappearing into the hallway, lost among the clinging of shackles and the feet dragging on the carpet. She was eight. She followed those words with a sigh of relief, as if having said them was itself a victory.

To this day, her intake form only reads "Katya Leticia" at the top, the last of the thirty-five parents we interviewed that morning.

CHAPTER 6

─ ·─·─·─

Family Petition

(1994–1996)

M iddle school was a new beginning for me. New school,
new teachers, and a new uniform—dressy khaki pants and
button-up shirt with a black tie—signaled to the world that I wasn't
a child anymore. Every teacher now addressed us as *jóvenes*, like
Miss Bertha had, but here it was true.

I performed well during my first year there. I wasn't the stel-
lar student that I had been in elementary, but I was still among the
disciplined and studious, not the troublemakers. At least not yet. By
the time I started my second year of middle school—the equivalent
of eighth grade—the plan to join my father in McAllen was closer
to becoming a reality.

By then, we had already obtained a tourist visa, so we could
visit him. We had applied for a tourist, "non-immigrant" visa at the
American Consulate in Monterrey, full of doubts, not sure if it would
be granted. This was 1995, and obtaining a tourist visa to the United
States was much less complicated than it is today, but it was still far
from a given. Knowing what I know today, I am not sure how we
were approved for it. To obtain a tourist visa one has to show proof

of a stable, good-paying job, enough money in the bank to justify the "tourist" visit to the States, and no strong family ties in the U.S., lest that make the officer suspicious that this is an attempt to join those relatives permanently. And even then, the decision whether to approve depends largely on an officer's discretion.

When we showed up to the consulate that morning, we met practically none of the requirements: my father was living and working in the United States, my mother was a stay-at-home mom, selling Cokes from her kitchen fridge to generate what income she could. As far as I knew, my parents didn't even have a bank account. Héctor and I were ten and twelve years old, respectively. Any consular officer could have suspected that there was a decent chance this family had plans to migrate to the United States, not simply visit as tourists. I remember my mother saying that if we were lucky and the officer who called her number was in a good mood, we had a chance. Since then, I've always marveled at the immense influence that one single government official can wield on families' lives. An applicant can be honest, hard-working, and fully qualified, but if the interviewing official is having a bad day, none of that matters. Luck must have been on our side that day, because the officer was in a good mood, and he approved our visa.

I have wondered many times, had we not been approved, had the officer been in a different mood that day—would we have stayed in Allende? Or would we have "EWI'd," like my brother Leoba had done a few years before? "Entry without inspection" is the euphemistic phrase the Immigration and Nationality Act uses to refer to entering the United States without being inspected by an immigration officer, whether it is by rafting across the Rio Grande into Texas or trekking for days across the Arizona desert. EWI'ing at a port of entry—such as by hiding in a vehicle's compartment—has become less and less common as sensors and industrial X-ray machines, used to inspect every vehicle entering the country, have become the norm. Notably, the vast majority of people without lawful status in the United States did not EWI; most entered with a valid visa in hand, like us, and simply overstayed the term of their visa.

Although entering the United States to visit my father was a defining moment, I do not have a specific memory of when we crossed that first time. I wonder if I was asleep in the car. To this day, I can doze off with remarkable ease within minutes of a vehicle starting to move if I'm riding in the back seat. It must have been through the McAllen-Reynosa Bridge, in the small town of Hidalgo, Texas, but I do not recall that specific moment. By contrast, I do recall the first meeting with a *notaria* to discuss moving permanently to the U.S.

Notarias and *notarios*—notary publics—are renowned in border states for the unauthorized practice of law. In most U.S. states, including Texas, the most common role of notary publics is to certify that a signature is in fact by the person whose name appears on the document; a notarized document is one signed in front of a notary. But in Mexico and other countries in Latin America, notary publics play a role equivalent to that of attorneys in many legal proceedings. They can officiate real estate transactions, prepare wills and trusts, and draft documents to create corporations and other legal entities. Due in part to this confusion of roles, many unsuspecting Mexican immigrants recur to notaries in the U.S. thinking that they can offer legal services that would normally be provided by a lawyer, but at a much lower price. My family was one of those.

We visited *la notaria* at her office in a strip mall in Brownsville, about one hour east of McAllen. The glass door had a sign reading simply "NOTARIA," and my father pushed it open to let us in. The small lobby had a potted fern by the corner and two burgundy armchairs already occupied by other families waiting to be called.

We leaned against a wall to wait our turn, standing straight and in silence. I looked at the potted plant and avoided eye contact with anyone. Nobody talked.

The *notaria* herself called each family one by one. When it was our turn, my father carried his naturalization certificate in a large, yellow envelope. He was always careful not to fold or otherwise wrinkle or damage the precious document bearing his black and white photograph. The notary—I never heard her name—was in her forties or fifties, with long curly hair, tied in a loose bun held together by a blue ballpoint pen. She held her reading glasses in her hand, putting them on and taking them off as needed to review documents or look up at my father. Her carpeted office was a complete mess. There were papers all over, files on her desk, on chairs, on the floor, stacks and stacks of forms held together with rubber bands, others simply thrown around with no apparent purpose or system. At the time, having no point of reference, I thought this must be what all notary public offices were like, disorganized and overloaded. Now I wonder if the disorder may have given my parents pause. Even if it did, there was no way around it. This notary was the one who had been recommended and the one they could afford.

What I remember most vividly about that day is not the visit itself, but the painful silence during the drive back to McAllen. We left the notary's office, and no one inside my father's Chrysler Fifth Avenue said a word for a long time. Héctor and I were in the back seat, suppressing our excitement that the day when we would live with our father was closer and closer, but the air inside the car was heavy, and I felt as if the entire plan was now in question. The problem, which my parents hadn't appreciated and the visit to the notary had revealed, was that we would need to surrender our tourist visas the moment we submitted the family petition, and that would mean that we wouldn't be able to leave the U.S. while our application was pending. We would need to wait until we received our green cards, and that would take years. At least five, according to the notary. Worse yet, she couldn't tell us exactly how long the process would take. The prospect of not seeing our relatives for years was existential, especially for my mother. My father would be able to visit, he was a U.S. citizen after all. But my mother, Héctor, and I would have to go all those years without seeing the family left behind: in the case of my mother, a brother, five sisters, and her father. For Héctor and me, it meant not seeing our aunts, uncles, grandparents, dozens of cousins, and our two sisters. The silence as my father drove was overpowering, drowning my hopes of all of us living together soon.

In the middle of that silent predicament, and perhaps because of how difficult the situation felt during that drive, I was unaware of how fortunate we were. Thousands of families try to come to the United States from all over the world every year, leaving everything behind, some fleeing violence or persecution, others in search of a better future, like us. In many ways, merely contemplating the possibility of visiting family, remaining connected to our roots and our loved ones, was a privilege that most immigrants do not enjoy and that I did not appreciate at the time. Most have no choice but to forgo their families and life as they know it, leaving their birthplaces never to return, often with no real plan and very little notice. I had no idea how intimately familiar I would become with that reality years later.

By the following January, my parents had decided that we would leave Allende. They didn't set a specific date, or if they did I never knew it, but I had a growing sense that the move was imminent.

One morning that month, *la maestra* Isabel, our young social studies teacher, began a lesson on world history by writing something on the blackboard. Like in the U.S., middle schools in Mexico divide their daily curricula into a set number of periods, each period dedicated to instruction on a different subject. But unlike in the U.S. (or at least in Texas), in Mexico it is the teachers that change classrooms from period to period, while the students remain in the same classroom all day. Professor Pablo Livas Middle School was a two-story school with a large open area completely laden with cement, where every Monday morning we would sing the national anthem. Behind the classrooms, there was a volleyball court lined by mature live oaks and ash trees that was often co-opted for a pickup game of soccer. Next to it was a small dispensary where sandwiches, Cokes, and candy were sold during recess.

Inside the classrooms, there were no seating assignments. Boys and girls sat where we pleased, generally interspersed among the various rows, unless you were a troublemaker or excessively talkative, in which case you were assigned a seat near the front of the classroom, next to the teacher. In my classroom, we all wound up sitting in the same spot every day anyway, functionally creating a fixed-seating arrangement. I sat about halfway back in one of the middle rows, close enough to have a good view of the chalkboard, but not so close to the front that my interest in the material would be too noticeable.

Miss Isabel had joined our school recently, and she quickly earned a stern, no-nonsense reputation among the students. This class period, she was telling us about the Code of Hammurabi and the Babylonian dynasty. She spoke with a firm voice whose cadence revealed that she had practiced this lesson before. My friend Alahyn, who was also my neighbor from down the street, sat in the desk immediately behind me, and Joel, one of my new friends, sat in front of me. Joel was one of the popular kids in class; he even had a girlfriend already, and she was older than him, which gave him even more status.

As the teacher explained Babylon's expansion to the rest of Mesopotamia, I heard murmuring from others sitting around us, and I turned around to check out what was happening. Alahyn had pulled out a white Bic lighter with a red tip. He lit it up and put it out a few times, each time risking that the scratchy flick of the flint hitting steel would alert Miss Isabel. As she continued her exposition, I saw Joel quietly rip a sheet of paper off his notebook in front of me. He crumpled it into a loose ball, and passed it back to me, setting it on the top right corner of my pupil's desk, careful to stay out of the teacher's sight.

When Alahyn saw Joel's move, he placed the lighter over my right shoulder.

"*Préndela*," he whispered, asking me to light up the sheet of paper.

I hesitated, the lighter resting on my right clavicle as Alahyn waited for me to take it from him. I thought about what might happen if I did, how things might unfold, trying to gauge the risks. Before I could figure out my thoughts, Alahyn urged me again. "*Dale, préndela*." C'mon, light it up.

I sat forward, and grabbed the scrunched-up ball of paper with my left hand. I didn't take the lighter from Alahyn, and instead held the piece of paper out to my left and slightly back, and turned discretely to Alahyn. He understood my cue, and promptly lit it up. I was facing forward, looking at the chalkboard and Miss Isabel, but I heard the flick and knew the paper would combust. As soon as I felt the heat reach my fingers, I quickly tossed the ball of fire left and forward. It landed slightly in front of Joel's desk.

Then it was just a matter of seconds. The sheet of paper burnt up before Miss Isabel noticed, but the smoke lingered. That smoke, and the giggles of several students, caught her attention. She stopped mid-sentence and walked a few steps in the direction of our row, remaining at the front of the classroom. She seemed alarmed at first, perhaps thinking it might be a real, threatening fire, but quickly realized this was something else.

"*¿Quién fue?*" she asked sternly, conveying frightful authority.

She stood in silence, waiting for an answer to who had done this, her crossed arms signaling impatience. A few seconds went by, and nothing. Nervous eyes looked around right and left, but nobody said a word. The entire classroom sat still, and time seemed to freeze. I was not expecting such collective, impromptu solidarity. In Lope de Vega's 1619 play, *Fuenteovejuna*, an entire village in central Spain named Fuenteovejuna claims responsibility for the killing of an abusive commander. When asked who the killer was, villager after villager repeats, even under torture, "Fuenteovejuna did it." Our classroom did not have this level of communal self-attribution, but our collective silence conveyed the same unshakable resolve.

Miss Isabel quickly lost what patience she had left. She took a couple of steps forward and addressed us again, this time with a thunderous, intimidating voice that I didn't know she had.

"*¿Me van a decir quién fue? ¿Sí, o no?*" Will you, or will you not, tell me who did it? I felt my chest stiffen, and the entire room stopped breathing. Our Fuenteovejuna spirit remained strong, or so I thought.

Then, out of my right ear, I heard the deep, throaty voice of one of my classmates who hardly ever spoke.

"*Se me hace que fue Efrén, maestra,*" I think it was Efrén, she said. I don't know if she had seen the entire ordeal, but she must have seen me toss the fiery piece of paper.

Miss Isabel wasn't expecting that, and she quickly turned to me. "*A ver Efrén, ¿fue usted?*" Was it *you*, she asked me pointedly.

I was so nervous, my throat so dry, that I blurted out a half-mumbled "no." Even I knew, from the moment I heard the indecisive word leave my mouth, that it wasn't credible.

"*A ver…Efrén,*" she added, pausing as if to emphasize that she was about to ask something of crucial importance. She took another step toward me, and I felt her exasperation on my skin.

"*¡Sea hombrecito y dígame si fue usted!*" Be a little man and tell me if it was you! she commanded in a decisive, frightening tone, the deliberate cadence of her order reverberating in the otherwise motionless classroom. Even the wind outside seemed to have stopped swaying the trees. She was irate by now.

Only Miss Isabel was looking at me, with her piercing, ominous stare, but I felt dozens of eyes waiting for me to answer.

"*Sí, fuimos Joel y yo, pero el encendedor era de Alahyn,*" I finally said, surprised at the confidence of my own voice. It was Joel and me, but the lighter was Alahyn's. I didn't even think about my answer, it must have been pressured out of my being by the teacher's directive to show I was a man. I went from one extreme of half-heartedly denying my responsibility, to the other, confidently sharing everything I knew; not just taking responsibility for my own actions, but also snitching on my two accomplices, unprompted. I could have simply said, "Yes, it was me," but perhaps not telling the complete truth would not have fully shown that I was a man.

"*¿Es cierto, jóvenes?*" She turned to my co-conspirators and asked if it was true. They both assented in silence. "*Límpienme bien ese mugrero, y se van a quedar los tres sin recreo lo que resta del año,*" she declared. Our punishment was to sweep up the ashes and clean the floor, which seemed perfectly reasonable, and we would lose our recess privileges for the rest of the school year, which seemed disproportionately unreasonable.

But what worried me most—much more than losing recess privileges—was telling my mother and having to explain myself to my father the next time he visited. What was I going to say? That I tried to start a fire? That I was part of a prank in history class?

I didn't know where I would even begin. Losing the recess break was much less of a concern in comparison. Plus, by then I knew that we would most likely be moving to McAllen before the end of the school year, so I wouldn't even serve my full sentence. Telling my parents was not even part of the punishment, but it felt like the most serious consequence emanating from that fire, one I hadn't considered in the few seconds I held the burning sheet of paper in my hand.

Later that week, as we wrapped up Spanish class with Miss Laura in the period right before recess, she noticed that Joel, Alahyn, and I weren't packing our things to head out. By then, word of our pyromania had spread, and she knew that we would be staying in the classroom through the recess break.

"You're going to be here the rest of the year, so get used to it," Miss Laura remarked as she packed her own things and grabbed her purse to head out.

"Well, not Efrén," one of my classmates noted as she exited the classroom. She was one of the few who knew that I wouldn't be there by the end of the school year. Her mother was friends with my mother, so she must have heard about our impending move.

For reasons I never fully articulated to myself, I was still uncomfortable sharing too widely that I would be leaving the school. Perhaps it was embarrassment at some level. Maybe I was ashamed that we *had to* leave, that my family hadn't been able to make a living in Allende like all the others. The other families were staying there to continue their lives; they didn't have to leave everything and everyone behind. Perhaps it was that I didn't have the words to explain what was happening or why. I was excited to be with my father again, to be a regular family with everyone living under the same roof like all my other classmates. But beyond that I couldn't express why I had to leave my school, why I had to leave my friends, my relatives, and my life as I knew it and as I had always expected it to remain. Whatever the reason, only a couple of my closest classmates—and none of my teachers—knew that I would soon be leaving the school.

So Miss Laura did not know. She set her purse down on her desk and looked at me. "*¿Por qué? ¿Te vas a cambiar a otra secu?*" she asked, concerned, if I was going to move to another middle school.

On top of the fire fiasco, for which I now felt wholly embarrassed, I was in no mood to explain that my family was about to emigrate to McAllen. Miss Laura waited for my answer as more and more students filed out of the room. When I realized she wouldn't leave until I answered, I simply looked down, saw the backpacks on the floor, each one resting against each student's desk, shook my head and mouthed a soft "no." It was a nervous, uncertain shake, but she seemed satisfied with my response, and I was relieved at not having to explain further.

Day after day since that moment, I missed the opportunity to correct my half-truth. I kept telling myself that it was fine, that what I had indicated the day she asked *was* true—I wasn't moving to another middle school after all, which was what my teacher had asked—and that I would simply clarify it tomorrow as soon as I had a chance.

Then, one day, I didn't come back to Pablo Livas. The day had come for us to move, and I never explained myself to Miss Laura.

CHAPTER 7

— · — · — · —

Have We an Orchestra Here?

(June 18, 2018)

Like most mornings, I arrived at the gym about a minute before class started. Trying to squeeze all the sleep I could out of the night, I had timed the drive from home so well—including the four traffic lights along the way—that I could set my alarm for 5:40, leave the house at 5:51, and be walking into "the box" at 5:59, in time for the 6 a.m. class.

This morning, I noticed a new member in the gym. With thinning, graying hair, seemingly in his early fifties and in good shape, this guy had never been to class before. At about 5'9," he wasn't exactly "short," but his shorts below the knee made him look shorter than he was. A teenage girl was with him. She looked like she was of high school age and appeared to be his daughter.

I had been going to this CrossFit gym for a little over a year by now, and I was sure I had seen him before, but not here. I just could not remember where. Was he a lawyer? Had I seen him in court, maybe? That is often my first thought when I see a familiar face that I can't place. But no, that wasn't it. Was he from Valley View, a teacher or employee perhaps? Sometimes when I see people I have

111

not seen since high school, it takes me a while to make the connection. But that was not it either. Maybe it was the clothes he was wearing that were different, navy-blue basketball shorts and a gray T-shirt. Maybe it was the place we were at that was different, an old building converted into a gym, with remnants of the old red paint still showing in some sections of the walls. Or maybe it was my foggy mind, still half-asleep at this early hour.

As we followed the coach's instructions, doing lunges, Spider-man walks, and butt-kicks up and down the gym, I glanced at the new gym member again and stopped for a split second halfway through a lunge when I remembered. I could see him clearly in my mind now, wearing his perfectly ironed olive-green uniform, with his shiny gold badge on the left side of his chest, holstered standard-issue handgun and taser, and military-style black boots, laced all the way up above the ankles. The new guy in class was a Border Patrol agent, Manuel "Manny" Padilla, Jr., Chief of the U.S. Border Patrol's Rio Grande Valley Sector.

For years, Border Patrol has described the Rio Grande Valley Sector as the busiest of its nine sectors along the border. It comprises thirty-four counties across Southeast Texas and covers an area that is roughly 34,000 square miles. The sector's area of responsibility is lined by 277 river miles and 317 coastal miles, stretching from Starr County along the border, all the way up the Gulf Coast to the other side of Harris County, where Houston is located, with its more than two million residents. Its terrain ranges from sparsely populated dry brush in Jim Hogg and Duval counties, to the coastal shorelines of Brownsville and Corpus Christi, to densely populated urban centers, such as Houston and Galveston, and including the Port of Houston, one of the busiest ports in the world. In 2018, the RGV Sector employed almost 3,100 agents, and Padilla was their chief, directing their land, air, and marine operations across nine stations and three immigration checkpoints. In the federal government's fiscal year 2018, which ran from October 1, 2017, to September 30, 2018, Border Patrol reported to have apprehended more than 396,000 people for crossing the southwest border without authorization. Over 162,000 of those apprehensions, some 40 percent, took place in the Rio Grande Valley.

Border Patrol often highlights the increase in apprehensions of unaccompanied children (which Border Patrol refers to as "Unaccompanied Alien Children," or UACs) and families (which Border Patrol refers to as "Family Units"). It has never been clear to me if there is a legitimate reason to refer to immigrant families as "family units." On its statistical information pages, Border Patrol explains that a "Family Unit represents the number of individuals (either a child under 18 years old, parent, or legal guardian) apprehended with a family member by the U.S. Border Patrol." How is that different from a "family"? Beats me. What is clear is that referring to them as "family units" others them, makes them somehow different from "families." Language matters, and labeling them "family units" makes them different from us. You visit your family on Thanksgiving, not your family unit. People travel to Disneyland with their family, not with their family unit. In Border Patrol's parlance, immigrants do not travel as families—they travel as units of the family kind.

According to the agency, Border Patrol agents apprehended more than 107,000 "family units" along the southwest border in 2018. In 2019, the number reportedly jumped to more than 473,000, a 342 percent increase. Purporting to put these numbers in context, Border Patrol focused on the increase in recent years, but it did not mention that in 2005, the number of apprehensions at the southwest border almost reached 1.2 million. In 1986 and again in 2000, that number surpassed 1.6 million. The number of apprehensions was thus hardly unprecedented based on Border Patrol's own statistics, and yet neither the Bush, Clinton, or Reagan administrations enacted Zero Tolerance or widespread family separation policies. These ups and downs in the number of people crossing the southwest border are more reflective of the cyclical nature of immigration flows and the conditions in the immigrants' countries of origin, than of any reaction to U.S. immigration policy.

The bare statistics also hide an important detail about how most of these "apprehensions" take place. Every parent I interviewed in federal court told me that as soon as they crossed the river, they sought out a Border Patrol agent to turn themselves in. The government's own accounts of the apprehensions corroborate this. The majority of immigrants who cross into Texas through the river are not trying to hide or run away from the agents. Instead, they are seeking them out, seeking their help so that they can apply for asylum or other type of protection.

With that as the backdrop, in mid-June, Padilla could not tell Gayle King on *CBS This Morning* that he disagreed with the Zero Tolerance policy and with taking children away from their parents.

"I do agree that we have to do something," he said in his perfectly ironed olive-green uniform. "We created this situation by not doing anything," he said.

When King pushed him regarding the stories she had heard directly from separated parents, Padilla called her "Ms. Gayle" and complained that there was a lot of "misinformation" being disseminated about the separations. He reassured King and the viewers that if only "we look at this without emotion, and without politics...if we look at this objectively," we would all understand.

What exactly was it that we were supposed to understand and how could we possibly understand it without emotion? Without the parents' emotion? The children's? Hearing these words, it was impossible not to think of Viviana and Leonel and Patricia and Arturo and so many others. They were the first people whose emotions came to mind. Maybe it was because I had spoken to them in the days prior and the emotion with which they answered my questions was still raw. Or maybe it was because, in the back of my mind, I did not see myself as so different from them. I did not see my father as so different from them.

Listening to Padilla attempt to explain away the actions of his agents, I could not get on board with his call to view the separations "without emotion." I could not get on board with an attempt to distance the viewers of the show, and the American public in general, from the separated parents. Our emotions—and our understanding of our emotions—are what makes us human, and I was not about to erase that from these parents, or from myself. I could not allow myself the comfort of viewing these parents in any way other than how I had encountered them: as humans with hopes, with flaws, with histories, and certainly with emotions.

The interview wrapped up, and Padilla did not specify whose emotion he was suggesting should be suppressed, but I think he meant the TV viewers'. A viewer could have interpreted his words as permission not to think of these parents or their terrified children with empathy. To not put ourselves in their shoes and feel their pain. To not imagine how they would feel in this situation. To not think of them as fellow human beings, but as "other."

Over the next few weeks, I saw Padilla at CrossFit several times a week. I saw him arrive at the gym with his daughter. I heard him grunt and saw him sweat doing deadlifts, clean and jerks, and box jumps. I saw him leave the gym with his daughter. As far as I could tell from those limited interactions I witnessed, they had a loving relationship. It was hard to think that the agents he directed were separating "family units" in cold cells during the day, and then coming home to the warmth of their own families at night.

On the same day that Padilla was on *CBS This Morning*, in the afternoon people around the country heard for the first time the cries of children in cages. *ProPublica* and local digital outlet *Neta RGV* published an eight-minute audio of a group of children, mostly young girls, crying and begging for their mommies and daddies, apparently at the Ursula detention center in south McAllen where Secretary Julián Castro had spoken at the rally just a day before. By the sound of it, an anonymous witness had recorded their sobs and whimpers—maybe on a cell phone?—gotten a lawyer, and then gone to the media.

Since early June, I had been telling Georgina and Roberto at the office that I hoped someone would leak a photo or a video of the separated children or their parents. Maybe seeing the way children were being caged would stir up public outrage, more than a thousand words could. My hope was for a Border Patrol agent, a conscientious one, someone with direct access to the *hieleras* and detention centers to have a conscience and be willing to risk their livelihood and their career in order to show the country and the world what was going on inside. But the days became weeks, and if anyone with direct access to the children had a conscience, they did not act on it until that day.

I was surprised that it was an audio that leaked. In 2018, when cell phone pictures and videos had become ubiquitous, it had not crossed my mind that all that might get out of those cages would be sounds. A leaked audio had a Watergate tape feel to it, somewhat anachronistic in today's image-frenzied world of livestreaming, Instagram, and Snapchat. But that was all the anonymous recorder was able to get out of there. The sounds.

When I first saw the *ProPublica* headline, Listen to Children Who've Just Been Separated From Their Parents at the Border, I couldn't help but read it in the imperative: like an order, telling me to do it, to listen to it. But reading Ginger Thompson's opening lines of the article made me want to do anything but:

Many of them sound like they're crying so hard, they can barely breathe. They scream "Mami" and "Papá" over and over again, as if those are the only words they know.

It wasn't hard to find something else to do instead of listening to the painful recording. With more names, dates of birth, and countries of origin to enter into our ever-growing spreadsheet, I quickly found something I "had to" do to justify to myself, albeit subconsciously, that I did not have eight minutes to spare to listen to an audio. Hours later, when I left the office for the night, I had not finished reading Thompson's piece.

When I walked into court the next morning, Azalea made a beeline toward the entrance of the courtroom as soon as she saw me. As she walked briskly in my direction, I quickly glanced around the room. The scene had become the norm by now: the crowd of defendants, sardined elbow-to-elbow filling every bench and looking confused in their dirty, ragged clothes, the interpreters testing equipment, and the public defenders and investigators passing files around getting ready to interview their clients. I might have described what I saw as a beehive of activity, if I thought what was going on was industrious. But instead, it would be better described as an automated factory, with dozens of mindless parts on an assembly line, each doing its job with spaced-out faces in a coordinated rote to churn out the product, in this case tens and dozens and hundreds and thousands of charged, convicted, and sentenced immigrants.

"I'm so upset," Azalea grumbled when she got to me, struggling to keep her voice down through clenched teeth.

One of the guards, she said, referring to the GEO Group employees who escorted the defendants to and from court, had been playing the leaked audio on his cell phone, showing it to his buddies on the bench at the very back. It was his company phone, so he was allowed to bring it into the courtroom. The guard had been playing the audio quietly— or so he thought—in the back of the room, but it was loud enough for Azalea to hear it at counsel's table, and therefore also audible for every single defendant, including the separated parents of the day.

"I had to go over there and tell him to shut it off," she chided.

I shook my head, pursed my lips, and looked up at the defendants crowded together. I got the impression Azalea assumed I had already listened to the recording. I did not tell her that I had not yet brought myself to do it.

I walked up to one of the counsel's tables and pulled out the stack of blank intake sheets from my briefcase to start interviewing the separated parents of that morning, with no time to dwell on what that guard might have been thinking. He had played the sound of crying children in front of those who could well be their parents, or who likely had been separated from their own children. Was it an unintentional, reckless disregard for how the parents in the room might react to hearing those cries? Or was it in fact a deliberate attempt to *make them* react?

When I got home that night, Karla was already cooking dinner. "Pasta ñaña," Julián's babbly attempt at *pasta naranja*, was his current favorite: spaghetti with tomato sauce. He especially loved making a red saucy mess all over himself. After we ate and cleaned the red smears he made, Karla gave Julián his bath before bed, and I sat at the edge of our dining table, tired, staring blankly at my computer screen.

I had avoided listening to the audio for over a day now, telling myself there was no need, asking myself what good is that going to do? I was becoming increasingly numb to hearing the stories from the parents, but why hear the cries and pleas directly from the children, especially when I felt there was little I could do for *those* children. They were at Ursula, a mere four miles from my home, but as much as I wished I could, simply walking up to the entrance and demanding that they be freed and reunited with their parents was not an option.

I rubbed my eyes and opened up Thompson's article on the Pro-Publica website. In retrospect, I pushed myself to listen to the audio in part because I felt it was my duty to hear those cries, since I was the lawyer representing their parents. I needed—I must have thought— to hear my clients' children cry in order to fully understand what the separation was doing to them. At a slightly more conscious, explicit level, I convinced myself of what I had said in one of the interviews: the federal government was carrying out this policy in our name. Regardless of which way one votes, in a representative democracy like the United States, government officials are meant to represent the will of the people, our collective will. That will had now been twisted and mangled to the point that it led to those cries and pleas escaping from the cages at Ursula.

I clicked play thinking I knew what to expect. From the bits I had overheard at the office when others played the recording, I expected mostly unintelligible cries. When the audio started rolling though, a black screen came on for a brief second, and then an image of a Latina woman and a child, both smiling shyly at the camera in what appeared to be a selfie taken on a cell phone. The woman had dark, wavy hair, with equally dark eyebrows, and the little girl, who looked like she was five or six years old, wore a white blouse with black polka dots and a pink collar. There was an introductory text at the bottom of the screen:

Six-year-old Alison Jimena Valencia Madrid was separated from her mother last week at a U.S. Customs and Border Protection facility. The following is an audio recording of Alison and other children as they spoke with border patrol agents and consular officials.

I did not recognize the name, but I thought—had I or someone from our team interviewed her mother in court? Later, scanning through our intake forms, I would find the intake form for her mother. She had gone through federal court less than a week earlier, on June 13. Her name was Cindy, twenty-nine years old, from El Salvador.

El Salvador is the smallest of the seven Central American countries, slightly larger than Massachusetts. With a population of about six and a half million, it is also the most densely populated. A Spanish conquistador gave it the name "The Savior" in the early 1500s, but before that the territory was inhabited by the Lenca, Mayan, and Pipil indigenous peoples, and the largest domain was known by its indigenous name, Kuzshkatán, or Cuzcatlán, meaning the place of precious jewels. In early 1980, in the midst of a leftist insurrection, a "death squad" assassinated Oscar Romero, the Archbishop of the capital, San Salvador, while he said Mass, in what many identify as the beginning of the country's civil war. A U.S.-backed and -financed military junta ruled the country during the twelve-year deadly conflict in which some 75,000 people were killed, according to the United Nations' Truth Commission for El Salvador. In one of the most gruesome episodes of the war, known as the Massacre at El Mozote, a U.S.-trained battalion of the Salvadoran Army raped dozens of women and girls and murdered more than 800 civilians, over half of whom were children. In 1992, peace accords brought the conflict to an end, and a year later the Salvadoran legislature passed an amnesty law covering all acts of violence during the war. Since 2001, the U.S. dollar is the country's official currency. For years, international human rights organizations have reported on the alarming crime and homicide rates in El Salvador, which are directly linked to the activities of gangs with ties to sophisticated transnational criminal organizations.

The unintelligible cries I had overheard at the office started fifteen seconds into the recording. I lifted my gaze past the computer screen and stared at the white wall in our dining room. A small crack where the otherwise empty wall met the ceiling caught my attention for a split second, and then the clearly intelligible voice of a young girl pierced my ears.

"*¡No quiero que me separen de mi papá, no quiero que lo deporten!*" I don't want to be separated from my dad, I don't want him to be deported.

The screen went black again, screams of "¡Papi!" "¡Papi!!" drowned by cries and more sobbing. The voices kept crying, crying, crying, their volume raising and then lowering again as the recording device got closer and then farther away from them. Their cries were accompanied in the audio by a constant grainy, staticky sound in the background, probably the result of cloaked recording in an enclosed space.

It was one thing to imagine what children might be going through, to pretend to know how they might be suffering without their parents. It turned out it was quite another to actually hear it directly from them. In his 1819 poem "Ode on a Grecian Urn," John Keats mused that heard melodies are sweet, but those unheard are sweeter. His imagination could conceive of a beauty much greater than what his senses could perceive. Nearly two centuries later, my imagination did not adorn reality in a romanticized, pleasant way, the way Keats's had. For me, it was quite the opposite: What I had

121

imagined was not nearly as horrifying as what I actually heard that night. For weeks, my imagination had been unable to come up with anything as raw as what was coming out of my computer speakers. The unheard cries of the children had been painful to imagine, but those I heard were excruciating.

As I was enduring the girls' continuing cries, the authoritative voice of an adult male appeared out of nowhere, as if he were walking onstage from behind a curtain.

"*Bueno, ¿aquí tenemos una orquesta?*" he said in a Caribbean Spanish accent. Well, have we an orchestra here? He was probably Cuban or Puerto Rican, as he characteristically rolled the "r" into an "l," making it sound *olquesta*. One of the children asked, confused and barely intelligibly among the nonstop cries, "*¿qué es una orquesta?*" What's an orchestra?

"*¡Faltaba el maestro!*" We're missing the conductor! The voice exclaimed at another crying child, unwilling to let go of the sickening analogy.

Fading into the background, the voice could be heard saying "*no llores*," don't cry, and it almost sounded compassionate as it dissolved into static. What could that agent have been thinking as he heard the children cry? All he did was elaborate on his sinister orchestra analogy and offer them a tepid *no llores*. Did he not see himself, or his family, his ancestors who came to this country before he did, in the faces and the cries of these children? Did he see himself as Cuban American or Puerto Rican and therefore "different" from these Salvadoran and Guatemalan children? The people in the Administration—especially his bosses pushing forth the Zero Tolerance policy—did not appear to care much about that distinction. Or did he simply see himself as "legal" and these children as "illegal" and that was enough to distance himself from the sobbing children, although they spoke the same language, shared some history and culture, and maybe had the same skin color?

Despite the voice's dull requests that they stop crying, the children couldn't help but continue crying, their sobs breaking free out of their cages when their bodies could not. I pushed myself away from the table and hit pause.

By now this audio had gone viral, and I was a day late to the furor. Listening to the children cry out of my computer, I started to grasp fully the power this recording was having around the country, and beyond. My team, others, and I had been sharing the stories of these children and their parents for weeks now, explaining the details of Section 1325 and ICE detention and Office of Refugee Resettlement (ORR) shelters. But this audio needed no explanation. It needed no editing, no introduction, no analysis. The children themselves came through.

When I hit play again, the agent's voice reappeared, on the back end of a conversation. "Houston is seven hours from here," he said. "It's close."

"Where are you all from," the voice asked.

"I am from El Salvador," one of the children said between cries. "And you?"

"Guatemala," another one responded, unable to keep the name of her country of origin from turning into the tail end of a sob, in crescendo. The voice made no mention of the orchestra this time. *No llores*, is all the voice repeated.

"*Quiero ir con mi tía*," another girl cried. "*Sólo una llamada*," she begged. I want to go with my aunt. Just one phone call.

"She can help you if you have the number," the voice told her.

She kept on crying, and it took her a second to process what the voice had offered. "I do have her number," she managed to say.

Another cry interrupted this dialogue, and it was not clear if it came from a boy or a girl. *Papá*, this child cried. *Papá, Papá, ay Papá,* that turned into more cries.

The girl who wanted to call her aunt came back. By now I knew this was Jimena, the girl introduced at the beginning of the audio. She had calmed down, and asked the consular official about the phone call: "Can you call my aunt so that she can come pick me up after lunch?" Her voice was young, childish, but confident and mature in the conviction with which she asserted her request. She posed her question so innocently, so genuinely, as if it were truly a possibility.

The cries had been going on for a full five minutes when Jimena came back on. "I know the number by memory," she said. "34 72..." and her voice faded into the background.

"Will you call my aunt so that she can come pick me up? And then so that my mommy can come as soon as possible." To her six-year-old mind, it was that simple: call her aunt, so that she can come get her. And then take her to her mom right away. Of course her aunt would come. Of course her mom would come as soon as possible. Why wouldn't they? They surely wanted to come get her. Surely as soon as possible.

Then the consular official appeared again. "The girl who wants to talk to her aunt... can I make that phone call?" she asked.

"If she is from El Salvador, yes," a female voice responded. Another agent. The cries continued in the background, but this voice did not mention anything about an orchestra.

"Yes, she is from El Salvador," the official answered.

"Where is the girl who was... from El Salvador... her?" the consular official asked around, turning away from the voice.

"Give me the number," she said, and it was clear she had found the little girl.

Jimena responded immediately, instinctively. "Thirty-four, seven-..." and then a beep muted her voice, *ProPublica*'s redaction to keep the number private.

"And then after my aunt comes to pick me up, my mommy will come as soon as possible so that I can go with her," Jimena repeated after reciting the number by heart.

The audio came to an abrupt end after almost eight minutes of cries and sobs. But it was clear that the cries did not end; the children remained trapped in those cages, asking for a phone call, crying for *Mamá* and *Papá*, their voices reaching the world only through this recording.

During the entire duration of the recording, not a single one of those children asked the agents to let them go, to free them. I had expected them to beg the agents to let them out, but none of them did. All of them were calling for their moms and their dads to come get them. Not a single one asked why they had been separated.

By this point I had been interviewing separated parents for almost four weeks and had interviewed over a hundred of them, but this was the first time I had gotten a glimpse into the children's side of the experience. Some parents would break down crying during the middle of the intake interview in court, and after a few minutes Georgina or I almost always managed to calm them down, reassuring them that we would try our best to find their children as soon as possible, even if I knew it might take weeks. But all these children were hearing was *no llores*, don't cry. No reassurance from anybody, not even the consular officials. I only heard those eight minutes, but I was sure the crying and sobbing continued all night.

At the age of six—Jimena's age—the prefrontal cortex of the brain is not fully developed, and children have a hard time rationalizing their emotions. This part of the brain is responsible for, among other things, reasoning, logic, problem-solving, and the ability to appreciate different points of view. Before the prefrontal cortex is developed at all, toddlers throw so-called temper tantrums, unable to reason with frustrated parents. Without a developed prefrontal cortex, young children often have a hard time controlling their emotional reactions. Experts say this part of the brain does not fully develop until adolescence, and perhaps into our twenties. Before the age of ten, it is undisputed that the prefrontal cortex is not fully developed. This explains why children are often unable to interpret what is happening in their surroundings other than through raw emotions, which often involve crying.

Jimena's undeveloped prefrontal cortex thus could not really make sense of why her mom could not come pick her up. She was certainly not throwing a tantrum, but she could not understand that her mother was being prosecuted under Zero Tolerance, that she would likely plead guilty to illegal entry, and that she would be processed for expedited removal within a few hours. In Jimena's brain, it was a simple and straightforward emotion: call her so that she can come pick me up. Her six-year-old brain did not yet know about international boundaries, their consequent hierarchies, and the violence enacted to preserve them. She stood outside it all, and she could not understand why the adult in the green uniform would not help her be reunited with her mother. Her six-year-old self did not yet understand the imposed difference between American and Salvadoran, either real or imagined. The Border Patrol agent's uniform did not yet signify to her what it signified to her aunt and all the other grown-ups who had crossed the border just like her. Her brain was still oblivious to the effect that this traumatic experience would have on her psyche, perhaps for the rest of her life. Jimena was still years away from the inevitable realization of a world divided by lines on a map, and of the violence wielded to enforce those lines in the name of sovereignty. In some ways, it is a realization and a trauma we all eventually come to, in varying degrees, of this world divided into nationalities and borders and exclusion and violence that we manage to normalize as, simply, our way of life.

I closed my laptop. It felt as if closing my computer screen would contain that reality and make it go away.

I got up from the table and walked down the hallway into our bedroom. I caught a glimpse of my bloodshot eyes in the bathroom mirror as Karla carried Julián out of the bathtub tightly bundled in a gray bath towel. He loved bath time and was still all smiles.

"*¿Listo?*" I asked him as I tickled him softly around his neck. Ready?

"*To*," he said, mimicking the last syllable of the word, and his smile grew into a chuckle.

Karla unwrapped the towel, and handed Julián to me. I hugged him a little tighter. I put a clean diaper on him, and changed him into his nighttime onesie. As I pulled the onesie over his head, he smiled widely when I acted surprised to see his head emerge again. He did not look sleepy yet and was eager when Karla picked him up. I turned off the bedroom lights, and Karla sat with him on the rocking chair in the corner by the nightlight. As if on cue, Julián rested his head on her chest and cuddled comfortably. He nursed peacefully and slowly dozed off into a restful, calm sleep.

Those days it was hard not to let work spill into my home life, especially the mental and emotional part of the work. Every bit of advice I had gotten about "self-care" and "work-life balance" said to "work at work" and "be home at home," but I failed at both that summer. And especially that night, seeing Julián resting on Karla's chest, undisturbed the way all toddlers should be, I couldn't help but make the connection with what I had heard just a few minutes before. The father in me felt fortunate, blessed, to have Julián there with us in the safety and warmth of our home. The lawyer in me felt powerless for the children who were not sleeping with their parents that night, and who did not know when they might be.

That summer was of course not the first time children and families had come to the United States in significant numbers. Neither was the summer of 2014, when the arrival of thousands of "unaccompanied minors" from Central America to the Texas border prompted the Obama Administration to first declare a humanitarian crisis, then swiftly proceed to outfit immigrant detention centers to hold entire families (in a classic act of governmental euphemism, the Administration labeled these facilities "family residential centers," but immigrants' rights advocates were quick to dub them "kiddie jails").

Some of the earliest foreign-born individuals to come to this country, of course, after the first white settlers from Europe, were the Africans who were brought against their will on slave ships to build this country with their unpaid, coerced labor. Forced separations of enslaved parents and children have been well documented, as mentioned earlier. As for immigrants in the more conventional sense, in January 1892, the very first person to register at Ellis Island was Annie Moore, a fifteen-year-old girl from Ireland who had traveled across the ocean alone. In the fifteen years after Annie Moore's arrival, thousands of children—orphans, refugees, and others headed to join their parents in the United States—arrived in New York, mostly from Europe. At the time, those opposing the arrival of immigrants and refugees claimed that Italian and Jewish émigrés would "mongrelize" the United States, blaming them for bringing disease and their inferior way of life.

Children of Ellis Island, a photographic compilation by Barry Moreno, librarian and historian at the Statue of Liberty National Monument and Ellis Island Immigration Museum, chronicles the all-too-familiar stories of immigrant children arriving in the United

States to mistreatment and confinement. It paints a picture of early twentieth-century New York that is eerily reminiscent of the situation at the southern border in the early twenty-first. The book's images depict hurricane-fence cages not unlike the ones that were widely publicized in 2018. A 1904 *Washington Post* article told of hundreds of detained children, including "black-eyed Italian bambinos, fair-haired 'Polacks' in quaint dresses that touch the ground and hide their bare feet, Romanians, Austrians, Syrians, Arabs, Turks, Slavs, Huns, Finns, Swedes, Russians, West Indians, Welsh, Scotch and Germans." An untold number of children arrived in New York Harbor in the first decade of the century. By 1907, the furor resisting the passage of hundreds of thousands of immigrants through Ellis Island led to the enactment of the Immigration Act, which restricted immigration of all "idiots, imbeciles, feebleminded persons, epileptics, insane persons, and persons who have been insane within five years previous; persons who have had two or more attacks of insanity at any time previously; paupers; persons likely to become a public charge; professional beggars; persons afflicted with tuberculosis or with a loathsome or dangerous contagious disease," among others. Despite the United States being characterized as a nation of immigrants since its inception, there were many immigrants who were not welcome. This was some one hundred and thirty years after the American Revolution and fifty years after the end of the Civil War. The rejection of certain immigrants who came to this country was still part of an effort to control and define what groups could aspire to become "American."

In 1915, the *New York Times* reported about two unaccompanied Colombian children, ages fifteen and seven, who arrived at Ellis Island without a parent or legal guardian. In an appalling normalization of the detention of a seven-year-old child that borders on the burlesque, the article noted that even though "the children were detained[, t]hey were eating bananas and seemed very happy." Nearly one hundred years later, the *New York Times* would again romanticize the detention of immigrant children, reporting in 2012 that "[i]t is not unusual for youths to recall the detention centers... as some of the best times in their battered lives." (In July 2018, Matthew Albence, the acting deputy director of ICE, told the Senate Judiciary Committee, under oath, that family detention centers were "like a summer camp," astonishing lawmakers and advocates alike. Children crammed inside a warehouse with chain-link fences dividing them from the adults, sleeping on concrete benches with a Mylar blanket for cover, and going outside maybe once per day— this is hardly any reasonable person's idea of a summer camp.) During World War II, when tens of thousands of school-aged children of Japanese ancestry—U.S. citizens and immigrants alike—were sent to internment camps, an untold number of families were separated, with children sent to one camp, father or mother to another. At different times and using different laws and policies as justification, immigrant children in cages have been more commonplace in the United States than many would like to acknowledge.

What was different this time was that cell phones were everywhere, and one of those omnipresent devices had been inside Ursula to record the children and send their sobs directly into millions of computer screens and living rooms. The release of the recording caused widespread public outrage. *ProPublica's* and *Neta RGV's* (a local youth-led digital outlet) posts of the audio garnered millions of views online, and the nightly news covered it extensively. The audio seemed to tug at people's hearts and guts in a way the previous three weeks of talking heads covering the separations had not. The stories we had been able to share—from Viviana fleeing after her husband's murder to Patricia and her son with medical needs—had received significant coverage, which helped, but they had not led to generalized uproar the way this audio did.

Fortunately, it was only the audio that leaked, and not a photograph or a video of the children. Those cries were more effective at evoking widespread indignation than a video or a still image would have been. And as much as it pains me to admit it, that is because when we hear those children cry, we cannot see the color of their skin. Of all the people who heard the children cry, nobody saw what they look like. Had it been an image or even a video, it would have been easier to "other" the children, to view them as different from us, seeing their deeper skins, their darker hair. But all children cry the same, regardless of their country of origin, the language they speak, or their immigration status. Those cries allowed anyone who listened to hear the children's humanity, their frailty and innocence, their despair, all contained in less than eight minutes of audio, without the comfort of viewing them as different. And although many fault the parents—well, they broke the law!—it is not as easy to place the label of "criminal" on crying children.

When I hear those children cry, I still hear Julián. Julián cries just like those children did when he wants to be with Karla. Hearing them cry made many people think *that could be me, that could be my child.* Then and only then did widespread condemnation erupt.

It seemed as though even for proponents of "tough" immigration and border policies, those cries embodied a moral line they were now unwilling to cross. A moral line that, although it had been there all along, they had been willing to cross before, before they heard what crossing it sounded like.

The recording and the pressure it unleashed would become a turning point that summer. Two days after the audio was leaked, President Trump signed an executive order purporting to end the separations and scaling back the harshest part of the Zero Tolerance policy. At the time, seeing that the Administration had to change course—against the wishes of its obstinate hardliners—felt like a victory, one that just a few short weeks before had seemed beyond our reach. Along with many other advocates, attorneys, and an outraged public around the country, we had, we thought, managed to put an end to the separations against all odds.

Soon, we would find out how wrong we were.

_. _. _. _

CHAPTER 8

At Night

B efore I knew it, I found myself in the middle of a vast expanse, approaching a small, unfinished house. It was at the edge of a clearing where instead of mesquites, live oaks, and other large trees, knee-high blades of grass carpeted the ground. Even a few sunflowers could be seen. The brush here was not as thick, which allowed our group to walk briskly but quietly into the house. The house was either abandoned or still under construction, its cinderblock walls partially covered in gray cement that had not yet been painted, and maybe never would be. The roof had not been built yet, so the sun shone brightly into the house.

We rushed into the house as quietly as we could, mothers and fathers holding their children's hands. Some mothers pressed their index fingers against their lips, signaling to their children to stay silent. We crouched down against one of the walls, avoiding the square openings where windows would go, and I heard some voices in the distance, but couldn't make out the words. I peeked outside, and did not see anybody. I was relieved not to hear any K-9s either. The Border Patrol agents must be on their own, I thought.

I crouched back down and continued hiding. I noticed the skirt that one of the women was wearing. Long and colorful, red and yellow and orange and green, it reminded me of the skirts I had seen indigenous women wear in Guatemala. Maybe it was even handmade, adorned with beautiful patterns that contrasted with our predicament.

Then the thought crossed my mind as I looked around the house, still trying to catch my breath: I could make a run for it. The agents would soon come upon the clearing and find the house, just like we did. If I ran now, away from the clearing and through the brush, I would probably make some noise that would alert them to me and to the house, but that seemed inevitable. They would probably find it on their own eventually anyway.

But if I ran now, no one else would be able to come with me. I would have to leave them behind, and the agents would find them all. Finding them in the house, the agents would most likely not leave a group of immigrants to chase after me, a lone runner. In my mind, there were two agents out there looking for us, but I could not be sure. Our group was about a dozen.

Or they could all leave quietly. I could try to convince mothers and fathers to leave this hiding place and venture yet again into the thick, thorny brush, with kids in tow, as quietly as possible, while I ran in the opposite direction to create a distraction. The chances of making it seemed lower under this option, especially for me, but at least they stood a chance.

My heart pounded, frightened. I couldn't make up my mind, but I needed to decide quickly.

As I was trying to peek through the window again, sweat dripping down my face, my body was overcome by fear. I was paralyzed. I desperately wanted to move but couldn't. I felt the physical manifestation of my indecision.

Then, suddenly, I heard footsteps approaching outside. My heart stopped. I gasped and looked up. Before I could see anybody, I woke up. I looked around in the dark, as if to confirm where I was. Karla and Julián were sound asleep, and the sound of birds chirping outside signaled that the morning was near.

CHAPTER 9

They Will Go See Her Tonight

(June 21, 2018)

The morning after the president signed the executive order that was supposed to end family separations, I arrived at the courthouse expectant about what I would find. The president had signed the order in the Oval Office mid-afternoon on Wednesday, June 20, about eighteen hours earlier. Surely, I thought, there had been enough time for any directives emanating from the order to make their way down to McAllen. Still, I decided it was necessary to go to court in person and verify.

It was a hot Thursday morning, four weeks to the day since Georgina and I had first gone to court. It did not even register that it was the summer solstice, as the days had been feeling very much like summer for a while now: scorching heat interrupted only by a couple of days of torrential rain. The previous four weeks, in particular, had compounded that heat with the chaos of the separations, yet we had managed to interview over 360 parents separated from their children in McAllen alone.

During that time, our team had developed a system to try to locate the children and assist in their release and reunification. The first step involved calling the Office of Refugee Resettlement to see if the child was at a government shelter. We quickly learned that the shelters would not provide the information to just anybody who called—for the safety of the children, they said. It was both fascinating and frustrating how many things were supposedly done "for the safety of the children," but nobody seemed to consider the safety of the children when they took them from their parents, without any serious tracking system or process, without any plan to reunite them. Since we could not confirm whether the child was at a shelter on the first call, we would leave our name and number, as well as the child's identifying information, and wait for a case manager to return the call, typically, they said, within one to three business days. All these delays took on a different meaning, because every "business day" meant one more day that Sandro and Miriam and Alessandro, and countless others, were who knows where, but not with their parents.

Alexis, Georgina, and the rest of our team would call ORR, sometimes wait for an hour on the line, and finally leave the information with the operator or the answering machine. The call back would sometimes take longer than the promised three days, and sometimes it would not come at all, so we would have to call ORR again. When somebody did call back, all the case managers would typically be able to share was whether the child was "admitted" or "not admitted," meaning that the child was at a shelter or not. Only after we provided proof that we were the attorneys working with their parent did they provide more information.

By this point into our efforts to locate the children, Alexis and the team had figured out a way to find them more quickly. After dozens of calls to ORR, they had spoken to the same case manager a few times, and once this case manager—whom I will call Manuel—realized who we were and what we were doing, he agreed to help. Manuel would help us search for children more quickly, and would sometimes also share if the child was not yet at a shelter, but en route, or whether the child was already being processed to be released to a parent or other family members.

A small percentage of families were actually reunited quickly, if the children were still at a Border Patrol station when the parents returned from court. Fortuitously, due to logistical and other delays, those children had not yet been transferred to an ORR shelter, and therefore a longer separation was averted. Those reunifications happened inside a Border Patrol station, with only other immigrants and agents to witness them. Parents and children were oblivious to how close they came to being separated for so much longer. But those were a tiny fraction. Some parents had been deported without their children, having been shoved through the "expedited removal" process in a matter of days. Others had been deported together. Most children, though, remained separated from their parents, scattered across the country in a web of shelters for "unaccompanied" children, temporary foster families, and other government agencies. At the time, estimates spoke of more than two thousand children separated around the country, but nobody knew the exact number. About a fifth of all the separated families had come through McAllen.

The ORR hotline had not been successful at locating the children of all of our clients. Many of them, including the children of three of our clients from our first day in court—Rivaldo, Jorge, and María's three children—were still showing up as "not admitted," which meant they had never made it to a shelter. Similarly, we had not been able to locate their parents, which could mean one of two things: ICE had either released them from custody in the U.S. or deported them. Whether they had been reunited with their children, we could not know. The inability to find out more information about our clients added frustration to an already extremely cruel and dysfunctional process.

But it was through this process—by calling ORR and waiting for a call back from the case manager—that our team was able to confirm the whereabouts of Alessandro, the six-year-old boy who had swallowed fluid at birth, and who we worried was not receiving the medical assistance he needed. After the separation, he had been driven to a shelter in San Antonio, while Patricia, his mom, remained at the Port Isabel Detention Center near the border, along with many other separated mothers and fathers. Built in 1950 and significantly expanded in 2007, the Port Isabel Service Processing Center, more commonly known as PIDC, is a dystopian compound surrounded by empty fields in rural Los Fresnos, Texas, about fifty miles from the TCRP office. Barbed wire and high watchtowers with threatening light fixtures surround the sprawling facility. Its detention capacity exceeds twelve hundred people, and we quickly learned that hundreds of immigrants prosecuted under Zero Tolerance passed through there before being deported. Patricia was locked up in the women's wing, with no information about her son's whereabouts or whether he was receiving his medicine. Every time she asked about him, guards told her that they did not have any information about him—which may not have been a lie—but she had no one else to ask.

I did not know for sure how severe Alessandro's condition was, and I worried about him and Patricia every day. Our team called ORR more than once to plead with the case managers to reunite them. As long as his mother remained detained, they told us, they had no authority to release Alessandro to her. Desperate and running out of options, we turned our focus to figuring out a way to secure her release.

The morning after the executive order was announced, I walked into the misdemeanor courtroom, and the scene was the usual. The air again smelled of clothes that had been worn too long. But this time I noticed there were more men in gray and black suits than before. I surmised they must be U.S. Marshals. There was usually only one or two of them on any given day, and today I counted four. The Marshals were gathering a group of about a dozen immigrants, directing them to get up from their seats and line up against the wall near the entrance to the courtroom. Sometimes the Marshals or the GEO Group security guards would rearrange the defendants in their benches for reasons I did not fully understand and preferred not to know. I assumed this was one more such reshuffling.

I took out a stack of intake forms from my briefcase and approached Azalea. She was the assistant public defender in charge that morning, and she was walking around the room making sure things were in order and setting up her own workspace at counsel's table to interview the defendants. I asked her if anybody had been separated from a child.

"I don't think we've asked yet," she said. "But there shouldn't be any after that executive order, right?"

Right.

The robust U.S. Marshal in the gray suit who had been gathering the group of immigrants waved at Azalea discretely. She met his gaze and walked deliberately in his direction.

"These sixteen are going to . . ." he started to tell her as she got closer to him. I could not make out the end of the sentence from where I was standing, on the other side of the courtroom. She flipped through her docket and made notes on it while they had a brief conversation I could not hear.

A moment later Azalea motioned in my direction, signaling me to come over. As I walked across the courtroom toward the wall where she and the group were standing, I nodded lightly at the seated immigrants who made eye contact with me, a sort of greeting.

"They are going to dismiss these cases," Azalea said.

These were the separated parents of the day, sixteen of them. Their names were on the docket, but they were not going to formally file criminal charges against them. Their names were listed with a case number like all the others, but these sixteen were not going forward. They had gotten lucky: prosecutorial discretion.

Someone, somewhere between Washington and McAllen, must have made a last-minute decision not to file charges against the separated parents as a result of the executive order. It turned out the directives emanating from the order had not made it to McAllen in time after all. Deliberately or not, officials in Washington had not passed along the message down the chain quickly enough, and that was why these sixteen parents had been woken up before the sun was up, loaded on a bus handcuffed and shackled, shuttled to court, and their names were listed on this morning's docket. But just moments before their hearing was set to take place, they were called back, their names crossed off the docket, their case numbers cancelled at the last minute. Just like they had been shuffled into the courtroom, they would be shuffled out. Just like they had had no say as to why their children were taken from them or where they were taken or by whom, they now had no say as to why their cases were called off. Someone else in the system had decided for them.

"Do you still want to interview them," Azalea asked.

"Yes," I responded instinctively. I did not know what this meant for the parents. They wouldn't be prosecuted under Zero Tolerance, but would they be reunited with their children that afternoon? Unlikely. By the time the parents were taken to court, they had been separated from their children typically for a day or two. In that time, Border Patrol had categorized the children as Unaccompanied

Alien Children (UAC), the same category as anybody under the age of eighteen who crosses the border alone. In categorizing them as such, Border Patrol agents all but erased the parents with a few keystrokes on the computer when they processed the children and labeled them as UACs. Just like that, the parents ceased to exist, and their children, after having traveled thousands of miles by their side, suddenly became "unaccompanied." "Unaccompanied minors" are the responsibility of the Office of Refugee Resettlement, and by now, the children of these sixteen parents were likely either at an ORR shelter, or en route to one. This was our only chance to collect their names and dates of birth.

"Yes," I repeated. "We need to get the kids' information."

The sixteen parents looked as confused as I was. They looked at each other, exchanged a few timid words, and then looked at the other defendants sitting and waiting to be called. One of them struggled to scratch the back of his head, the handcuffs making it nearly impossible. For these parents, it was confusion on top of confusion.

A political decision by the president the prior afternoon had completely changed the course of their cases this morning. After we interviewed them, another U.S. Marshal ordered them out of the room and into one of the elevators. As the elevator doors closed and the parents disappeared behind them, I imagined they were still trying to wrap their minds around what this meant for them, and for their children. For their children, who were already on their way to a shelter, perhaps nearby, perhaps hundreds of miles away, that decision by the president had likely come too late. The immigration system and the criminal system had shifted suddenly yet again for reasons they did not understand, scattering them around like billiard balls after a violent break, bouncing off the rails and against each other, powerless to control in which direction they were going, scratching and bruising themselves up in the process.

One evening the following week, I received a frantic call from Georgina while I was driving.

"Efrén! Viviana just called," she said, ecstatic, as soon as I picked up.

We had been trying to locate Viviana since we first interviewed her more than a month earlier, on May 24. We had found her son Sandro soon after that, at a children's shelter in South Texas. But there was no sign of Viviana. Not on ICE's online detainee locator system, not on the immigration court's hotline, nowhere. We worried she may have been deported without Sandro, but we could not confirm that either. Georgina had given Viviana her business card on the day of the interview, so Viviana had her phone number. And tonight, more than a month later, she had finally called.

Georgina was so excited to finally receive Viviana's call that she could barely contain herself. ICE had sent Viviana on a plane to an immigration prison called the Northwest Detention Center, and someone had told her it was close to Seattle. She had heard nothing about Sandro and had no idea how far she had been taken away from him and from McAllen. Her initial asylum interview, the Credible Fear Interview—known simply as the CFI—was scheduled for the next day at 1 p.m. Viviana had questions about that, but mostly about her son.

I was still running through potential scenarios in my head when I put the car in park—was there any way we could possibly help Viviana at this point, when her CFI was to take place in less than twenty-four hours, thousands of miles away?

I stepped outside the car and walked past a flagpole into the Las Palmas Community Center. I was here to speak on a panel titled "The Legal and Moral Issues of Separating Families," which had been advertised as a "thoughtful, nonpartisan, interfaith dialogue about the legal and moral perspectives of separating families at the border." I walked into the lobby and immediately noticed a pair of open doors leading into a big ballroom, where the event would take place. I walked in that direction, greeted the two volunteers welcoming attendees, and stepped into the large venue.

The place was reminiscent of a high school gymnasium, with shiny linoleum flooring, walls the color of caffe latte, and what appeared to be a stage at one end, its long burgundy curtains drawn shut and nearly touching the floor. A few dozen chairs were orderly lined up facing the curtains, and some people were still making their way in slowly. At the foot of the curtains I spotted a foldable table, with a royal blue tablecloth and chairs neatly arranged for the panelists. The place made me feel as if a high school pep rally was about to take place, not a panel about immigration policy.

At the opposite end of the room, I noticed the lone security guard. A man in his sixties with pale skin and thick eyeglasses, he wore dark blue pants and a light blue security-guard uniform shirt that made him look like a cop at first glance. His watchful gaze scanned the room slowly in one direction and then the other. His left hand loosely held on to his right wrist at the lower abdomen, his arms resting across his round gut forming a wide V, a high fig leaf position.

Before the panel began, standing next to the foldable table, I pulled out my phone and started a group text in a Hail Mary attempt to help Viviana. I contacted the immigration attorneys I most trusted to reach out with an urgent request: Claire Antonelli and Lauren Joyner, with Texas Rio Grande Legal Aid, and Carlos García. Unlike Carlos, Lauren and Claire were transplants to the Rio Grande Valley, but after living in South Texas for so many years, the border had become their home. The three of them had volunteered, on different days, to help us interview separated parents in court, so they were familiar with what we were facing.

"Urgente. Do you have s contact at north western detention center?" Autocorrect turned my "urgent" into *urgente*, but did not care to correct my "s" into an "a."

Lauren responded first, suggesting an immigration attorney in the Seattle area. Carlos also chimed in: "I know folks at NWIRP," referring to the Northwest Immigrant Rights Project, a Seattle-based organization that provides services to immigrants.

When I asked whether NWIRP attorneys might be able to do CFI preparation for Viviana, Carlos didn't beat around the bush: "Dude, the CFI is tomorrow! When are they going to prep her?"

That was my fear too. I was hoping they had *already* done the "prep" with Viviana—telling her what kinds of questions to expect in a CFI, how important it was to include as much specific detail as possible, and to tell her story in a chronological, coherent manner. I sent Carlos Viviana's full name and A-Number anyway, just in case. Carlos was well aware that with such short notice and the CFI looming, there was little else we could do. "I don't think it's worth it," he texted, "but who knows."

More people were coming into the ballroom, and reporters had set up their cameras aimed at the panelists' table. The volunteers walked around the ballroom, making sure everything was in order and making small talk with the attendees. All the speakers had arrived and we were about to begin, so even though I was anxious about trying to find some help for Viviana, I put away my phone, took a sip from my water bottle, and took my seat.

When the presentation was already underway, I felt my phone vibrate against my leg. I tried to pull out my phone discretely to look at it under the table, trying not to be rude to the presenter, but when I saw that it was a message from Carlos, I quickly opened it.

"HOLY SHIT!" popped up on my cell phone screen. I wasn't sure if Carlos's expletive was due to good or bad news.

I waited impatiently while he typed another message. I lifted my gaze from the blue table, trying to casually make eye contact with the audience, then looked to my left at the presenter discussing the mental health impacts of family separation, then back down at my phone again.

"They'll go see her tonight," read Carlos's second message.

I sighed in relief. Some good news, at last. At least Viviana was going to have a lawyer explain to her what a "credible fear interview" was. She would be much better prepared than the vast majority of asylum seekers who face the CFI alone, unrepresented, and without any guidance about the process. The news gave me some hope she might pass. These moments of hope were so few and far between, and often turned out to be ultimately unsuccessful, that I usually preferred not to get my hopes up. I did not want to be disappointed later when things did not work out.

As the other panelists gave their presentations, I looked at the security guard in the back of the room as he adjusted his glasses. He took a couple of steps sideways and crossed his arms, his body language betraying skepticism. When it was my turn, I covered as much detail about the parents' ordeals as I could fit in the seven minutes I was allotted. I went through the details much more mechanically than I had at the beginning of the summer, and I could hear myself beginning to sound desensitized. It was becoming harder and harder to tell Viviana's story, and Arturo's and Patricia's, and so many others, with the same level of outrage and disbelief as the first time I had recounted them. My voice was starting to show the signs of compassion fatigue.

I hadn't been sleeping well that week, and the round-the-clock news about family separations had begun to take a toll on my concentration. After going to court in the mornings, I would spend the day at the office trying to coordinate our efforts to locate children, on the phone with family members who had questions about their loved ones (parents or children who were still unaccounted for), or on the phone with ICE agents. It had been a month since we had started working with the families, but it felt like much longer. I was physically exhausted. And every now and then, a particularly difficult case took an emotional toll too. All this on top of my regular civil rights caseload, which I had tried to put on pause, but some cases still had upcoming deadlines. I had begun to think this pace was not sustainable for much longer, but the adrenaline, the urgency of the work, and unhealthy amounts of coffee, kept me going.

"The only other country in the world that I am aware of," I said, at the end of my remarks, "the *only* other country that punishes children for what their parents do—in addition to the United States today—is North Korea."

I made a long pause, staring at the attendees. "Thank you."

The comment was meant to provoke a reaction from the audience, but it was also true. I knew that political prisoners in North Korea spend their entire lives in forced labor camps, and if they have children while there, their children will die without ever leaving the camps. For me, the comparison to the family separation policy was true at its core: like North Korea, the United States Government was punishing children for something their parents did—and what their parents did was often simply cross a border, perhaps in hopes of applying for asylum. Like North Korean children who didn't know why they couldn't leave those camps, the thousands of immigrant children separated from their parents at the border had no idea why their parents were violently taken from them.

I looked up and scanned the audience for reactions. A lady sitting near the front instinctively covered her mouth with her hand. A few others lowered their heads and shook them in disapproval. The security guard in the back shifted uncomfortably in place. I was looking in his direction when my thoughts were interrupted by a new vibration against my leg: another text message. I waited for an opportunity to pull my phone out of my pocket.

It was Carlos again.

"Guess what?!" his message read. "She has a pro bono attorney to attend her CFI and has been prepared."

I could hardly believe it. I wanted to high-five every co-panelist, with both hands. Viviana would have a lawyer with her at the CFI! Now she *really* had a shot. The CFI passing rate of asylum seekers who have a lawyer with them during the interview is much higher than that of those who are unrepresented—the vast majority. I wanted to clap my hands together in excitement. But instead of doing any of that, I simply looked at Sister Norma, one of the other panelists, as she explained that we were all children of God, all brothers and sisters, and I nodded. "ICE agents, Border Patrol agents, we all take communion together," she said. Sister Norma Pimentel, a Catholic nun from South Texas, had made national news in 2015 when the "respite center" she founded in McAllen to assist unaccompanied children received a live-streamed call from Pope Francis himself.

Her comment startled me. As far as I could tell, Sister Norma's remark was an attempt to get the audience to see the agents as fellow human beings, to not deny their humanity. I got that. But it was still hard for me to hear her say that when I was seeing day after day at the courthouse how many of these agents were not seeing the humanity of the immigrants they apprehended. I agreed with her comment in the abstract, but sitting in that chair, I struggled to get past the fact that many of the agents who took communion on Sunday were taking children away from their parents on Monday. I was thinking of the parents sitting in a cold cell and the children at a shelter, alone, wondering where their parents were. Did the agents think of *them* as brothers and sisters?

After the presentations and the Q&A wrapped up, I walked around the ballroom, making my way toward the door to head home. Before I could reach the exit, the security guard who had been listening in the back approached me.

He walked slowly, hesitantly, as if embarrassed. I stopped and smiled, greeting him. Up close, his pale skin showed reddish patches, signs of damaged skin and old age, perhaps from long hours in the sun. His short gray hair was neatly combed.

"Hello, sir," he said respectfully. He pushed his thick, heavy glasses up his nose and adjusted his belt.

"Hi, how are you?"

"You know," he said. "I'm just the security guard here, but I was listening to the presentations. Regardless of what my views on immigration might be, I feel for those children you were talking about, I really do. But you know, their parents broke the law. . . ."

I had heard this line before: their parents are criminals, the separations are their fault. The parents had been sentenced to "time served" for breaking the law, for crossing the border without authorization. When U.S. citizens are convicted of a misdemeanor that does not result in prison time, they go home and their families are there waiting for them; the government does not take their kids away. In sharp contrast, weeks after being sentenced to time served, hundreds of immigrant parents still had not seen their children. The separation was punishment *on top of* the judicial sentence. Not to speak of the punishment on the children. I was always interested in the moral acrobatics necessary to resolve the cognitive dissonance and make the separations seem acceptable.

But rather than get into the fallacies of his argument as we stood there, a couple of feet from the exit, I told the guard that I disagreed with the family separation policy for people who crossed the border illegally, even for people who had crossed it multiple times. He clasped his hands and rested them on his belt as he heard me say that I disagreed with the policy even for people who had a criminal record. The separation amounted to extra-judicial punishment, I tried to explain. It was a matter of basic human rights.

"It's not that I don't feel for the children, because I do," he insisted. I got the distinct impression that he was looking for a sign of approval from me.

I wanted to stop his explanation and ask: Would he accept the policy of taking children away from American citizens because they had committed a misdemeanor? Would he be okay with a white American child being forcibly taken from her mother because she had, say, run a stop sign at the Pentagon, which is a federal misdemeanor that carries the same penalty as crossing the border illegally for the first time?

Despite his emphasis on how he *really* felt for the children, he was so quick to dismiss them that I wondered how much he actually felt for them. In the same breath he said he felt for the children, he also said that their parents had broken the law, immediately qualifying any sympathy he may have felt. Not to speak of the parents, for whom he did not say he felt anything. When speaking of the immigrant children and their parents, he referred to "them" in a way that made it seem as if he was putting "them" in a certain category I couldn't quite put my finger on, a category to which he did not belong. In our discussion, he did not raise anything about *us*. Even if the parents had violated Section 1325, did that justify *us*, as a government, as a society, taking another human being's child away? Did that justify our taking the parents away from the children?

Despite how much he tried to say that he "felt" for them, it was clear to me he did not see immigrant parents and children as he saw himself, and that prevented him from truly putting himself in their position. That was why it was possible for him to come up with a version of the situation that was acceptable to his moral compass. He may have been capable of feeling sympathy for the children— he repeated time and again he "felt bad" for them—but he came short of empathy, of truly putting himself in the place of the parents and the children. Only when we consider the other person a human being equal to us, when we literally see them like we see ourselves, deserving of justice and compassion and respect for the simple reason that they too are a human being, are we able to transcend the material differences of our circumstance—place of birth, nationality, skin color, language, criminal history, poverty—and feel true empathy for one another.

I looked around the room, and more than half the attendees had already left.

"And," the security guard added, "I know you're trying to be provocative and whatnot, but, you know, I'm a veteran, I served in Vietnam." He paused for me to react, and we exchanged glances as I nodded.

"Don't you think it's a little much when you say that our country is like North Korea?"

He felt the need to tell me he was a veteran before voicing his uneasiness with the comparison to North Korea. As most other times I had uttered it, that line had caused discomfort. It was hard for him to conceive of the United States and North Korea— arguably the most repressive dictatorship in the world—as similar in any way. It was simply too jarring to think of North Korea as having anything in common with the country for which he had risked his life.

"I didn't say they are the same," I told him. "I said I am not aware of any other country that punishes children for what their parents do, and I am not."

He was less than satisfied with my response. He adjusted his belt pulling his pants up slightly, uncomfortably, and pursed his lips. The mere mention of the two countries in the same sentence seemed to him preposterous, offensive, as an American citizen, perhaps even more so as a combat veteran. Perhaps his notion of patriotism made it difficult for him to criticize the current government of his country, even long after he had retired from the armed forces and the president had stopped being his commander in chief. Perhaps his notion of good citizenship translated into an unflinching allegiance to America and its policies. Perhaps his experience as a veteran made him see those who come from other countries without papers as enemies, as threats.

I had no such notions. For me, the best way to support a democratic form of government was to call it out—loudly—when it violated human rights. When the government violated the fundamental rights of the men, women, and children who came to its shores, staying silent would amount to complicity. And if calling it out meant criticizing the country where I lived, where I made a living, and where I was raising my family, then so be it. That was the best way I could conceive of being a responsible member of society. More than that, I saw it as a way to speak up for the parents and children who could not speak for themselves. Or if they spoke, they were not heard. I could be a voice for them, a tiny fraction of their voice, this evening, in this community center, in front of this security guard.

Viviana's turn of events was unlikely. Every year, thousands of people wishing to apply for asylum face a Credible Fear Interview; the vast majority do it alone, and most of them fail. In the last twenty years, some 45 percent of asylum applicants represented by a lawyer have won their asylum cases. For those facing the process alone, the success rate is barely over 10 percent. It is almost inevitable that, alone, they will fail. Viviana's case was an anomaly, to say the least.

After all she had lived through in Guatemala, traveling more than a thousand miles to get to Texas, and then having Border Patrol agents take Sandro away from her in McAllen, she had ultimately been "fortunate" to have a lawyer represent her at her CFI.

The NWIRP attorney who represented Viviana at her CFI also agreed to handle her bond application, to try to secure her release. Against all odds, the immigration judge (IJ) set a bond, and an anonymous donor came up with $13,000 to pay it. Thirteen thousand dollars. It still escapes me what notion of justice requires a person fleeing death threats and seeking refuge and protection to come up with that amount of money. What was that IJ thinking? Did he set that bond amount thinking that Viviana wouldn't be able to pay it? If he considered Viviana not to be a flight risk or a threat to the community, why require her to pay any money at all? That bond amount certainly signaled a desire to keep her locked up, or more perversely, an attempt to make money off a widowed, destitute asylum seeker who had been begging to see her son for weeks. But again, the stars and volunteer attorneys and good Samaritans all lined up from McAllen to Seattle, and Viviana was released a few days later.

Most immigrants are not that fortunate. Thousands of Vivianas are deported every year, many to places where they will be harmed or killed, because our immigration system is designed to deport, not to protect. They are deported because every actor in the system—from Washington to McAllen—is doing their part to deport as many people as possible, as quickly as possible. Every cog in the bureaucracy, from field agents to IJs, is pushing the deportation conveyor belt along, never mind if they are themselves the descendants of immigrants from another era. If the country's doors were open when their parents and grandparents arrived in Ellis Island, they have been fiercely shut for the parents and grandparents arriving today at the Rio Grande. It may be different shores, but those showing up at our borders come for the same reasons that people have migrated to this land since before the country's founding: to seek safety and opportunity. And why are the doors shut to them? It is not really because they come to take others' jobs or pose a national security risk, as anti-immigrant hardliners would have us believe—those arguments have been made for years, always to mask the real reasons non-white immigrants have historically been unwelcome to this country: because they do not fit the mold of what those bigots view as the "real" Americans.

Later that month, sitting in my office, I finally got ahold of Arturo, the father who had made up the summer camp story for his daughter. We tried to update our spreadsheet of parents every day with any new information, after calling parents, siblings, distant relatives, pastors, doctors, family friends, and anyone else whose contact information the parents had given us in court. We often found ourselves calling family in Guatemala or Honduras if there was no one else in the United States. For the most difficult cases—say a father deported without his son, and no working contact information for any relative anywhere—we reached out to Justice in Motion, a nonprofit organization that specializes in locating individuals deported to Mexico and Central America.

I dialed the number Arturo had given me for his sister in Santa Barbara, and she put him on the phone.

"*Hola Arturo, buenas tardes,*" I greeted him gleefully.

"*Buenas,*" he said, and I pictured him smiling softly like he had done in court.

I asked if he remembered me, adding that I was the lawyer who interviewed him about being separated from his daughter Miriam. "You told me about summer camp," I said, recalling our conversation.

"*Sí*," he said. "*Sí me acuerdo.*" He remembered.

When I asked if he had been reunited with his daughter yet, he went quiet.

"*Sí, sí, ya,*" he said tersely.

He and Miriam had been transferred to California, and then released together days after they arrived. They had been separated for a shorter period than most other parents, but I still sensed he did not want to go into the details. All traces of a smile disappeared from his voice, and his answers became short and curt. After having been abandoned by his wife when Miriam was only three years old, he had now come very close to losing her too. But his laconic responses made it clear that he did not want to discuss the separation, or even the reunification, and I respected that.

I asked about his immigration case, and he said his sister was helping him find an immigration attorney to represent him and Miriam. That gave me some measure of hope.

"Well, that's good. And I'm glad Miriam is back with you," was all I could say.

"*Sí, sí,*" he said. We then said a quick goodbye, and never spoke again.

CHAPTER 10

Together Again

(1996)

M y mother, Héctor, and I arrived in McAllen on a Thursday in early February 1996. The night before, in Allende, Héctor and I had helped pack our clothes into two small suitcases. My parents had sold most of our furniture, or stacked it up in the laundry room out back, the same place where Silvia had written out the alphabet for me on a toy chalkboard ten years earlier.

Héctor and I were excited to be with our father again, as we had fantasized for years at the breakfast table. I imagined my mother was too, but she didn't say much. She simply put our photo album and a couple of VHS tapes in a box, and took them to the room in the back.

When we had visited my father months earlier for the appointment with the *notaria*, he and my brother Leoba had been staying in a tiny room next to Tía Tila's house, my father's older sister, on Chicago Street. I was surprised when I saw where they lived. I had never seen a house set atop cinderblocks like Tía Tila's. It was toward the back of a rectangular lot, and the room where Leoba and my father slept was detached from the house, also resting on cinderblocks. Multiple lawn mowers lay around the lot with their engines partially taken apart, some pieces missing, as if a mechanic had been working on them and stopped halfway. Discarded tires, cigarette butts, and empty aluminum cans littered the lot, which was mostly bare dirt except for the few patches of yellow, shriveling grass. I did not see roses or geraniums anywhere.

When I first saw the room where my father was staying, I thought it was abandoned. We climbed the two wooden steps and opened the screen door to walk inside, its hinges creaking like an old swing set. The entire place was poorly lit even in the middle of the day, and the smell of dust was stronger inside than outside. To the right, next to a small bed, my father's clothes were neatly folded and arranged on a makeshift wooden shelf no taller than the bed. There was no closet. The left end of the room, which served as a kitchen, had no stove, only a small fridge and a portable electric grill, the kind with two coils that shine bright orange when hot. The place seemed clean, but the dusty smell made it feel dingy, unkempt. The floor squeaked painfully every time my parents and Leoba walked around the room. Héctor and I were still too light to disturb the floorboards enough for them to make a sound.

There was only the one bed, and I worried about where my mother, Héctor, and I would sleep once we moved in—the floor seemed like the only alternative. My father must have noticed the worry on my face, maybe my mother's face betrayed concern too.

"No se preocupen," he said. "Don't worry, when you all come, we're going to rent a different place, a bigger and nicer place."

My surprise grew when I heard that they were renting this room. I didn't think this was a place anyone would pay to stay in.

In the intervening months between that visit and the time we moved for good, my sister Tania also left Allende for McAllen, to stay with Leoba and my father. They had found somewhere else, like my father had said, an apartment down the street. It wasn't much bigger, and it wasn't much nicer.

Because Tania was my father's daughter from a different mother, the *notaria* suggested that she file her immigration application separately from the one my father filed for my mother, Héctor, and me. That was better under the law, she said, and my father heeded the advice. I never heard him or Tania bemoan this decision, having to file separate applications, even though we were now part of the same family, living under the same roof. That was how the law worked, the *notaria* explained, and that was what we had to do.

The apartment at 2023 Chicago Street was a long, rectangular unit. I had never seen walls like these, white like the clouds but thin as if made of cardboard, instead of the hard cement of our house in Allende or the cool adobe of my grandmother's house in Loma Prieta. Every room was connected to the next, and there was no hallway, so that to get to the kitchen and the bathroom all the way at the back, you had to walk through the length of the apartment: a "living room" by the entrance; a small room with a closet next, which we used as the bedroom; and the kitchen at the far end of the rectangle. Leoba and Tania stayed in the living room, near the entrance, sleeping on a sofa, while my parents, Héctor, and I stayed in the middle room with the closet. The first time I walked into the apartment, I noticed that the wall dividing the middle room from the kitchen did not reach all the way to the ceiling, so that there was an opening between these two rooms. That feature seemed odd, as if that wall hadn't been finished, or had been added as an afterthought to divide these two rooms, as if this apartment had never been meant to house an entire family. The opening on this wall also meant that the smells from the kitchen permeated the entire apartment morning and night.

That first night in the apartment, Héctor and I discovered that we would sleep on a thin foldable mattress in the middle room. The mattress was rough against my skin, and the sheet my mother put on it wasn't thick enough to shield my back from its scratchy surface. Tiny specks of its coarse outer fabric fell off the next morning when my mother lifted it off the floor. Every night my mother brought out that mattress, and every morning she put it away in the closet, folding it into a trifold, a few more scraps of fabric falling off each time. In Allende, Héctor and I had each had our own bed. There was no backyard here either, and we did not know any of our neighbors. Still, I was content to be here, scratchy mattress and all. The lack of physical comfort was more than compensated by the intangible comfort of knowing that Héctor, my mother, and I were not by ourselves anymore.

Héctor and I were not allowed to attend school until we could present the piece of paper showing that we were fully vaccinated. When my mother produced our Mexican vaccination cards, they showed that we each needed a couple more. Just like not having the visa before to visit my father, not having the proper vaccination card kept us from starting school and fully entering our new life. It was again a document that dictated whether we could belong. After years of waiting, we were finally physically here in McAllen, but inoculation was a last step we needed to take in order to fully "arrive." My mother worried that we would not start school for weeks, until we received the additional shots. Héctor was eleven and I was thirteen years old, and she was concerned that we would fall behind in our education. There was no way around it, my father said. *Ni modo.* That was what the school required, so that was what we had to do. His matter-of-fact acceptance of the way things had to be confounded me. About a month later, my brother and I finally received our additional shots at a county clinic. One poke on each arm was our last passport, and we were ready, safe to step into a school on this side of the Rio Grande.

That same night, like every other night, my father set the alarm clock for 5:45 a.m. Except unlike prior mornings, the next morning Héctor and I would also have to get up when we heard the alarm clock buzz, its bright red digital numbers announcing our wake-up time. With the four of us crammed in that middle room—my parents sharing a mattress on the floor, Héctor and I sharing our asperous foldable next to them—it was hard to ignore the loud buzzing. The timing was such that the alarm would go off at 5:45 a.m., we would leave the apartment by 6:00 a.m., arrive at the big parking lot where all the school buses were neatly lined up by 6:20 a.m. or 6:25 a.m., and my father could punch his card before 6:30 a.m. To be awake and ready to go in fifteen minutes, Héctor and I did like my father: we readied our clothes the night before, set them on the kitchen table, pants folded over the back of a chair, socks on top of the shoes under the chair. At first I did not understand why my father would even pass his belt through the pants' belt loops the night before, but I soon learned that those precious seconds were key to being ready in time.

On that first drive the next morning, I did not see any of the bright lights I had pictured so many times in Allende. Héctor and I got in the car and I dozed off for the entire drive. If we drove past any McDonald's arches or Walmart signs, I did not see them. We arrived at the school bus yard some twenty minutes later, and I struggled to stay awake as I dragged my feet toward the one numbered nine, the predawn darkness broken only by the headlights of a bus whose engine was already running. Like all the rest, the bus my father drove was parked diagonally, with its back impossibly close to the short cyclone fence that encircled the entire yard. Héctor and I climbed on and dozed off again, each of us in a seat across from each other near the front, while my father started the engine. He opened its enormous yellow hood—I had never seen a hood so big or that opened in this way, away from the windshield—to check the coolant and the brake fluid, and made sure all brake and turning lights were working properly. Every few minutes, the roar of another engine coming alive would startle me, the sun slowly rising, its timid morning rays shining faintly to reveal, one by one, giant mustard-colored vehicles readying for the day.

In my grogginess, I recalled a story my mother told so many times, and with so much pride, about my first day of elementary school in Allende, when I was six years old.

Like most nights when I was that age, I had made it to my parents' bedroom in the middle of the night. I could never remember that sleepwalk, but I was magically in their bed by morning.

"*Ya es hora*," Mami said in a soft voice, her hand gently rubbing my shoulder, as if trying to wake me and not to disturb me all at once. It was time. "*¿Todavía tienes sueño?*" She noticed my struggle and asked if I was still sleepy as I turned in the bed. The neighbor's parakeets chirruped from their cages confirming that it was morning.

"*Sí tengo sueño*," I said, "*pero no quiero llegar tarde.*" Yes, I was sleepy, but I didn't want to be late. So I still woke up, and my mother was immediately pleased at my commitment and dedication. "You were always such a good student," she would say later when recounting the anecdote, and so little, *tan chiquito*. My mother has repeated that story so many times, with those exact words and beaming pride, that I am no longer sure if it's truly a memory of mine, or the memory of hearing her story over and over again. It's as if her satisfaction at my demonstration of discipline at an early age grew every time she repeated the story. Like the main character in the Argentinean film *The Secret in Their Eyes*, I don't know if it's a memory, or the memory of a memory that is left. *Y ya no sé si es un recuerdo, o el recuerdo de un recuerdo lo que me va quedando.*

Another memory that has receded into that same category of uncertainty—is it my own childhood memory or a memory that I have constructed as an adult into the idea of a childhood memory after hearing it so many times—is being asked which of my parents I loved more.

"*¿A quién de los dos quieres más?*" Mami would ask, in the most endearing way, with the loveliest of smiles, as if daring me to choose one over the other, but knowing full well what I would say in response.

The first time she asked, I was not genuinely thinking whether I loved one of my parents more than the other. I was thinking whether I could *say* that I loved one more than the other. I didn't dare choose one. I couldn't.

"*A los dos igual*" was my invariable answer. Both the same.

"But you *must* love one more than the other, no?" She would insist, her jesting smile growing wide.

I did not waver, repeating that I loved them both the same. No matter how many times she insisted, I remained steadfast in my answer, making Mami so very proud, especially if someone was around to see me remain firm in my impartial expression of love. Once I figured out that the answer "both the same" not only got me out of having to choose either of them, but was also a celebrated response—despite not really answering the question—I went along with the repeat performance as many times as I was asked.

Other memories are so vivid that I can still see them unfolding, as if they were happening anew. On a late summer afternoon in Allende, after my father had moved to McAllen, Héctor and I were playing with two neighbors to see who could jump the farthest. To mark the distance of the jump, we set two pieces of wood on the ground, parallel to each another, in the middle of the street in front of our house. Once all four jumpers cleared the initial distance, we moved one of the markers a little farther away and tried again, and so on each time. My mother watered her roses and kept an eye on us, glancing up every few minutes to make sure we got out of the way if a car drove by. Cars would slow down as they approached, and we simply stepped to the side, leaving our markers in place, lest we lose track of where we were and who was winning. Once the distance to jump became considerable, a couple of centimeters could determine the winner. We were aspiring long jumpers leaping over rough asphalt and gravel instead of soft sand.

One of the markers was a broken piece of a broom's handle. In what was perhaps our most amateur move, we placed that cylindrical marker at the landing side of our jumping area instead of at the take-off side. When it was my turn and the distance seemed to me like several meters—surely this had to be some sort of record—I walked back a few extra steps to pick up speed before the decisive jump. With the sun at my back over the Sierra Madre mountains, I could see my shadow stretching long in front of me, always one step ahead. I took a deep breath and sprinted down the street as fast as I could toward the jump, fists clenched and arms swinging, the faint breeze hitting my body harder with each step. When my right foot reached the take-off marker, I leapt with all the strength in my body. My arms swung up and forward, propelling me into the air, and I flew high over the asphalt. In the fraction of a second that I was in the air, I felt my body stretch its full length trying to land as far out as possible. In my mind I was nothing short of the Olympic long jumpers I had seen on TV.

And then I landed. My heels touched down on the round piece of broom handle, thrusting it forward violently and sending me sliding sideways and scraping the outer side of my right thigh. When my body came to a stop, heat ran up the side of my leg, my shorts bunched up from roughing against the ground. I sat up slowly, holding back tears and dusting my hands off. I slowly turned my leg inward to see the damage. No major bleeding, but my thigh burned badly as soon as I stood up and tried to walk.

My mother heard the commotion. I limped slowly in her direction, as she put down the hose and walked briskly toward me, worry in her face.

"*A ver, a ver, ¿qué fue?*" Mami asked. But before I could answer, she added, "*no fue nada, no te pasó nada,*" as she inspected my leg and I tried hard not to cry. She picked up the hose again, poured some water on her hand, and used it to wash off the loose gravel and dirt from my chafed leg, all the while repeating tenderly, "it was nothing," "you're fine."

And what was most remarkable: it worked. The more I heard Mami repeat those words, the less pain I felt, the burning sensation slowly subsiding. She was right, it seemed. It was nothing. I was fine.

For most other falls or scrapes, my mother repeated some version of those words. Years before that jump, when I had rammed my yellow too-big-for-me bicycle into a blooming crape myrtle, banging my head against its trunk and knocking off more than one of its buds, her "*estás bien*" had assuaged my bulging skull. I was okay. And years before that, when I was learning how to ride a bicycle and rode it straight into a parked Grand Marquis—I had explained to her between sobs that it wasn't that I couldn't ride straight, I simply hadn't seen the car—Mami's cradling words had brought me peace. "*Levántate mi amor,*" get up sweetie, "*no fue nada,*" it was nothing.

I always heard her words as coming from a place of profound love. I would wipe my tears and hold any pain I may have been feeling tightly closed inside. Unexpressed, it would go away, and I learned to overcome physical pain by telling myself that it was nothing, that I was fine. With time, I have come to realize that what I had considered my "natural" predisposition to not express unpleasant feelings and emotions may not have been so natural after all, and instead may be related to the way I learned to tame my pain. The repeated instructions to make it not hurt, to not cry, to be fine, were also consistent with my father's deadpan manner. I hardly ever saw him cry or express any kind of affliction. Especially when it comes to pain, anguish, or other emotional burden, I still deny it until it fades away.

"*Listos*," my father said, more a statement than a question, as the bus inched forward, the sun shining bright by now. He was ready, we were ready, the bus was ready. When our turn came, our bus exited the yard, heading away from the fence and toward our first day of school.

When I first entered Valley View Junior High School, it was like the schools I had seen on TV. The first thing that struck me was the air-conditioning. *Everything* was air-conditioned. Not only were all the classrooms at a perfectly cool temperature—I had never been in such classrooms—but even the hallways were air-conditioned. The doors that led to the outside were always closed tight, a piece of soft rubber sealing every space between the doors so that not a drop of cool air could escape. In Allende, the hallways that connected one classroom to the next were all outdoors, exposed to the weather of the day, and if it was raining, you got wet. Here, the entire place was like a giant bubble, cool and pleasant and shielded from whatever was happening out in the world. The chilly air followed you around to the library, to the cafeteria, to the principal's office, to the nurse's office—I couldn't believe there *was* a nurse's office at school. Everywhere you went, everything was cool and clean.

The floors in particular were always shiny. After finishing his morning shift driving students to school, my father joined the other janitors. To get the floors to shine so clear that you could see your reflection on the large tiles if you looked closely, my father used what looked like a large electrical mop with huge handlebars at the top, and a big round yellow brush at the bottom that spun nonstop when the thing was on. The machine had a long power cord so that the electrical mop could be pushed long distances to clean and shine every inch of the hallway. Between classes, I would see my father and other janitors slowly make their way around the school pushing the electrical mop, a couple of steps at a time, then across the full width of the hallways, so that when we came out of the classroom, we wouldn't have to step on even a speck of dust. I went from seeing my father only once every few weeks and only for a couple of days at a time, to seeing him every day, even at school, in between classes and especially after school. I didn't go talk to him while he was working because I didn't want to disturb him, but knowing he was there was comfort enough.

Math quickly became my favorite subject. When I walked into the classroom and saw "Ms. Gonzalez" written across the chalkboard, I breathed easy, expecting her to be fully fluent in Spanish. I had always seen Gonzalez spelled "González," with an accent mark on the letter "a," but she omitted it. This "chalkboard" with her name on it wasn't like the ones I was used to in Allende. This one was white, and there was no chalk anywhere, its surface so smooth and shiny and easy to erase on. All the chalkboards at Veteranos and Pablo Livas had been green, their surface always dusty from stubborn chalk that would not come off completely, even after the teacher used a wet rag at the end of the day to wipe it off. This board was silky clean, math problems coming off as easily as they had gone on there, leaving no trace.

Ms. Gonzalez greeted me like she was truly happy to see me. Her short hair fell just above her shoulders, her beige slacks and a perfectly ironed blouse dressed her petite frame.

"*O-la,*" she said, her friendly smile revealing the whitest teeth. "Effrin?" she asked, tilting her head indecisively. Her soft voice was amiable, but I was confused at the way she said my name, with a question mark at the end, like running into somebody you haven't seen in a long time and don't recognize.

I didn't know what to say. This was the first time I had heard my name pronounced like this, with an English-sounding R and the emphasis on the first syllable. That wasn't really my name. Or was it? For her it was. I smiled back, attempting to mirror her gleefulness, and tried my best at a "hello" in response.

"Welcome, Effrin," Ms. Gonzalez said, pleased with herself. Once I took my seat, I tried to say my name in my head the way Ms. Gonzalez had said it, and I simply couldn't do it. Even in my head, silently, it came out as Efrén each time, the way it always had, the way everyone had pronounced it before, up until that day. Up until that day, it had never crossed my mind that our move to McAllen would entail changing not only houses and schools, but also my name.

My parents picked my name based on the day I was born. The Roman Catholic calendar of saints, which assigns saints to almost every day of the year, set "San Efrén" for June 9, and that's how I came to be christened Efrén. Had I been born a day before, I could have been a Medardo, a day after and I would have been Asterio. San Efrén, often spelled Ephrem in English, was reportedly an ascetic who lived in the fourth century in present-day Syria. When the town of Edessa was suffering a devastating famine, he was tasked with brokering the distribution of grains to the poor and administering aid to the ill. He wrote poetic hymns in Aramaic about suffering and austerity and is believed to have died on June 9, 373.

That moment in math class was not the first time I wished I had a different name. A "normal" name. From the time I entered kindergarten and met other children whose names I had heard on TV and elsewhere—*Juan, Edgar, Luis*—I wished I had a more common name, a name easy to recognize. I would have been perfectly happy being a *Daniel* or a *Pablo*, but no, my name was a thing most people had never heard before. A thing I almost always had to repeat at least once so they understood it. For most people I met, I was the first Efrén they met, and I had to correct them saying no, it's not Efrain, it's *Efrén*. And that day in Ms. Gonzalez's class, I wished again I had a different name.

Ms. Gonzalez's presentation at the front of the classroom interrupted my thoughts. When she started her lesson, I couldn't follow. She looked in my direction a couple of times and gave me the same smile she had when she had given me my new name, but no matter how nicely she looked at me or how much she slowed down her speech when looking at me, I simply couldn't understand the language. I knew the numbers up to ten and a few loose English words, but it wasn't enough to follow along.

When she started drawing on the whiteboard, everything changed. She drew four straight lines to form a square, and then the number six next to the line on the right and another six below the bottom line. On the right-hand side, she wrote "area: L x W =" and continued her explanation. I could not understand the words length and width yet, but I recognized the problem. What a lucky coincidence, I thought, the English word was so similar to the Spanish *área*, oblivious to the world of cognates.

For the rest of the school year, I was able to follow in math class based on the numbers and shapes Ms. Gonzalez drew on the board. I had learned the concepts at Pablo Livas months earlier, and that gave me a confidence that carried over into other subjects where I could not yet follow the lessons in the same way, like Texas history and life sciences. Every day I looked forward to math class, where numbers and shapes became the keys that unlocked the language.

One morning a few months later, Ms. Hernández, the school's middle-aged counselor, brought me into her office. Down the hall from the principal's office, her small room had only one chair for the visitor, like a therapist's office meant to see only one client at a time. The bright white light overhead was, like everywhere else in the school, that artificial light emanating from two bars behind a plexiglass covering. I sat down, the seat squishy underneath me, as if many students had been in my place before.

"*¿Cómo te va?*" She greeted me with a smile, taking off her glasses.

I had never had a school counselor before and did not really understand her role. Ms. Hernández's Spanish was flawless, but I had never heard her accent. On her desk, she kept a framed photograph of two girls that I guessed were her daughters. Next to it were a wooden cross and a small flag with two horizontal royal blue stripes, a white stripe in the middle, and a coat of arms in the center resting on a laurel wreath. I had never seen the Salvadoran flag or heard the Salvadoran accent, but I guessed both had to be from a Latin American country.

The first time I had been in Ms. Hernández's office, on my first day at the school and accompanied by my father, she had been the one to break the news: Since I didn't speak English, I was going to be placed in seventh grade, even though I had been in the equivalent of eighth in Mexico. This wasn't bad, she had said, it would allow me to learn English and "catch up" with the material. Héctor wasn't being held back, so I didn't understand why I had to be. My father had assented and nodded along, and I, standing next to him, hadn't voiced the "but" in my head, withholding all my questions, unsure if the decision was even up for discussion. Every day since then, Ms. Gonzalez's math lessons had been a constant reminder that rather than catching up, I was reviewing in English what I had already learned in Spanish.

"*Bien,*" I smiled back at her this morning, nodding lightly.

"I hear that you're doing really well with Ms. Gonzalez. *¿Te gustan las matemáticas?*" She looked at me eagerly, as if waiting for an emphatic "yes, I love math," in response.

I didn't particularly love math, but I had enjoyed it since coming to Valley View. It was the one class where I could follow the material, and being familiar with most of it made it even easier. The confidence I found in math gradually overcame the disappointment at having been held back a year. It was not something I thought about every day, but each time I remembered, I couldn't help but think that our move had set me back in a very concrete way, and wondered if I would ever make up that lost year.

"You're also doing well in ESL," Ms. Hernández added, raising her eyebrows joyfully. English as a Second Language, with Ms. Velasco, was meant to teach us English, but I felt I was learning more from Ms. Gonzalez and her numbers.

"Will you be ready to enter regular English classes next year?" she posited, as if asking herself, looking at the paperwork in front of her.

I wasn't so sure. Texas history had been especially challenging—I kept confusing stagecoaches with Nacogdoches—and I feared the following year classes would be even more difficult. I shifted awkwardly in my seat, the cushion offering little comfort.

"*Yo creo que sí,*" she looked up and answered before I could say a word, her smile widening across her enthusiastic nod. "You just need to pass this vocabulary test," she added confidently, "and you'll be ready to go." I had hardly said anything the entire time I had been in her office, but she seemed to be enjoying the conversation with herself.

She rolled her chair back and pulled out a large book from one of her drawers. She laid it out in front of me, its pages thick like a baby's board book.

Each page, she explained, had four images. "All you need to do is name one of them, any one." *Facilito*, she quipped. Piece of cake.

The images on the test were also reminiscent of the drawings in children's coloring books. Colorless outlines of a pair of pants, a house, a tree, and a dog, all sitting on the page for me to name. A book, a pencil, a pair of scissors, and a *sacapuntas*, the sharpener that I still couldn't name. Every time I named one of the images, Ms. Hernández would make a note on a sheet of paper and then turn the page. As the test progressed, the images became less childlike and more difficult for me to identify. I recognized the *semáforo*, *desarmador*, and *tuerca* right away, all simple enough in Spanish, but I hadn't come across them as traffic light, screwdriver, or bolt nut. Still, I was able to name at least one of the images on most pages.

"Okay," Ms. Hernández said when she turned to the last page of the book. "*Ésta es la última, vas muy bien.*" It was the last question, and I needed to get it right in order to pass.

I looked down at the images on the page one by one, and drew a complete blank. Top left, top right, bottom left, and bottom right. Nothing. I pushed myself up and back from the chair's plastic armrests, and then pulled the chair forward to look at the images again. I lifted my gaze and met Ms. Hernández's confident smile as she adjusted her glasses, her expression trying to project reassurance that didn't quite reach me.

I went through the images again, wished for a miracle as I glanced up at the cross on Ms. Hernández's desk, and then looked down at the page one more time. Nothing still. A faint herbal aroma that must have emanated from the potted plant behind her desk intensified the longer I stared at the images, incapable of coming up with a name. I later learned it was rosemary, and more than once that smell has transported me to that office and that test.

After a long while, when Ms. Hernández must have sensed

my hopelessness, she leaned forward and got close to the book in front of me. Holding a pen between her index and middle fingers, she pointed at the image on the bottom right. It was the drawing of a zipper, like the one on a sweater, depicted by itself, halfway unzipped, with a large pull tab in the middle. It was a zipper, I had no doubt. But I had no idea how to say zipper in English. I looked up at Ms. Hernández, my nervous eyes trying to say I *know*, but I *don't know*.

She nodded and, smiling, tapped the image again with her pen a couple of times, as if confirming the instruction she was trying to convey. Our eyes met and she nodded again like saying c'mon, go for it.

It was clear she wanted me to say—to guess—the word for zipper. I had no clue, so I did the only thing I could.

"See..." I hesitated for a second, Ms. Hernández still nodding. "See...per?" I finally said, full of doubt.

"*¡Eso!*" she exclaimed, delighted. "*¡Excelente!*" And her smile grew into outright laughter.

I had said the Spanish word I knew for zipper, trying to make it sound like English, and wishing for the best. Luck was part of it too—had I been from Spain, where zippers are known as *cremalleras*, or even from central Mexico, where most people know them as *cierres*, the ploy wouldn't have worked. But I was fortunate that I had grown up calling zippers by the anglicism *zípers*, and Ms. Hernández's nudge, smooth and precise like the scalpel of a trained surgeon, worked perfectly. I did not appreciate all the implications in that moment, but thanks to that nudge, I passed the vocabulary test. Thanks to that, I entered regular English classes at the beginning of eighth grade that fall. And thanks to that, I was able to follow the standard curriculum and eventually pass the state's standardized test at the end of middle school.

The help Ms. Hernández gave me set in motion a chain of events that propelled my academic path into high school. Those two soft taps of the pen were more consequential than she likely ever knew. As with my sister Silvia, who exposed me to the alphabet ahead of my peers, I was now indebted to Ms. Hernández for giving me that little push, for putting out a small ladder for me to step on and forge ahead.

CHAPTER 11

Dime que no es tu hija

(July 9, 2018)

I heard Alexis before I could see her, storming into the office lobby and causing commotion. She rushed straight into my office carrying her car keys in one hand and the intake sheets in the other. She didn't even stop at her cubicle to drop off her things, but stopped cold at the door, embarrassed, when she realized there was somebody else in my office.

Alexis had grown up in the Rio Grande Valley, the daughter of Cuban refugees, and had a pleasant, outgoing personality, which came in very handy when interviewing parents in court. Her Spanish was not exactly fluent at the beginning of the summer, but after interviewing dozens of Central American parents in the last month, it had improved significantly. She had spent one year of law school in Miami, reconnecting with the Cuban American community in South Florida.

When she burst into my office, I was at my desk, sitting across from Laura Peña, our new temporary attorney on her first day on the job, this Monday after the Fourth of July. I was explaining to her our work with separated families when Alexis stood at the door, almost tipping over as she held on to the door frame before she burst out: "The thing is, there was a separation today, and you had told us to flag it right away, since they are not supposed to be happening anymore."

Executive orders emanate generally from Article II of the Constitution, and at their simplest, they are presidential instructions directed at officials within the executive branch. Whether those directives are followed depends, in large part, on the willingness of the officials' superiors to oversee compliance. That is, if the president's office does not follow up to ensure that a particular executive order is fulfilled, there is no guarantee that it will be. Unlike what happens with judicial orders, for example, courts will typically not mind themselves with whether an executive order was in fact fulfilled. That is the job of the Executive.

The order to end family separations called for the Department of Homeland Security to "maintain custody of alien families during the pendency of any criminal improper entry or immigration proceedings involving their members," to the extent permitted by law. That was legalese for keeping the children in the custody of Border Patrol—which is part of DHS—while the parents were prosecuted, so that the family could be reunited after the parents' criminal hearing, albeit in detention. To my dismay and that of many other advocates, the order said nothing of reuniting families who had already been separated. Even if every federal agent complied with the executive order to a T, that would do nothing to bring separated children back to their parents. It became immediately clear that the directive did nothing for those families. We needed to keep searching for the children, call Manuel and other case managers at ORR, reach out to the Guatemalan, Salvadoran, and other consulates nearly every day, strategize with Justice in Motion and its contacts in Central America, and try to reunite them.

Still, I had thought, it was some comfort to know that no more families would be ripped apart going forward. Our list of parents had grown to 382 in under a month, and this was only in McAllen. We had been going to court twice a day for the morning and afternoon shifts, interviewing so many separated parents each day that simply keeping track of them left little time to contact the Office of Refugee Resettlement to try to locate the children, much less to really get to know each parent's story, why they fled their home country, where they were headed in the U.S., and if they had any family. The pace at which parents were detained, separated, and prosecuted in court made it nearly impossible for us to understand their individual stories in any meaningful sense. Many became simply a number on our list. Parent number 347, Row 285, on a color-coded spreadsheet. After the executive order came down, I had some comfort that maybe now we could slow down and begin to get to know our 382 clients and their children.

But that comfort was shattered the instant Alexis rushed into my office fumbling her keys. As soon as Laura heard the account of what had happened in court that morning, she was eager to jump on Mario's case. Mario Pérez Domingo had traveled all the way from Tojlate, a tiny indigenous village in the outskirts of Colotenango—a small town about the size of Allende—in the mountains of western Guatemala. He had been traveling with his daughter, Oralia, not yet three years old. That she was so little distressed me immediately. She was the youngest separated child we had encountered all summer, and in fact we had not seen anyone younger than five until now. It took me a while to wrap my mind around how Border Patrol agents would look after a two-year-old, alone, at a border station. My son Julián was one and a half, and I couldn't imagine him being alone anywhere, much less in a cage inside a Border Patrol station.

Mario had turned twenty-four less than a month earlier. Like the rest of the residents of Colotenango, he spoke Mam, a Mayan language, and very little Spanish. Oralia didn't speak much yet, and the little she understood was Mam, not Spanish. Mam is one of twenty-one Mayan languages spoken in Guatemala, and close to half a million people still speak it, mostly in western Guatemala and the southern Mexican state of Chiapas. With twenty-seven consonants and ten vowels, the language has multiple dialects, which are not always mutually intelligible, given the limited contact among the inhabitants of the more than sixty communities where it is spoken. Mario, we would later learn, spoke the "Mam of Huehuetenango" dialect, a relatively common variety. His command of Spanish, however, was extremely limited.

Mario and Oralia had made it to the border on July 4. As millions of Americans barbecued hot dogs with their families and enjoyed fireworks to celebrate liberty and justice for all, Mario had been preparing to cross the border. They crossed together on a raft the following day, according to the government's complaint, and turned themselves over to the first Border Patrol agents they saw, near Mission, Texas, just west of McAllen. When Alexis interviewed Mario in court on the morning of July 9, Mario and Oralia had been detained for four days in a Border Patrol station, and Oralia had been taken the day before. Border Patrol agents had told Mario that they were taking her because she was crying.

That much was largely consistent with the hundreds of stories we had heard since May. But the rest of Mario's story was different, and it immediately gave us concern. When Alexis had asked Mario if he had been told why he was separated, he struggled to explain in fragmentary Spanish. The agents, Alexis gathered, for some reason thought Oralia was Mario's niece, not his daughter. Like many immigrant parents, Mario had Oralia's birth certificate with him, but the agents were still not persuaded. Apparently the agents had believed the birth certificate was forged or otherwise fraudulent.

Standing in court that morning, handcuffed and sleep-deprived, Mario had been alarmed, desperate to find out anything about his daughter, and frustrated by the language barrier. When he tried to explain to Alexis and the federal public defender what had happened, Mario repeated in exasperated broken Spanish what he had told the agents tens of times: "mi hijo, mi hijo." My son. The Spanish words for son and daughter differ only by one letter, hijo and hija, respectively. Mario made such a basic mistake that immediately gave away that he did not speak Spanish fluently. If Mario struggled to explain to Alexis what had happened, how could he possibly have understood the agents' interrogation about his daughter? Was this simply a problem of things lost in translation? Even if his answers in erratic Spanish were unconvincing to the agents, Oralia's birth certificate, which would have been in Spanish—showing him as the father—should have been the proof they were looking for. I thought there had to be something else to explain what had happened.

Alexis handed me the intake form. On the right side of the page, in hurried penmanship, she had scribbled "hija, but they think it's my niece."

The myriad possibilities ran through my head like flickering sparks on a live wire. My gut told me that Mario was likely telling the truth and this was yet another unlawful separation; but at the other end of the spectrum, my mind was telling me it was possible that Oralia was not really his daughter. We needed to corroborate what he had told Alexis.

"Any relatives in the U.S.?" I asked.

"His cuñada lives outside Atlanta," Alexis said. A sister-in-law.

Earlier in the summer, we had edited our intake form to ask whether the person had any relatives in the United States. Most of them did. If not a relative, most immigrants at least knew somebody, a friend of a friend, a pastor at a church, somebody to connect with at their destination city. We would take down that person's name and number, and—if the number worked—that usually allowed us to get in touch with the rest of the family, either in the United States or in their country of origin.

Later that morning, I dialed the phone number Mario had given Alexis as I poured myself another cup of coffee. The phone rang and rang, but Martha, Mario's sister-in-law, did not pick up. The call did not go to voice mail either. I double-checked the number, and dialed again. Nothing. This was not unusual, especially during business hours. Relatives were typically at work, and we tended to have better luck reaching them in the evening and on weekends.

I tried Martha via WhatsApp, the messaging application, and I confirmed that a person with that phone number had an active account. As I was typing a message to her, she called back.

I told her I was contacting her regarding Mario and his daughter, and she confirmed that she was Oralia's aunt. In calls like this, I would typically leave out a detail, in an attempt not to feed all the information to the person on the phone. In this case I had left out Oralia's name, and the way Martha referred to Oralia by name, almost instinctively, gave me some confidence that they were indeed likely related. Mario and Oralia had been headed to Atlanta to go live with her, she said.

I told her that, unfortunately, they had been separated at the border, and that government agents did not believe Oralia was Mario's daughter. Martha stayed quiet for a few seconds. I imagined her trying to process what that might mean, brow frowning through the silence hanging over the phone line.

"Pero él sí es su papá de la niña," Martha implored me, as if I was the one who needed to be convinced that he was really her father. Martha's Spanish was intelligible, but it was clear it was not her native tongue either, the chopped grammar betraying her. Her voice broke a little when she spoke, perplexed at having to state the obvious, pleading to be believed.

I explained that I was not with the government, a common misconception when we first contacted the families. There was no need to convince me, I was trying to help find Oralia, I said, and any way to confirm that they were really father and daughter, especially with documents, would help.

Any chance you can send me a copy of Oralia's birth certificate? I asked her in Spanish.

"Sí, sí, yo se la mando, cabal." Yes, she would send it over.

Before noon, I had an image of Oralia's birth certificate on my phone. I had no way of knowing if this was the same document that Mario had shown the Border Patrol agents, but at least now we had *a* birth certificate that showed Mario as Oralia's father, and the dates of birth on the certificate matched what Mario had told Alexis. If we could get it admitted as evidence, this document could be solid proof in court. This could be the key to reuniting Oralia with her father.

As soon as I confirmed that the names and dates of birth on the birth certificate matched the information Mario had given Alexis in court and the document did not otherwise appear obviously fraudulent—it had a file number and an official-looking seal of the Registro Nacional de las Personas (RENAP), Guatemala's national civil registry—I picked up my office phone.

I had met officials from the Guatemalan, Honduran, Salvadoran, and Mexican consulates in McAllen in 2015. We had filed a lawsuit against the state of Texas for refusing to issue birth certificates to the Texas-born children of scores of Central American mothers. Since the mothers lacked an official government ID—they were undocumented—the state had claimed that it could not issue their children's birth certificates, even though the children had been born in the United States, *jus soli* again. We argued discrimination against the U.S. citizen children. The case eventually settled two years later, after the state agreed to issue the birth certificates, and I got to know the consuls well in the process.

Since May, we had been in frequent contact with consular officials again, this time regarding separated families. Officials there often received calls from family members looking for their loved ones who had crossed the border in South Texas, and consular representatives would call us to ask if we had encountered them in court. We, in turn, would often contact them when we needed to confirm the authenticity of a document, like today.

Consul Claudia Anguiano was a pleasant, middle-aged bureaucrat. She was always polite and eager to help but, like many government officials, often struggled to see a way around the red tape.

I explained the situation we were facing, and asked if she could confirm whether a document with this file number existed on the Guatemalan national registry, and whether the information on their registry matched the information on our document. If so, we would have a strong case that the birth certificate was authentic. In my eagerness, I gullibly expected her to say she could search on her computer right then and there and give us an answer on the spot.

"The consul does not have that capability, unfortunately," she said. I always found it interesting that many consular officers speak in this way, referring to themselves in the third person, like some politicians. When I pressed her and asked if there was any other way to confirm the document's authenticity, I heard my own exasperation. She said we would have to contact RENAP directly, in Guatemala City.

"Is there any way your office can help us do that?" I asked, surprised at the unintended beseeching tone in my voice.

"Let me see what I can do," she replied. "It may take me a couple of days."

A couple of days. That could mean a week in bureaucrat-speak, or even longer. Mario and Oralia would be separated for days, despite the executive order, and there was nothing we could do. A familiar sense of impotence came over me. I recognized the feeling, my shoulders drooping as I hung up the phone and sighed heavily. I had lost count of how many times I had felt this way over the summer, but the familiarity did not make it any easier to process. It was the same impotence I had felt when I sat in my car after Georgina and I left the courthouse that first day back in May. It felt like a lifetime ago, and yet, despite an executive order, a federal court ruling out of California ordering that families be reunited, hundreds of families encountered in court, dozens of pleas on TV and radio interviews, here was this same, detestable, heavy feeling of powerlessness. Like every time before, I did not know how to overcome it. The feeling came over me and stayed until I could no longer sense its presence.

That same Monday afternoon, we learned from the public defender that Mario's criminal hearing for illegal entry had been postponed to Friday. Mario would be detained in a U.S. Marshals prison until then. But what about Oralia? Where was she?

Following the methods we had set up and improved over the previous weeks, Alexis tried to locate her every way she could. Contacting ORR always took a while, often days, but it was the most trusted source of information.

"Not admitted," Manuel, the friendly ORR case manager, told Alexis. But he was able to confirm that Oralia was en route to El Paso. She was so young, he explained, that it was likely that she would be placed with a temporary foster family. "So that her living situation can be as close to normal as possible," he added.

As normal as possible, I thought. I tried to imagine who this temporary foster family might be, what their house might look like, if there were other children in the house, their ages. But I was all but certain that a temporary foster family in El Paso was not going to speak Mam, and their house would not be anything like Oralia's village in the mountains of Colotenango.

"For her own well-being," Manuel added. And there it was, again, the notion that there was some actual concern in tearing a child away from her father, while he sat in a prison hundreds of miles away, each wondering where the other was. Manuel and the other caseworkers really did seem concerned about the children's well-being. For us it was too raw to hear caseworkers say things like this, after we had heard the children's parents cry in court. At the end of the day, both the ORR caseworkers and the Border Patrol agents who separated the children were federal employees, pawns of the same administration.

The vast majority of separated parents over the summer had had their criminal cases completed in a quick hearing in the morning or afternoon shift. The few minutes we had to interview them in court before their hearing was the only chance we had to meet with them in person. In many cases, that was the only time we ever spoke with them. This was how Zero Tolerance was designed to work—to deprive immigrants and asylum seekers of any meaningful chance to interact with attorneys or any kind of legal representative. But since Mario's criminal case had been reset from Monday to Friday, that gave us a brief window to try to meet again with him and do a proper, full-length interview. While he awaited his rescheduled hearing, he was locked up in a federal facility one county over, some forty-five minutes away, and we could go visit him there.

Laura was eager to get involved in his case from the outset. It was what she came here to do, why she left private practice in San Francisco to return to the Rio Grande Valley all these years later. In her midthirties, Laura is tall with wavy hair, and wears eyeglasses when she sits at the computer. She was a good fit in our office from the start. She got along well with Georgina, Roberto, and Alexis, and with me. I heard rumblings that TCRP employees in other offices were appalled that we had hired a former ICE trial attorney, someone who had been deporting families for a living during the Obama Administration. I owned up to the criticism but had a hard time seeing any other option. When I received Laura's email on Father's Day and saw that she had immigration law experience, I didn't think for two seconds which side she had been on. I was so desperate for help that her past at ICE was something I could overlook, as long as she was now willing to help reunite families and guide asylum seekers through the process.

Having two lawyers in the office was a game changer. Laura and I could split the work and the day's tasks, and this literally doubled our legal capacity. On Thursday that week, Laura attended a meeting with Border Patrol and other community organizations at the Ursula detention center—where the pictures of children in cages had been taken and gone viral—while I went to visit Mario.

The Willacy County Regional Detention Facility is a sprawling, orange brick complex surrounded by concertina wire in Raymondville, Texas, population ten thousand. The facility is run by another private prison company, Management & Training Corporation (MTC), which is one of the GEO Group's competitors and whose slogan is: "A leader in social impact." The effrontery of their slogan raised eyebrows each time someone heard it. "Willacy County," as the facility is known, has capacity for over 550 detainees in federal custody, most of them awaiting their criminal hearings, like Mario.

This was my first time visiting, and I was struck by how the complex stood out off Highway 77, in the otherwise barren South Texas landscape.

When I arrived, Roxana was already at the parking lot, waiting for me. She was the public defender's investigator assigned to this case, and since Mario's criminal case was still pending and he was still technically their client, Roxana had arranged for this visit.

The lobby of Willacy County felt old. There was a low counter on the left side, a guard-turned-receptionist behind it, and a metal detector that looked much newer and fancier than the rest of the furniture. The white vinyl counter was worn out, showing where people had rested their hands and forearms countless times when they walked up to it, smudges of grease and dirt forming indentations over the years. A dusty smell at the entrance gave way to the scent of cleaning products as we walked in. Three plastic chairs with rusted legs and cracked seats were set against the wall, waiting for strangers to lay their weight on them. The black pen for visitors to sign their names in the visitor logbook was broken off the chain that had once attached it to the counter. Everything in that lobby seemed like it had seen better days, except the metal detector. Its bulky, shiny, white frame and multiple lit-up buttons made a statement that even if everything else in that place was broken, not even a paper clip would get through that thing undetected.

A guard escorted us through wide, silent hallways until we made it to the tiny interview room, where Mario sat in a chair by the corner wearing a prisoner's navy-blue jumpsuit. His slumped body perked up when the guard wrangled the keys to unlock the door and let us in. I had seen a picture of Mario and Oralia that his family sent us from Guatemala, a cheeky Oralia pouting and Mario crouching down on one knee, his left forearm resting on his other leg, and his face betraying the slightest grin in front of a bed of colorful flowers. Seeing him now in the flesh, in prison uniform and his smile gone, immediately made an impact on me. His deep skin revealed stark indigenous features; black hair, a wide, flat forehead, and wide lips, the space between his teeth showing every time he spoke. His black, shy eyes had not smiled for some time.

As we greeted him, it became immediately clear that Spanish was not his native language.

"Hola Mario, buenas tardes," I said. It was around 2:30 in the afternoon.

"Mhmm," he said, smiling and nodding.

We had arranged to have an interpreter available by phone. I was instructed to call the interpreting company and, after punching in the confirmation code, a Mam-speaking voice was supposed to appear. When Roxana and I introduced ourselves to Mario before calling the interpreter, he had a hard time following even the pleasantries and small talk. It threw me off to see Mario and hear him clearly unable to speak Spanish, and I found myself in a type of unintended double bind. On the one hand, here was a man whose name was Mario Pérez, and who "looked" like his native language had to be Spanish. On the other, it was clear that he could not form complete sentences in Spanish, no matter how hard he tried. The contradiction in my brain did not resolve right away, such is the power of the false narratives of indigenous peoples as something of the past and only the past. Perhaps the Border Patrol agent who processed Mario had experienced the same dissonance I was feeling, and that was why he had refused to provide him an interpreter, even though Mario had tried to ask for one in his broken Spanish.

I pulled up the phone that the guard had set on the desk and dialed the 1-800 number. As soon as Mario heard the Mam interpreter come in through the speakerphone, his face brightened with excitement. He pulled up his chair closer to the phone and leaned forward into the speaker. I did not understand the words, but I could sense the urgency in his voice. Hearing a familiar language finally come through that phone seemed to give him hope that someone might at last understand him and be able to help him find his daughter.

Through the telephonic interpreter, I asked Mario to please walk us through what had happened when he and Oralia were detained. What did the agents tell you? What did you tell them? Tell us everything as best as you can remember.

After taking his name, his photograph, and his fingerprints, the agent had started asking about the baby.

"Es mi hijo," Mario had said—again mistaking the *a* for the *o*—and from that moment on the Border Patrol agent had changed his tone. I imagined the agent, in his olive-green uniform, adjusting his gun and taser on his belt, sitting up straighter and hardening his face.

When Mario pulled out the birth certificate, the agent had looked at it quickly, and then dismissively put it to the side, Mario recounted through the interpreter.

"Dime la verdad," the agent had told Mario. Tell me truth. "Yo te puedo ayudar." I can help you.

Over the next few minutes in that interview room, Mario repeated the same phrases in Mam into the phone over and over again. Mam has a choppy cadence to it, with frequent hard "h" and "ch" sounds. It also uses sounds that do not exist in English or Spanish as stand-alone letters. One of those resembles a click of the tongue, and another sounds like a brief pause, the sound one hears in the middle of *uh-oh* between the vowels. As it turns out, the latter is the glottal stop—phonetically represented as ʔ—and exists in several indigenous languages throughout the Americas, as well as in Hebrew, Tagalog, some Polynesian languages, and others.

Even though I did not understand their meaning, I could tell Mario was repeating the same phrases again and again. The interpreter interrupted him to relay the phrases to us in Spanish: dime la verdad, yo te puedo ayudar, dime que no es tu hija. Tell me the truth. I can help you. Tell me she's not your daughter.

Tell me she's not your daughter.

It took a while for that to sink in. The agent had asked Mario repeatedly to tell "the truth," but he had decided, independently of Mario, what that truth was: that Oralia was not his daughter. Again and again the agent repeated that if only Mario said she wasn't his daughter, he could help them both. This had gone on for a long time, Mario wasn't sure how long, but thought maybe two hours. Oralia had been crying nonstop when the agents took her from him.

"How was he going to help you?" I asked Mario through the interpreter.

"I don't know," Mario responded. "I asked him the same thing... Help me how? And he kept saying help you, help your situation, help you with the little girl. Help you. I can help you, I can help her."

Mario paused in the conversation, his gaze fixated on the phone as if waiting for it to vocalize the answers he did not have.

"And what did you say?" I asked after a while.

"I kept saying no no no, she is my daughter. But he kept saying no no no, tell me she's not your daughter. I can help you. If you tell me she's not your daughter, I can help you. I can help her. Tens of times, that's what he kept saying."

I could hear his voice starting to break, even in Mam. He looked at me, and I saw expression in his eyes for the first time—fear, defeat, shame. His welling eyes looked back at the phone, and he spoke into it again.

"And then I said...fine, she's not my daughter," the interpreter said, crushed. Mario wiped a tear off before it could stream down his face.

Unable to grasp what kind of help the agent was promising, desperate for any help for himself and his daughter, after hours of hearing the same thing dozens of times, tired in a cold cell and uncertain about his future, Mario had finally been broken.

It is remarkable how a few words can become so consequential. After being called a liar, a criminal who can't be trusted, forced to prove with documents every single thing he says—from his parentage to the basis of his asylum claim—all of a sudden an immigrant's words alone became definitive proof that he was not really his own daughter's father. Mario was treated like a liar, a fraudster, a child trafficker; but the moment he uttered the words the agent had coerced him into uttering, his word suddenly, magically, became his bond.

These few words, four simple words spoken in chopped-up, incorrect Spanish took on an oath-like quality. Bueno, no es mi hijo, fine, she's not my son, became Mario's and Oralia's nightmare. After having repeated dozens of times that she *was* his daughter, the moment he said she wasn't, everything changed. Those four words precipitated a series of events that landed Mario here, at the Willacy County Detention Center, sent Oralia 800 miles away, and left him wondering where was the help the Border Patrol agent had promised.

After hearing Mario's story about the coerced "confession"—if it was a confession at all—obtaining the certification from the Guatemalan consulate became much more critical.

As consul Anguiano had promised, two days after we spoke I received a consular document certifying that a birth certificate existed, and it showed Mario as Oralia's father. The consular document was a simple one-pager bearing an official seal and the coat of arms of Guatemala, with a resplendent quetzal—the country's national bird—with its long and colorful arched tail posed royally over two rifles and a laurel wreath, and containing the critical information we had requested. Every piece of information on it matched the information on the Guatemalan registry. We had what we needed.

In my inexperienced trial lawyer mind, I pictured a Perry Mason moment in court. When the judge called Mario's case and asked his lawyer if there was any proof to challenge the government's assertion that Mario had confessed to not being the father, Azalea, the public defender, would rise from her chair, wave the certifications in her hand, and shock the prosecutor and the judge. Everyone in the courtroom would gasp, and the judge would bang his gavel and deliver justice. The certifications would be the definitive proof that Mario had been telling the truth all along, he would be declared innocent, and he and Oralia would be reunited that same day.

What actually happened was much less dramatic and much more upsetting. Early that Friday morning, before Mario's case was called, the prosecutor dropped all charges against Mario for crossing the border illegally. Even with Zero Tolerance in the books, Mario wouldn't be prosecuted. Mario was at the Bentsen Tower, we were told, but he wasn't even brought up to the courtroom on the eighth floor because the charges were dropped. Just like that, the prosecutor dismissed his case "without prejudice," meaning not that Mario wasn't affected or "prejudiced" by it, but rather that the government reserved the right to re-file it at a later time. Still, Mario was off the hook for now.

Surely, I thought, this meant that he would be reunited with Oralia right away. But instead, when Mario asked about his daughter, the guards told him that they did not know anything about that.

The prosecutor had simply dropped the charges for reasons we did not understand, but what became clear was that they did not want to engage on the issue of the separation. "That's a separate matter, I have no control over that," the prosecutor had said.

I was puzzled. Why would they drop the prosecution for illegal entry? Regardless of the separation and of whether Mario was Oralia's father, he *had* crossed the border without authorization. They could likely get him convicted of that. They simply chose not to, and promptly closed the case, "for the stated reason that the government no longer wishes to prosecute said cause," said the order's boilerplate language dismissing the case. There was no mention of Oralia at all, not in the complaint, not in the motion to dismiss, and not in the order closing the case. No mention of what the agents had done, who had taken Oralia, where she was now, or when she might be returned to her father. For the system, it was as if she did not exist. It felt as if the government bureaucrats in the room wanted to keep us from even coming into contact with Mario and pursuing the reunification with his daughter.

Back at the office, Laura and I scrambled to try to find Oralia and Mario. As far as we knew, Oralia was still in El Paso with a temporary foster family. And Mario, now that his criminal case was dismissed, would likely be transferred to ICE custody and could be deported quickly under the process known as "expedited removal."

Adopted in 1996 and signed into law by President Clinton, expedited removal allows immigration officers to summarily deport immigrants who entered "without admission" and who have been physically present in the United States less than two years. On paper, the law exempts from this process people who seek asylum or express a fear of persecution in their home country. In practice, expedited removal has been applied wholesale. Immigrants subject to expedited removal do not go before an immigration judge; the line officer can "order" them removed. The law was initially applied only to immigrants seeking admission at official ports of entry, but in 2004, the federal government issued regulations that allowed it to apply expedited removal to any "alien" apprehended within one hundred miles of the border and who entered without inspection in the fourteen days prior to their arrest. It is the immigrant's burden to prove otherwise.

Some two-thirds of the U.S. population live within this 100-mile zone, as the swath also extends inland from the coastline and encompasses metropolises such as New York, Los Angeles, Houston, and Chicago, the country's most populous cities. Expedited removal has become such a pervasive method to expel hundreds of thousands of immigrants and asylum seekers every year with no process at all that it's easy to forget it has been around for less than two decades in its current form.

When he was arrested, Mario met the criteria for expedited removal, so he could be removed without ever getting to see an immigration judge. Would the government deport him without his daughter?

Since our attempt at using the consular certifications in court had not worked, we tried a different approach. I had gone to law school thinking that the courts would be a place to address injustices, but this was yet another instance of those naive hopes being shattered. The government had simply washed its hands of Mario and his daughter, and our options within the legal system were vanishing. We had to look for justice elsewhere.

After consulting with Mario, we went to the media. Separations were not supposed to be happening after the executive order, and we thought the public outrage was still fresh enough that it could generate enough pressure to bring Oralia back from El Paso before Mario was gone. We issued a press release including the picture of

Photo credit: Mario Pérez Domingo and Texas Civil Rights Project.

Mario and Oralia in front of the flowers—her face blurred—and desperately called every reporter we knew.

National media outlet BuzzFeed covered the story. It allowed us to tell the story we had learned from our longer, interpreted interview with Mario, highlighting that the birth certificate showing him as the father was authentic. That same evening, Border Patrol issued a statement in response—the first time the agency had specifically responded to one of our cases—and reading their response, my blood started to boil: "there are instances where a child may be separated from an adult/parent solely for the child's welfare." There it was, that same line again. "Separation is a possibility under exigent circumstances in order to protect the child and to ensure the well-being of the child. . . ." All I could think of was Oralia with a family of strangers who knows where in El Paso. "Mr. Pérez Domingo initially stated that the child was his daughter. Mr. Pérez Domingo later admitted that the child he was traveling with was actually his niece and that he had retrieved a fraudulent document from a smuggler in Guatemala in order to support his claim." My mind returned to that interview room in Willacy County, Mario staring into the phone, waiting for the voice to speak to him in Mam, his eyes trembling with desperation and disappointment as he recounted how he had been broken.

The Border Patrol's statement made no mention of the consular certifications, or why the Border Patrol agent had not attempted to corroborate the authenticity of the birth certificate. After all, the agents have access to consular personnel directly from their stations. The agent could have picked up the phone and called the consulate, just like I did. It would have taken five minutes. But he chose not to. Instead, Border Patrol dug in on their false narrative, despite never having interviewed Mario with an interpreter or attempted any verification. No, they simply regurgitated the words they had coerced out of Mario back at him, and then some. It was repulsing to read that statement, full of such inflammatory allegations, devoid of any evidence, and in fact omitting evidence to the contrary.

Over the next few days, my anger gave in to frustration. I was at a loss. Reunification with Oralia felt so unreachable at this point, and the familiar feeling of powerlessness came over me yet again. Mario's sister-in-law, Martha, called or messaged me nearly every day, sometimes multiple times a day, and every time I had to tell her the same thing in a different way. I tried hard not to convey my own despair onto her, and instead tried to find a way to convey hope, resiliency. She had the same question every time: ¿Ya le dieron a su niña? Had they given Mario his little girl back. And no matter how I coated my answer, trying to explain that we were still trying, we were talking to government agents, every time the answer was, at bottom, no. They had not given Mario his little girl back, and we did not know when they would.

The following Monday, from my office, I called the number that Dagoberto had shown me written on his forearm in blue ink, his brother-in-law's. Along with Viviana, Dagoberto was among the five parents Georgina and I interviewed that first day in court, and he had been separated from his sixteen-year-old son, Jorge. According to our periodic searches on ICE's online detainee locator website since May, Dagoberto had been transferred from McAllen to the Stewart Detention Center in rural Georgia, from there to the Folkston ICE Processing Center near the Georgia-Florida border, and from there back to South Texas to the Port Isabel Detention Center. The constant and senseless runaround was always puzzling to us. While Dagoberto was being shuttled from one detention facility to the next, his son remained in South Texas, near the ORR shelter where Sandro, Vivana's son, had been held.

I called Dagoberto's brother-in-law in the late morning, accounting for the time difference and waiting for it to be later on the West Coast. He picked up on the first ring.

I explained who I was, and the reason for my call. I was used to these calls by now. But Dagoberto's brother-in-law would not even give me his name.

"Mhm, yes…" he said, and I sensed skepticism.

I sat down, somewhat disconcerted at his lack of trust. After a while, I gave up trying to convince him that we were trying to help, even if I understood his distrust. At the end of the day, he and I had never met, and I had no idea about his immigration status. Especially in those days, he was right to mistrust a stranger calling him on his cell phone and asking questions about his family.

MY BOY WILL DIE OF SORROW

"Está bien, I understand," I said, politely. I explained that I was part of an organization trying to locate separated children and parents, and that a federal court had ordered all separated children be reunited with their parents. At the end of June, in a lawsuit led by the American Civil Liberties Union known as *Ms. L v. ICE*, a judge had ordered a stop to the separations and that separated families be reunited within thirty days.

"The only thing I am trying to find out is if Dagoberto and Jorge are together now," I said in Spanish.

"Ok," he said.

"¿Ya le entregaron a su muchacho?" I asked if the government had returned Dagoberto's boy to him.

"Yes," he said, tersely.

I asked him if he knew any details, but he said he did not know anything beyond that.

"Ok, muchas gracias," I thanked him.

After we hung up, I pulled up ICE's online detainee locator website on my computer. I typed in Dagoberto's A-Number, and the search returned a hit: he was now at the Karnes County Residential Center, south of San Antonio. This was yet another immigrant detention facility where, at the time, ICE was detaining fathers with their children. I shook my head, upset that Dagoberto and Jorge were still detained, but I had enough information to believe that they were together.

When I typed the A-Numbers of the other three parents we had interviewed the same day as Viviana and Dagoberto—Antonio, Leonel, María—no hits came up. According to this website, none of them was in ICE custody. We did not have contact information for relatives either—these had been our very first interviews, and we had neglected to ask those questions that first day. All we had to go on were their A-Numbers, and they were not yielding results.

We did not know where their children were either. Alexis and the team had been calling ORR for weeks, and as of late July, the children were still "not in the system." The *Ms. L* reunification deadline was only days away, and on our spreadsheet, the "reunification status" column for these three families still showed the ominous "unknown."

If the ICE website was to be trusted, this could only mean they were either deported or released in the U.S. Without an attorney, it was unlikely they would have been released. I feared they had been deported by now, almost two months after their apprehension. In the intervening weeks, it was all but impossible that María, Antonio, and Leonel had gone in front of a judge. If they had been deported, we had no way of knowing whether their children had been deported with them.

The Inter-American Commission had not yet ruled on our human rights complaint, and the government had provided no information about these families, even within that formal legal proceeding. The immigration court's automated 1-800 number had no information about their cases either. I felt at a dead end. It had been nearly two months since Georgina and I encountered them in court, and I was starting to lose hope of ever finding them, of knowing what became of them. I feared that we never would.

Weeks later, we finally learned of their fate from consular records. María and her three children were sent to Alabama, where they were reunited and continued on their journey to their family in Missouri. We had enough information to confirm they had been reunited about a week after they were separated, and eventually reached their destination. I remembered María's apparent dissociation that first day in court, and I hoped that she would be doing better now that she had reunited with her husband.

Leonel and his son, Daniel, were also reunited. According to the consulate, by the time Leonel made it back to Ursula, Daniel was still there. He was among the few children that had not been transferred to ORR quickly enough, and so, by a stroke of luck, he was reunited with his father within a few days in one of those cages that made national headlines. They eventually made their way to the Pacific Northwest, and their immigration case remains pending in Portland, Oregon.

Antonio Bol Paau and his son had a different turn of events: Antonio was deported to Guatemala, while his son, Rivaldo, remained in the U.S. I was aghast when I first learned this, and over time, it came to light that there were many other families in the same situation. When we flagged Antonio's case to the attorneys working on the *Ms. L* lawsuit, we were met with the news that the court had not ordered that parents deported without their children be brought back to the United States. Rivaldo, twelve years old at the time of the separation and now labeled an "unaccompanied child," was transferred to a migrant children shelter.

Back at the office, another week went by. After countless automated messages and voice mails, Laura finally got ahold of a person on the phone about Mario's case. It was an agent with HSI, Homeland Security Investigations, the division within ICE that investigates alleged crimes committed in the interior of the country, not just illegal entries. A successor to various divisions within the former Customs Service, HSI took on its current form in 2010, and its mandate includes authority to investigate "all types of cross-border criminal activity," ranging from money laundering to cybercrime, to international art theft and transnational gang activity. Critically, its jurisdiction also includes human smuggling.

The agent explained to Laura somberly that HSI was preparing smuggling charges against Mario. They had enough, he said, to charge him with a felony. He harped on what Mario had told the Border Patrol agent, his "confession." Laura tried to explain that

Mario was not fluent in Spanish and had not been provided with an interpreter, to no avail. All they needed, the agent told Laura, was a DNA sample from Mario and Oralia. As soon as they received the results and confirmed that Oralia was not his daughter, they would move forward with the charges. If convicted, Mario faced up to ten years in a federal prison.

Laura and I were appalled. I sat in her office in disbelief. All of a sudden the stakes became much higher. From the moment HSI became involved in the case, we knew it wasn't going to be easy to reunite Mario, but we were shocked to hear that human smuggling charges were already in the works. We felt way out of our league. I had never handled a human smuggling case, and neither had Laura, at least from the defense side.

Laura and I called Willacy County, deposited money into Mario's account so that he could return the call, and desperately waited for a call back. It is not possible to call into an immigration detention center and speak to an immigrant directly, even if you are their lawyer. Detainees are generally not afforded a phone call. So the only way they can speak to someone on the outside is if they have money in their account, and almost no one does. Without money in their account, they can't call anyone, not their family, not their lawyers. Family members typically call, deposit money into their loved one's account, and then wait for a call. Over the summer, we had deposited $5 and $10 into dozens of accounts as we tried to communicate with parents regarding their children and the reunification process. Sometimes a call back never came.

It was around this time that I had started screening calls to my personal cell phone. I poured myself yet another cup of coffee, and walking down the hall from the office kitchen to my desk, I felt my phone vibrate in my front pocket. The vibration was a familiar feeling, and it had been triggering the same anxiety, expectation, and impatience for weeks. There had been more and more calls from "Unknown Caller" or "Private," and I knew those calls were coming from a detention center. Sometimes it was one of the parents we had interviewed, but more often it was somebody else asking for help. Calls to our office phone would always be answered, but calls to my personal phone started increasing, and my phone would ring at all times of the day. My personal number had been passed around in the detention center, and people would call asking for help. Any help, even if it was somebody we had not interviewed, someone who hadn't even crossed the border near McAllen. All they wanted to ask was, simply, was there anything I could do to help.

The lines between my work and my personal life became more and more blurred. I found myself taking one of those calls more than once when I was at home trying to play with Julián, the call bringing me back to the very reality I was trying to escape. Sometimes I couldn't take it, and I let some of those calls go to voice mail. My mental and emotional tanks were depleted, and I let some calls ring and ring unanswered even after I found out that the "Unknown Callers" may not be able to leave a message. If I didn't pick up, there was no one to press 1 when prompted, and therefore the option to leave a voice mail would not even be presented. I answered multiple calls a day, even into the evening and on weekends, but sometimes I couldn't bring myself to pick up one more. It was never a deliberate decision to not pick up the call, but rather I simply could not bring my hand to slide the green button on my phone and answer. I felt guilty, the weight of having no answers for yet another desperate mother was sometimes too much to bear.

Over time, the adrenaline-infused feeling of *let's help them all, let's take every call* was overcome by a feeling of *no matter how many we try to help, we won't be able to help everyone.* Sometimes I would ask myself why focus so much on this one individual when there were dozens, hundreds of others, just like her that we couldn't get to? There were hundreds of others just as deserving of justice that we would never even know about. Each one of them was a story like Mario's, like Viviana's, like Patricia's—or worse—a story that would never be told, silenced forever on a deportation flight. The human rights abuses that our own government was inflicting upon thousands of immigrant parents and children alike seemed so insurmountable, what difference would taking one more call make, in the grand scheme of things?

As we waited for Mario's call to explain the turn his case had taken, we planned to call a Mam interpreter three-way once we had Mario on the line. Mam interpreters are not easy to find in the United States, and they are especially hard to find in South Texas. But as it turned out, the very day we needed an interpreter, Oswaldo Vidal, a Mam interpreter based in Oakland, California, was three hours away in Laredo, Texas, interpreting for Mam speakers at an immigration prison there. He agreed to come to McAllen the next day, and I felt relief that something had finally worked out in Mario's favor since he crossed the border.

Oswaldo is fluent in English and multiple variations of Mam, and conversational in Spanish. He had immigrated from Guatemala to the Bay Area with his parents when he was four, and he had remained close to the indigenous community there. Now in his early twenties, Oswaldo was in college and frequently interpreted in immigration court. The growth of the Mam community in Northern California starting in the early 2010s spiked the demand for Mam interpreters, and Oswaldo is one of the few.

The following day, sitting in my office, we started conversing in Spanish. Oswaldo is about 5'7" and when we met, he wore dark pants and a button-up shirt with traditional indigenous designs—colorful flowers and geometric patterns—on the collar. He carried a small satchel over his shoulder where he kept his notepad. When I saw that he struggled in Spanish, we switched to English. He spoke slowly and softly in Spanish, but immediately became more confident speaking in his flawless, American-accented English. I was going over Mario's situation with Oswaldo, when I saw "Blocked Caller" pop up on my cell phone screen. I picked up right away, and heard Mario's timid voice on the other end of the line.

"Mario, un momento," I said, and handed the phone to Oswaldo.

Oswaldo spoke to Mario for a while, looking up at me every so often and nodding as he listened to Mario. Then he would respond to Mario, the choppy cadence and the glottal stops becoming more and more familiar to my ear.

"Yes, he says it's fine to do the DNA test," Oswaldo said after a while. "That she is his daughter." And there we were again, awkwardly restating the obvious, Mario repeating yet again what he had said so many times before to no avail.

The government had taken the position that since Oralia was in federal custody, the federal government could make medical decisions on her behalf. For us, it was important that Mario give informed consent before a DNA sample would be drawn from him or his daughter.

"Blood or saliva?" I asked Oswaldo. The HSI agent had not been able to confirm which type of DNA test they planned to run. He had told Laura that a blood test would be more accurate, but HSI had had trouble finding a lab to run a blood DNA test in South Texas. Every lab they had approached refused to work with the federal government in light of the family separation policy, and this had caused further delays for Mario and Oralia. The irony stung sharply.

"Yes, either one is fine," Oswaldo said, after asking Mario. "That she is his daughter," he said again, faithfully interpreting Mario's words.

Later that evening at home, well after dinner, Mario's sister-in-law called back. I took the call in the living room, and as soon as I said hello, Karla gestured to me to keep my voice down. Julián was already asleep, and even though he was in another room, the sound of my voice could carry. It's really a family thing—for a strange reason that none of us can explain, every one of us on my mother's side of the family has a tendency to raise our voice considerably when we speak on the phone. It might be a remnant from the times when landline phone reception was botchy and people needed to yell into the receiver, and over the years it has evolved into a genetic mutation or a Pavlovian family tradition. Whatever it was, Karla was worried that my additional decibels would wake our son.

I stepped into the garage to take Martha's call, but the heat was unbearable, even at this hour. I opened the garage door and stepped out into the street behind our house. The conversation I needed to have was important, and I couldn't focus on both the substance of the conversation and the volume of my voice. The street was empty and quiet, a hot moonless night covering the houses up and down the block. The faint yellowish glow of a streetlight illuminated the driveway as I apologized to Martha for my delay.

"Perdón, buenas noches," I said. "Hoy hablamos con Mario." We had spoken with Mario that day. I explained to Martha where things stood. The government was adamant that Oralia was not Mario's daughter, that he had been trafficking her, and the only way to prove that all of that was a lie was through a DNA test. Yes, I said, we showed them the birth certificate that you sent us. Yes, the Guatemalan consulate confirmed that it was authentic. Yes, we showed them the picture of Mario and Oralia too. I did not even get into how unfair it was to place the burden of proof entirely on Mario.

"So, the government wants to draw blood from Mario and from

Oralia," I continued. "Mario has given his consent, but I wanted to discuss it with you too."

"Bueno, sí, está bien," she said. It's fine, no problem.

"If they draw blood from both of them, what do you think the results will be?"

"Yes, she is his daughter," she responded, and I again felt silly for asking the question.

The problem is, I explained, that if the DNA comes back negative, Mario could go to prison for many years.

"Let me ask you something," I tried a different way. "We have worked with families with adopted children. Fathers who have raised their children from birth, but who are not really their children. I mean, they *are* their children, but a DNA test would come back negative, they're not their biological children....Is there any chance this could happen with Mario?" It was possible Oralia was adopted, and Martha did not know it.

"No, no, no, la niña sí es su hija." She is his daughter.

"And this is uncomfortable, but it's very important," I said, "because Mario could end up in prison. If that DNA test comes back negative, I don't think we will be able to help him. Or Oralia."

"Ok," she said, confused.

I struggled to find the right words to ask the question. "You know, when I was growing up in Mexico, sometimes I would watch telenovelas...." Martha chuckled lightly in confusion. In one of those soap operas, there was a father once who learned after many years of raising his son that the boy was actually not his. He loved and had raised his son his entire life, but then he learned that his wife had cheated on him many years ago, and the boy wasn't really his. If they had done a DNA test for that father and son, it would have come back negative.

"Mhm. I don't understand," she said. "What do you mean?"

"Is there any chance at all that Mario is not Oralia's father?"

"No, she is his daughter..." I could hear the puzzlement in her voice.

"Is there a chance Mario is not Oralia's father and you don't know? Is there a chance Mario is not Oralia's father and not even *he* knows it?"

A few seconds of silence filled the other end of the line, and I sensed that she understood what I was trying to say.

"Pero ella sí es su hija," she pleaded, repeating the same words. "I was there when she was born," she added in hesitant Spanish.

"So even if the risk is that he would go to prison for many years if the DNA test comes back negative, you agree that we should go ahead with it?"

"Yes, it has to be positive..." she said, in a contemplative tone, as if speaking to herself.

We hung up, and I was still lost in my thoughts about the possibilities. It has to be positive, I also told myself.

Weeks passed. Alexis would call Manuel every couple of days, and all he could do was confirm that Oralia was "fine," still with the same foster family in El Paso. Mario was now in ICE detention, and once we confirmed he was in a facility in South Texas, Laura visited him. She had no real updates to share, but wanted to check up on him, tell him we had not forgotten him, to try to convey some hope. I continued to field calls and questions from Martha via WhatsApp almost daily, every time responding with "not yet, we're still working on it."

Toward the end of July, HSI finally found a lab willing to run Mario's and Oralia's DNA test. Laura walked briskly into my office, her glasses in her hand, a faint smile on her face.

"I just got off the phone with HSI," she said, matter-of-factly. "The test was positive," and her smile deepened a little.

I had imagined this moment before. In bed at night, unable to sleep, I had imagined that if the test came back positive, everyone at the office would celebrate. We would high-five and hug and clench our fists high in the air. But instead, Laura and I exchanged glances of forbearance. Any celebratory mood was quickly muffled by a reminder, upsetting and unnerving as it was, that Mario had been telling the truth all along. That none of this needed to have happened. That all of this was illegal. Unjust. Arbitrary.

The thought of Attorney General Sessions at the press conference announcing Zero Tolerance earlier that year came back to me. "If you don't want your child to be separated, then don't bring him across the border illegally," he had said. Zero Tolerance had never been about "securing" our borders or about protecting children from smugglers and human traffickers. Like many other immigration policies, Zero Tolerance was not about national security or "protecting" jobs or public safety. These justifications were a facade. Zero Tolerance was always about "deterrence"—about inflicting the greatest amount of pain possible on asylum seekers, adults and children alike, as a way to discourage future immigrants from coming to the United States. The more they suffered, the less likely others would come. It was a way to dissuade Central and South American immigrants, in particular, from making the treacherous journey; we did not see cases of European immigrants being separated from their children. The message to would-be immigrants was about how ruthless the United States could be to them and their children, so that they would think twice before coming. The Trump Administration wanted to be clear that it would spare no effort, no matter how cruel, to keep Black and brown immigrants out of their vision of America. But of course, the Vilmas and Patricias of the world had no choice. Coming to the United States was their last, desperate effort to save themselves and their children from persecution, from brutal violence, no matter how long the odds.

I shook my head slightly, looking down. "Ok, so when are they going to reunite them?" I asked, looking back up at Laura.

"He said he needs to call ORR first, send the paperwork over," Laura said, her shoulders drooping in resignation. "It may take a few days."

It was now August 1. Mario and Oralia had been separated for nearly a month, unlawfully, in contravention of an executive order, in violation of a federal injunction. DNA tests had now confirmed unequivocally that he was her father, and it would still take "a few days" to bring them back together. It had taken a split second, four coerced words out of Mario's mouth in broken Spanish to rip them apart. And after all this, it would still take "a few days" to reunite them.

A familiar feeling of powerlessness came over me, and I could see that it had gotten to Laura too.

———·—·—·—

CHAPTER 12

The Pot and the Frog

(1999–2001)

A cackling burst of laughter caught my attention, and I peeked through the screen door. The mechanic's shop across the street had closed hours ago, but every night three or four men gathered there after hours to share forty-ounce beers, cigarettes, and the intermittent roar of chuckles. Like every other night after dinner, my mother was cooking the following day's breakfast and lunch for my father to take to work. A faint but unmistakable whiff of calabacita squash reached every corner of the apartment, only overtaken by the chorizo as soon as it hit the frying pan, the sizzling sound complementing the spicy aroma. I sat on the couch near the front of the apartment, the farthest I could possibly retreat from the kitchen, trying to immerse myself in Advanced Placement (AP) Government and Politics and avoid the odors and the chatter from the kitchen, and failing at both.

It seemed that the noise out in the street was less than inside the apartment, so I stepped outside, shut the screen door, and sat on the hood of my father's car, which faced the apartment. The car's front bumper was only a couple of feet from the coffee-colored front wall, so I was able to sit on the hood and, with slightly bent knees, rest my feet against the wall and use my lap as a desk. I brought out my white binder full of worksheets and the government textbook. The sheets took on an amber hue from the glimmer of the exposed lightbulb outside our door, while Frederick Douglass stared at me from the page, his black and white beard taking on a bronze shade in the subdued limelight.

"¿Qué estás haciendo acá afuera?" my mother asked, peering through the screen door. I didn't know how long I had been out here like this.

I looked up, lowering my feet and straightening my knees. "La tarea," I said, using the generic homework as shorthand for explaining what an AP test was.

"But why out here? Isn't it too dark for you?" She stepped outside, and looked over at the group that was still gathered across the street.

"No'mbre, it's fine," I put my pencil down as I looked up at the light, sliding my feet down from the wall. It was dim, but I could still make out the text on the pages, and even though the lighting was less than ideal, I was able to focus better outside.

I should come inside, my mother said, it was getting late. She took another look across the street and stepped back into the apartment.

Fortunately, my father's uniform was already ironed when he picked it up from UniFirst, the clothing servicing shop where he dropped them off and picked them up every two weeks. The navy-blue pants and light blue button-up shirt with a patch bearing his embroidered name—"J. Olivarez," characteristically misspelling our last name—were ready to wear every time. The entire concept was novel to me: that uniforms, or any clothes for that matter, would be dropped off at some warehouse, and they would return not only laundered, but perfectly ironed and neatly arranged, each pair of pants with a corresponding shirt, on a wire hanger and covered with a thin clear plastic, a paper twist tie keeping it all in place. I was amazed at how they simply gave away dozens, hundreds, probably thousands, of wire hangers with every batch of uniforms every two weeks. They never asked for them back when my father dropped off the dirty uniforms in a black garbage bag. Did they give them away to every bus driver? At every school? In every city? Where did so many hangers come from? We kept them all, and once we had enough for our own clothes, we stacked up the rest inside the closet, repurposing the twist ties to bunch the hangers together by the dozen. My father would then take them with him when he visited my grandmother in Allende. I never knew if he sold them or gave them away, but he always made sure that each bunch was a dozen, and counted how many dozens he was taking. For my mother, this arrangement Valley View had with UniFirst meant that she didn't have to iron the uniforms, and instead only had to prepare her own clothes to head to work the next morning.

Now that we had joined my father, my mother got a job sewing the waistline darts of pants at a Dickies factory in south McAllen, down Ware Road next to empty fields where, years later, the Ursula detention center would be built. Our immigration application was still pending, but she had received a permiso, an employment authorization document, and as soon as she did, she started looking for a job. Even with both of my parents working, it wasn't clear to me if we were better off now than we had been in Allende. We had moved into an apartment that was much smaller than our old house, Héctor and I still slept on the foldable coarse mattress, and my mother now worked outside the home. Subconsciously, I must have expected that once we moved, there would be an immediate and noticeable improvement in our material condition, but like the fable of the frog in the pot of warming water, I had adjusted to our new reality.

Every night after dinner, my mother washed the dirty pan and put it right back on the stove. She would then cook another large meal, the next day's lunch for my father, as well as a smaller egg-based dish—chorizo, potatoes, nopales—which she would invariably place into four corn tortillas, and wrap them in a piece of aluminum foil. In the morning, in the fifteen minutes that it took the rest of us to get ready, she would warm the tacos on the comal, and put them right back into the foil, so that they would stay warm until my father unwrapped them after finishing his morning bus routes. Héctor and I ate at school, but if we hadn't, she would have cooked for us too. She would then head over to Dickies for the day, and when she got back home in the afternoon, it was time to start cooking dinner again.

The day my mother received her first paycheck, the four of us went to El Globo to cash it. Two incomes, I thought, when we'd always had only one, should be a game changer. My father had been paying the bills with his lone paycheck, and now an additional one, even if it was less than his, was an extra boost. I imagined the possibilities. With my mother's pay, there would surely be money left over to buy something for Héctor and me. I wasn't tempted so much anymore by the candy bars from the stuffed shelves leading to the registers—I had outgrown that sweet desire with the passage of time and with being told next time again and again—but still, the thought crossed my mind that if we wanted one now, we could have it. My mother must have been excited too, to finally have some money of her own, though if she was, she didn't show it.

The aisles at El Globo Supermarket were wide and stale, the scent of Pine-Sol masking the dusty smells of months' old boxes of crackers and canned vegetables that lined the shelves. We were often here to buy beans and chorizo, always the San Manuel brand, always in bulk, which was twenty cents less per pound; we didn't need the packaging anyway, my father said. No matter what time of day we were there, the industrial lights on the ceiling blanched every corner of the place. The check-cashing window was near the entrance, on the right side as you came into the store, past the registers if you were walking out. It must have been payday for others as well because the line to cash checks stretched well into the baking goods aisle. When it was finally our turn, the lady at the window greeted my mother in Spanish and asked for an ID. Either her chair was too low, the window was too high, or she was very short—or a combination of all three—but for some reason her face barely reached the counter on the inside of the diminutive office. She was alone at the window, and said something to my mother as she handed her back her ID. The fluorescent orange "Checks Cashed" sign hanging above forced my mother to turn her face slightly away as she took the card back.

"¿Cuánto?" my father asked with restrained shock, overhearing the lady's comment.

That was the standard fee, the lady said. If you don't want to cash the check, that is fine, but that is the fee, and the line is long, so please make up your mind.

"No pues sí," my father said, resigned.

My mother grabbed the few twenty-dollar bills and some loose change from the counter, and we walked away. Before we made it out of the store, I saw my mother hand the money to my father without saying a word, like this had been the unstated plan all along, like they both knew this was the way it was going to be, like the money had never even been hers. No one ever mentioned what we might be able to afford with the extra cash.

I was relieved when, at long last, we received the letter we had been waiting for. The outside of the envelope was like others we had received before, the emerald lettering on the upper left corner—Immigration and Naturalization Service—bringing and then dashing hope each time. But the inside was different: this time, it finally contained the appointment for our permanent residence interview.

INS in Harlingen was a small single-story office near the highway. As instructed in the letter, we made sure to bring with us the results of yet another physical exam confirming we were still not infirm (we had had a prior physical exam at the time we applied), our vaccination cards, of course, and proof that we had been living in the United States since we had submitted our application years earlier: every single one of my father's and my mother's paystubs, and every one of Héctor's and my school report cards, dozens of them. My father had stacked them, methodical as he was, in chronological order and held them together with a rubber band. We brought our hopes tightly bound like that rubber band to the immigration office on Thursday, November 30, 2000.

By then, I had submitted college applications at the urging of Mr. Cerda, the eleventh-grade English teacher. The prior year, he had assigned us to research one of the "Ivy League" universities and write a paper about it. I wrote mine about Princeton, somehow it rang a bell, and I was further interested when I learned that Einstein had taught there. I had to learn what the Ivy League even was, and although it didn't entirely make sense to me, I was clear that it was a prestigious bunch. Ever since then, Mr. Cerda encouraged me—pushed me, I would say—to apply to those schools. Even after I moved on to twelfth grade, whenever I walked past his classroom in between class periods and he was standing out in the hallway, he would ask me if I had submitted the application yet. After a while, he wouldn't even say anything; he would simply raise his eyebrows as he lifted his head with a smile when we made eye contact, as if asking "done it yet?" His was never an obnoxious push. It was more like a constant encouragement, like saying I know you *can* do it, but you *gotta* do it, have you done it? I would reciprocate the smile, say I'm working on it, ya casi sir, almost there, and keep walking, until the next time I ran into him.

What I never told Mr. Cerda was that I worried about financial aid. I had submitted the Texas Common Application and had already been admitted to University of Texas–Pan American, the local university, but even they had asked for the Free Application for Federal Student Aid (FAFSA) in order to offer a financial aid package. When I had picked up a FAFSA at the counselor's office, I noticed right away that on page one, near the top, the form asked for a social security number, which I didn't have.

"Well," Ms. Torres had said, concerned, pushing her glasses up her nose, "if you don't have one we can look at other options." Our high school counselor was a short and stocky dynamo of a woman with a habit of using the Spanish filler "este" even when speaking in English, even when speaking in a formal setting, even when she spoke at our graduation. She couldn't help it, and it was so unmistakably hers.

I had told Ms. Torres that I wasn't sure when I would get a social, and she hoped that I would by the time the FAFSA deadline rolled around. "Some private colleges don't require it," she had said. "They may, este, offer you the options they offer international students...."

Was I an international student? I wasn't sure, but the possibility seemed less than ideal, even from the way she said it.

"If you were to go to Pan Am, or, este, UT, is there any way your parents can help you pay for it?" She must have noticed disappointment on my face, and added, "at least for part of it, if you're, este, unable to get it all covered by scholarships?"

I had lied and said I would ask. The same way I had wondered whether my father would attend my elementary school ceremony, or when I had questions about why I had to be held back a year in school and Héctor didn't, I didn't ask this time either, because I already knew.

When the immigration officer finally called our name at the INS office, we walked into a narrow hallway, past some cubicles, and into a small office where the agent asked us to take a seat. The high stacks of manila folders and paper-clipped documents on either side of his desk, along with his stubby mustache, made him the perfect portrait of a government bureaucrat. His navy-blue uniform was barely a shade darker than the uniform pants my father wore. A U.S. flag on a toy flagpole rose among the stacks of papers on his desk, and a smiling Bill Clinton looked at us from a framed photograph on the wall behind him. The officer pulled out our file and began reviewing our information.

"¿Dónde trabaja?" he asked my father, his face scanning the document in front of him.

"¿En qué grado estás?" he asked Héctor, and then me, his voice formal and curt. The windowless office was bright from the harsh, unnatural light overhead. The officer continued in this way for a while, asking questions to which he appeared to already know the answers. Where did my father work? What grade were we in? Did my mother work? Had we traveled outside the country? Had we committed any crimes? He did not seem interested in any of the answers, as if he was simply going through the motions, counting the minutes. He held a blue ballpoint pen in his hand as he questioned us and flipped page after page, without writing anything down. He would sometimes nod at our answers, mumble aha, mhm, and sometimes he would simply move on to the next question without even acknowledging the answers my father offered like a soldier on his first day of bootcamp.

When he was satisfied that he had asked enough questions, he pulled out a blank form. He began filling it out, starting with our names and dates of birth.

"Olivares with a Z or an S?" he asked my father. This had never been a question in Mexico, where everyone seemed to spell Olivares with an S, and nobody ever asked. Here, there seemed to be more Z spellings, and most people wouldn't ask, simply defaulting to Z.

"Ese," my father said, with no small amount of pride. He sat up a little straighter as he said it.

"Are you still at 2023 Chicago?" the officer asked, as if hoping only to confirm.

No, my father jumped in. We had moved that summer. Our new address was 807 South 42nd street. "Ochocientos siete, sur Cuarenta y Dos," my father said, translating our address literally.

The officer started writing the updated address on the form, and when he reached the 42, he stopped and looked up. He squinted, looking into the empty space, as if trying to remember something, and, unable to do so, he gave up and looked up at Héctor and me.

"Is that with a T-H or an R-D?" he asked.

It took me a second to register what he was asking. I tried to avoid Héctor's perplexed stare, sensing he was also in disbelief.

This man, the federal government personified, with his starch-ironed uniform and patches on his chest, was the gatekeeper of residency into the U.S. He held in that ballpoint pen the decision whether we got our green card, whether we got to call ourselves "lawful permanent residents," and whether I obtained that number to put on page one of my FAFSA. He who held the keys to a door we had been waiting for years to enter, he who wielded more power over our lives than perhaps he realized, could not spell "42nd." And it wasn't even the fully spelled ordinal, forty-second, but merely two numbers and two letters.

"I think it's N-D, no?" I finally said.

"Right, right," he said, jotting it down on the form as if he had remembered on his own.

Like the man at the consulate in Monterrey who had reviewed our visa application years earlier, this singular immigration official had so much discretion over our family's future, that it was impossible for me to reconcile that amount of power with his inability to spell something so simple. Individual immigration officers, whether the ones at the bridge as one enters the country, or the ones who decide a family petition, have broad—unfettered, some might say— discretion to refuse admission or reject a petition. They often make those decisions based largely on the papers in front of them, maybe a photograph, maybe a short declaration, documents that can never do justice to the lives summarized to their bare bones in a few pages. I sat there watching as the officer continued filling out the form, repeating *no mames* over and over again in my head—are you kidding me, how can he be the one who gets to say yes or no?

But he was, like a modern-day Julius Caesar rendering a verdict with his thumb in this Colosseum of an office. He completed the form, signed it, and looked up at us. He handed my father three pieces of paper, and told us these were temporary. We should expect to receive the cards in the mail in the next three to four weeks, he added.

"Congratulations," he said, shaking my father's hand and smiling at my mother as we stood up to leave. In shaking the officer's hand, my father bowed his head in a series of half-nods, as if kowtowing to reaffirm that the officer did have all the power, his misspelling notwithstanding.

When the principal called my name, I rose from my chair on the rostrum and slowly made my way to the podium to make my speech as the school's valedictorian. It had been just over six months since our green card interview, and I felt a different kind of nervous tonight, but the applause and the cheering drew a smile on my face. The loudest cheers came from the soccer players, with whom I had shared a perfectly mediocre season. In the first year of Valley View High School's soccer history, we had tied 50 percent of our games, and of the rest we had won half and lost half. I could barely make out my family seated in the packed bleachers in the distance, shading my eyes from the glare of the bright stadium lights that lit up the graduation ceremony. The Gulf summer breeze ruffled the sheets of paper in my hand as I set them flat on the podium.

The applause from the rest of my classmates was sincere too, I was sure, except for those few who thought they ought to be the ones giving this speech. More than once, I had been asked how come I went here and not to the school to which I was zoned in McAllen. That had been our original plan, for Héctor and me to attend Valley View for a few months—even though we did not reside in this district, we were allowed to attend because my father worked for the school—and then once we had learned English and settled in, we would transfer to our home district. That had been the plan even over the aired objections of my father's sister, who thought that this wasn't a good place for us. Too many Po'Boys and other gangs in Las Milpas, she had said, referring to the colonia where the school was located, a low-income unincorporated part of town where streets weren't paved, and many houses still lacked indoor plumbing. Po'Boys often wore khaki Dickies pants, white undershirts, and black short-sleeve shirts buttoned only at the very top, and went about their business with a supercilious gait, as if daring anyone to question what they were up to. I was puzzled when I learned that Po' was short for "poor," unsure why they chose to highlight that in the group's name. In any event, even over those objections, Héctor and I still attended Valley View. And once we learned English, we

did not want to change schools again, preferring to share the classroom with gang members over having to go through the ordeal of
meeting new teachers and making new friends a second time.

What no one said to me directly, but I overheard once in English
class, was that had I not come from Mexico, some of my classmates
would have ranked higher, and there was some resentment that I
had taken what they considered their spot on the class top-ten list.
"If he just hadn't come," Jasmine told one of her friends, "or if he just
went to the school where he belongs, I would be higher up." Her
voice carried a combination of wishful longing and hopelessness,
like wishing the sun wouldn't burn so hot in August—you don't like
it but there's nothing you can do about it. I pretended not to hear
from a few desks away, as the teacher went on about Frost and a
crow and snow and dust.

I'm not sure if this was the reason her comment stung so much,
but Jasmine herself had come from a town across the border a few
years before me. And she and I were not the only ones; a good
number of the students at Valley View hadn't started kindergarten
or even elementary there. The majority of us who had joined the
school later had come from Mexico, and there were a few from Central America. Of those who had been at Valley View since kindergarten, many of their parents or their grandparents had come from
elsewhere too.

That eavesdropped conversation would not be the last time I
would encounter rejection of newly arrived immigrants by those
who had arrived earlier—even if only a short time earlier—and felt
more entitled to claim this land as theirs. Jasmine's caustic remark
evoked in me the feeling that I was taking someone else's place, that
I didn't belong. It was as if the time when a person migrates across a
border creates a sort of moral legitimacy over membership in a community, and those who come later can no longer join on the same

terms. I wonder if those whose families had arrived a decade or a century earlier viewed Jasmine the same way she appeared to view me. How far back in time, or forward, does that claim over a piece of the earth extend? What is the meaningful difference between a Central American family arriving today and the pilgrims arriving at Plymouth Harbor in the early sixteen hundreds? Is length of time the relevant factor? Black Americans, whose ancestors have been in what is the United States today for more than four hundred years, were mostly brought here against their will on slave ships and are still treated as second-class citizens in many respects, excluded from the community of "real" Americans. I've never heard of a white second-generation immigrant being told to "go back" to England or Norway. Indigenous peoples have inhabited this land for centuries, long before the pilgrims arrived and long before present-day borders were even drawn. If length of time were the deciding factor, their claim to the land ought to be the strongest. But it is often the descendants of white settlers who claim an unassailable entitlement to this country, pointing to multiple generations in the United States as the basis for that claim. But even their ancestors, whether they like to admit it or not, were immigrants once.

Sometimes those who arrived earlier point to the "illegality" of how some immigrants enter the country as the relevant difference, arguing that their ancestors did it "the right way." In 2018, some descendants of immigrants blamed immigrant parents for being separated from their children—they chose to cross the border illegally, they would say, so it's their fault that their children were taken away. Putting aside the fact that the Trump Administration had made it impossible for would-be asylum seekers to apply at a port of entry, what counts as "legal" and "illegal" depends entirely on the laws in effect at a particular time, and those laws have changed time and again, sometimes dramatically. What in 2018 was considered "illegal

entry"—crossing the Rio Grande without being inspected, for example—in 1918 had been perfectly common, and in 1818 would have
been wholly inconceivable, as the border was then at a different lati-
tude altogether. And it's not necessary to go back hundreds of years
to find instances of sea changes in the law. The way somebody could
"legally" migrate to the United States was drastically different in
1964 than in 1965, when the Immigration and Nationality Act was
enacted. What would have been an inconsequential traffic ticket for
speeding away from an immigration checkpoint in 1995 became the
life-changing deportable offense of "high speed flight" in 1996, the
year Bill Clinton signed the Illegal Immigration Reform and Immigration Responsibility Act into law, labeling a broad range of conduct
as "aggravated felonies." Each subsequent law builds on the previous
one, and over time, the reality they create becomes the new normal. Like the frog in the pot of water, we become accustomed to this
metamorphosing reality, except by now the water is boiling.

I did not cover any of this in my graduation speech. Instead, I
talked about how we were all like droplets of water. We had traveled together for years, from tiny molecules of dihydrogen monox-
ide into fully formed condensation, becoming closer to one another
in the process, growing heavy like a gray cloud in April. And now
it was our time to rain down. We would rain and go our separate
ways, some of us flowing into streams and rivers, irrigating crops
and making flowers bloom, some pouring down far into the vast
ocean. Frankly, I was afraid some droplets would flow straight into
a sewer, but I had edited that part out in an earlier draft.

Ever since I delivered that speech more than twenty years ago,
I have asked myself many times why it didn't occur to me to read
at least part of it in Spanish. I included a "gracias a mi papá y a mi
mamá" near the beginning, but other than that perfunctory thanks
to my parents, I wrote and read the rest entirely in English. The two

people I most would have wished to understand what I was saying did not understand a word I was saying. I've regretted it ever since. Every time I found myself wondering why, I would tell myself that it must have been because I was too young to realize, that I simply didn't think of it, or that the crowd I was addressing were my class-mates and teachers, not really my father and mother.

Only now, as I write these pages, have I been able to reflect and realize that the comment I overheard a few months earlier in English class probably had something to do with it. Perhaps I read the entire speech in English in an attempt to show that I had learned the language, that I deserved to be at this podium, that I belonged in this community. And in trying to prove all that, I inadvertently alienated the two people I most wanted to be proud of me on that stage. I feel as if in my attempt to show that I belonged that night, I left part of me behind. What else have I left behind along the way without even realizing it? Must all immigrants give something up in order to be fully accepted?

One morning later that month, when students were already gone for the summer, I showed up at the principal's office. The empty halls were only partly lit, and they seemed wider now than when they had been bustling with student chatter.

I walked into the deserted reception as Ms. VanHort was about to exit. She had been our Geography teacher in tenth grade, and had since moved up the ranks to assistant principal. Cardboard boxes were scattered on the floor, reams of copy paper stacked up on the counter where the receptionist usually kept a sign-in sheet. Like the hallways, the reception was also half lit, giving the place a comfort-able warmth. Ms. VanHort was surprised to see me, but she greeted me with her characteristically welcoming smile.

"Hi, Effrin," she said. "What are you doing here, how can I help you?" She didn't walk me into her office, so we stood there amid the boxes and disarranged blue vinyl chairs.

I was there to pick up the money from two scholarships I had been awarded, I told her, one from the National Honor Society, the other from a local bank, fifteen hundred dollars in total. I showed her the two certificates I had been handed at the end-of-year pep rally back in May.

"No, I'm sorry," she said nicely. "We don't need the certificates, we need the receipt."

"What receipt," I wondered aloud. "This is all I got."

"No, the receipt from when you spend the money." She explained that I needed to spend the fifteen hundred dollars first, buy books or supplies or anything else I needed, then bring those receipts, and she'd be glad to give me my scholarship money. She added sprightly that the scholarship terms were so flexible, and that I'd have enough to buy anything I needed. Maybe even a computer.

Where am I going to get fifteen hundred dollars, I thought.

I was leaving for Philadelphia for the semester, I told her, hoping that this would help change her mind. I wouldn't be back until Christmas break at the earliest.

That was no problem at all, she said. They would safeguard the scholarship money for me for as long as necessary. I could pick it up whenever, so long as I brought the receipt.

I had been counting on that money to buy the plane ticket to Philadelphia. Without that money, I had no idea how I would buy it, and I had to leave in a few weeks.

Before exiting the building, I turned around and looked for Ms. VanHort again. Could she maybe give me the money for only one of the scholarships? Perhaps the one from NHS, the smaller of the two, for $500. I would bring the receipt in a few short days, but I needed the money to buy a plane ticket, I told her.

"Oh yes, absolutely," she said, her smile still there. "Your scholarship definitely covers that." But I had to buy the ticket first. Don't you worry, she tried to reassure me, your money will be right here waiting for you when you bring the receipt.

I dragged my feet out of the school holding the two worthless certificates folded in my hand. What was the point of getting a scholarship if I couldn't get the money? The financial aid package that the University of Pennsylvania had offered me had been the most comprehensive. It was not a full ride, technically, but it was enough to cover tuition, fees, and a dorm for the first year, which made the decision of which college to attend a no-brainer. If I got a job and kept expenses low, I figured I could make it work. But I needed to get there, and now I had no idea how I would do that. The semester would start the first week of September.

When I asked my father that evening, he shook his head. It was not a shake to say no, but to express the same resigned frustration that he had expressed at the check-cashing fee at El Globo. "Qué chulada," he said with a mix of irony and understated exclamation. Great. Sitting at the table, he pushed down the heel of his left shoe with his right, until the shoe came off and fell on the kitchen floor. The evenings at home had become slow-moving affairs, as my father arrived increasingly tired from work, resting his feet on a chair most nights to help with the periodic swelling. My mother would remove his socks, his feet taking on the pale complexion of ever poorer blood circulation.

He slid an envelope in my direction from the middle of the table. "See how much that one is for," he said, referring to the credit card offer inside it. The pre-approved Visa credit line was enough to cover the cost of the flight. He handed me a pen, and asked me to fill out the form for him, for me. The card arrived about two weeks later, and he nearly maxed it out with my Continental flight to Philly.

CHAPTER 13

Pro Bono

(July 2018)

The same year that my family came back together in McAllen—1996—President Bill Clinton signed the Illegal Immigration Reform and Immigrant Responsibility Act into law (IIRIRA). IIRIRA created a broad range of so-called criminal bars to immigration relief under the tough-on-crime sentiment that still dominated politics since the "war on drugs" had launched in the 1970s. The creation of low-level drug offenses in that period was now coupled with serious—sometimes permanent—immigration consequences for those convicted of the new offenses, leading to thousands of arrests and deportations that had not existed only a year prior. The newly created reasons to deport immigrants often resulted in family separations, including from their U.S. citizen children, and still do today.

After IIRIRA, a major reorganization of the immigration bureaucracy came following the September 11 attacks, when all immigration agencies were brought under the newly created DHS. Since that restructuring, ICE and Border Patrol in particular have doubled down on an agency culture that views immigrants as criminals, as terrorists, as inherently dangerous to the security of the nation, and that largely disregards human life. Since its founding in 2003, at least 214 people have died in ICE custody, and reports of physical and sexual abuse number in the thousands, prompting calls to dismantle the agency altogether in recent years. After a Border Patrol agent in El Paso shot and killed fifteen-year-old Sergio Hernández Güereca while he stood across the border in Ciudad Juárez in 2010, the Supreme Court ruled that the boy's family had no right to bring a lawsuit in part because the boy did not have sufficient ties to the United States. Even today, the ruling and the reasoning in that case are the law of the land, and a Border Patrol agent may shoot an unarmed child across the border with impunity.

From the Somali taxi driver to the destitute mother hoping to apply for asylum, officers at these agencies seem to function from the default of the Other as a threat. Amidst this bureaucracy and agency culture, the same department tasked with protecting the homeland from existential threats also evaluates applications for asylum and humanitarian protection. With two such markedly different roles housed in the same department, how can the latter not become infected with or distorted by the law-enforcement focus of the former?

Overt racism and white supremacist views have been part and parcel of immigration law and policy in the United States for more than two centuries. It is not as if there are a few historical breadcrumbs here and there that are hard to find, like Hansel and Gretel's, as we try to retrace the steps that got us here. Nor were these fringe positions that were discarded when laws and policies were designed. No, these views have made it directly into, and are evident in, our laws and institutions.

This is not merely to chastise the history of immigration policy in this country, as problematic as it is. Rather, this is to push the nation to be honest with itself about the history of how the United States has treated immigrants in the past, so that it may better understand why it treats immigrants the way it does in the present. And to ask ourselves, honestly, how far our compassion and commitment to human rights truly extends, especially when Black and brown immigrants show up at our borders. It is better to accept and face this difficult history head on, rather than tell ourselves feel-good stories about the past. Some say that it is not fair to judge past generations based on the values of today; after all, the concept of "human rights" hasn't been around as such for that long in the arc of human history. Perhaps, but we should also not romanticize or sanitize the history of past generations simply because they came before us. While U.S. history contains multiple "success stories" of individual immigrants, that history is also replete of instances when its laws and institutions have deliberately rejected non-white immigrants—from the Nationality Act of 1790 to the National Origins Act of 1924, to Zero Tolerance in 2018.

Understanding this history is a fundamental piece of understanding who we are as a country, a country where the faceless sobs of immigrant children inside a detention center turned public opinion against a callous policy, but where the pleas of their immigrant parents had made little difference before. A nation not of immigrants, but of the children of immigrants: in one sense, a nation so outraged at the abuse of the children of immigrants—children in cages, children ripped from their parents' arms, children crying inside the Ursula detention center—that yet condemned their very parents because they "broke the law." Time and again, adult immigrants are demonized, criminalized, and blamed for the country's problems. In another, historical sense, we are also a nation where almost every person—except for the descendants of its original inhabitants—has descended from someone who migrated or was brought to this land from elsewhere. In this sense, even the harshest anti-immigrant bigots are the children of immigrants.

*   *   *

The weeks leading up to Mario's and Oralia's DNA test results were daunting. As we worked on their case worrying every day about what the results might be, dozens of other families were supposed to be reunited before the end of the month. The court in *Ms. L* had ordered that all separated families be reunited by July 27, and since the government had been shoddy at best in keeping records, complying with that order became a chaotic undertaking.

For weeks, dozens of people around the country had approached us asking how they could help. We received emails, phone calls, messages on TCRP's social media accounts, and even some hate mail. Some people suggested protesting outside of the shelters where unaccompanied children were held, others wanted to come and do a hunger strike outside of the courthouse. Attorneys started contacting us too, asking if any of the families needed legal help. And they did. We had interviewed nearly four hundred families, and there was no way we could represent them all in immigration court. We started making a list of attorneys wanting to help, planning to match them with families as soon as possible.

One particularly hectic afternoon, Roberto wandered into my office and, alarmed, said that one of those attorneys was in town. She had flown in from California and had just called Roberto asking how she could help.

"She says she's here, in McAllen," Roberto added, worrying. "And I don't know what to tell her."

An idea popped into my head. "Can she commit to taking one of our cases all the way through?" I asked Roberto. "Please ask her if she can agree to take the entire immigration case, not just CFI prep or bond, but all of it—asylum or any other application, and appeals." I knew it was no small request, since immigration cases can take years, but that was the level of commitment we needed to be able to represent each family properly. If attorneys agreed to take only the early phase of a case, I was concerned the families may be left hanging on their own down the road, without representation to help them complete their asylum or other type of application.

"If she says yes, ask her to come over to the office, we have a case for her." We had been trying to place cases with attorneys, and had started creating a list of cases that were most urgent. Since the day of the interview in court, I would frequently think of Patricia and her son Alessandro. I really had no way of knowing how bad his condition was—all she had told me was that he swallowed fluid during birth—but they were at the top of our list. Now separated for weeks, we were unsure if Alessandro was receiving the medical care he needed at the shelter where he was being held. There was no way to know if he was getting any medication or therapy. It was our priority for reunification. Every child needed their mother or father, but of those who we confirmed were still separated, Alessandro stood out.

A few minutes later, a smiling Roberto was again standing at my door. "She's on her way."

Maggy Krell walked into our office less than a half hour later. She had traveled from Sacramento, California, looking for any way she could help. With her was Clara Levers, also an attorney and friend of Maggy's who was fluent in Spanish and came along mainly to serve as interpreter, since Maggy spoke little Spanish.

Maggy wore a gray skirt and a perfectly ironed button-up white blouse. She looked very much like a lawyer. She and Clara sat in my office, and commented on the pictures of a flower market in Guatemala hanging on my office wall. The pictures were from the time I visited Guatemala with a delegation from the Inter-American Commission on Human Rights. The colorful flowers contrasted with the tired faces of the women selling them, a common contrast one finds in Guatemala—rich natural beauty side by side with misery and extreme poverty.

I told Maggy and Clara that our priority case involved a Honduran mother separated from her six-year-old son. "This is our most urgent case because I don't know if he is receiving any kind of medical care at the shelter. He's in San Antonio. She is detained at PIDC, so you can probably visit her tomorrow."

"PIDC?" they asked in unison.

"Oh, I'm sorry, the Port Isabel Detention Center. It's about an hour east of here."

"Ok, ok," Maggy repeated, nodding softly, and seeming a little overwhelmed. Maggy's voice was now a little hesitant, contrasting with her initial eagerness to help with whatever we needed. It seemed to be dawning on her what taking the case would entail.

Knowing what they were getting into or not, Maggy and Clara agreed to take Patricia's case. Maggy was the General Counsel of Planned Parenthood of California, and she said her organization fully supported her doing this pro bono work. Clara worked for the California Office of the Attorney General, but she was doing this only in her personal capacity, and, she clarified, was here only in her role as an interpreter, not as an attorney.

Maggy and Clara needed to submit paperwork to ICE in advance in order to visit Patricia at PIDC. I contacted Carlos García, who had helped us interview families in court and often had clients at PIDC, to ask if he could get them a copy of the visitation forms that needed to be faxed and generally guide Maggy and Clara through the visitation process.

He responded right away. "I'm headed to PIDC tomorrow. Perhaps Maggy wants to go with me? Or follow me? Or meet me? Or we can just give her the form to fax in." It was Carlos's characteristic willingness to help.

When Maggy and Clara left, Roberto was sitting in his cubicle.

"If we could only get three hundred attorneys just like them, each willing to take a case..." I said, half-jokingly.

"I don't know about three hundred," Roberto responded, "but I have tons of emails in my inbox." Perhaps we could find enough attorneys willing to take the families' immigration cases, seeing each one through to completion, however long that took.

We had also tried to draw attention to the human suffering as an essential piece of our efforts to stop the separations and get the children back to their parents. In one of many sleepless nights, I had thought that a celebrity doing a hunger strike against family separations and demanding reunification might draw more attention to what we were seeing in court. But I did not know any celebrities. I had no way to make that happen. Someone suggested a concert at one of the international bridges—a protest concert à la the 1960s—and there was talk of having it in Laredo, but nothing materialized.

Then one Monday afternoon, I received an email from an attorney at Robert F. Kennedy Human Rights. Kerry Kennedy, Bobby Kennedy's daughter and the president of the organization, wanted to know if they could do anything to help stop the separations.

The hunger strike idea came back to me right away. Would she be willing to start a hunger strike until all the children were reunited? Organizing such a strike and drawing enough attention to it would require a lot more human power than our team had. We reached out to La Unión del Pueblo Entero (LUPE), a farmworkers' union turned into a community organization in South Texas. The LUPE staff were ecstatic about the possibility of a hunger strike. They called Dolores Huerta, the internationally famous activist for the rights of farmworkers, migrants, and the poor, and a longtime supporter of LUPE, to see if she would participate. Huerta, now in her late 80s, had been organizing farmworkers in California since her youth and had worked alongside César Chávez and Bobby Kennedy. In fact, she had been on the stage with Bobby Kennedy when he delivered his victory speech after winning the California primary in 1968, the day before he was assassinated.

In the sixties, Bobby Kennedy had joined César Chávez and Dolores Huerta in a hunger strike in support of farmworkers. The connection between Dolores Huerta and Kerry's father during the civil rights movement made the idea of a hunger strike appealing to Kerry and her team. A long-running hunger strike would be hard to pull off, and Roberto had an alternative idea: a sequential fast. Each individual would fast for twenty-four hours, and then pass on the fasting "baton" to the next person. The fast would go on for twenty-four days, symbolically seeking the reunification of the 2,400 children who had reportedly been separated at the time. A sequential 24-hour fast seemed more feasible than an ongoing hunger strike that could last for weeks or months. And people could participate virtually, fasting for twenty-four hours wherever they lived around the world. We were all on board with the plan.

I arrived at Archer Park the day I was to start my fast and parked on Broadway Street. A small and quaint park in the heart of McAllen's downtown, Archer Park is a mere three blocks from the courthouse and for years has been the focal point of protests and demonstrations. On weekends, children play by the dry fountain on the north side of the park. A kiosk in the center lends itself as a stage for speakers, and its mature live oaks provide shade and refuge on hot days like these in July. Cars were parked on the streets all around the park, and fasters, supporters, and onlookers would walk on one of the four arms of the X-shaped set of sidewalks that led from each corner of the park to the kiosk.

"Break bread, not families," was the slogan that The Robert F. Kennedy Human Rights Center (now rebranded as RFK Human Rights) team came up with. Every day at noon, a medal bearing that slogan would be passed from one person to the next, the symbol that one was fasting for the families. The person fasting would wear the medal for the twenty-four hours and then pass it on to the next faster.

As I was about to get out of my car, my cell phone vibrated yet again. "Unknown caller" stared straight at me. I slid the green button on the screen with my left thumb and answered as I stepped out of the car. I pressed 1 to accept the call, and the shy voice of a woman greeted me on the other end of the line.

"Buenos días, licenciado," she said. "Habla Ana."

I had spoken to Ana a couple of times before. I hadn't interviewed her in court, but my number had been passed around to her at the South Texas Detention Center in Pearsall, Texas, about three hours away. Ana had been traveling with her nine-year-old daughter, Juliana, from El Salvador, hoping to reunite with her husband and son in Colorado. Upon crossing the border, Border Patrol agents had apprehended them. The next day, a Border Patrol agent had come and taken Juliana, telling Ana that he was taking her for a bath. That was the last time Ana had seen her, and by now Ana hadn't heard from Juliana in more than a month.

Every single separation was cruel, but the level of deception involved in Ana's separation from Juliana made it particularly sinister. These painful details came to mind as I heard Ana's voice on the phone.

"Hola, Ana, ¿cómo está?" I felt silly when I heard the words leave my mouth asking how she was doing. Even asking that question, a mere formality in my daily life, felt like an immense privilege compared to Ana's predicament.

"Pues aquí," she said. Here.

While we tried to find pro bono immigration attorneys for Ana and Juliana, Alexis also contacted ORR to try to arrange for a phone call between them. We had done this for scores of families, a small sliver of information and hope in an otherwise vacuum of both. At least they could hear each other's voice, we thought, and know that the other was accounted for and okay, all things considered.

"Have you been able to speak with your little girl?" I asked.

"Bueno," well, she said. I thought I heard her voice starting to break, and at first I wasn't sure if it was the connection, as calls from detention centers were always unstable.

Then I heard her sniffle, and I was sure it wasn't the connection. She was weeping.

"No ha podido hablar con ella," I said, half-asking and half-stating that she hadn't spoken with Juliana, frustrated again that either ORR or the detention center had not facilitated a call between yet another separated parent and their child. This had been a pattern all summer, a combination of ORR staff claiming that they needed confirmation that the parent was in fact a parent, and the detention center staff doing the bare minimum, generally unconcerned about the requests of the parents they held in custody. Neither agency was designed to facilitate communication between children and the detained parents intentionally separated from them. Their staff, like most bureaucrats, were set in their ways, and it was a struggle to get them to do something that was not part of their protocols. If it was not part of their protocols, they told us, it couldn't be done. As usual, the bureaucracy was a one-way street that got in the way of sparing the immigrant additional suffering, but not of causing even more. Meanwhile, hundreds of parents and children had no idea where their loved ones were and did not know if they had been released, deported, or worse.

I tried to explain to Ana to please be patient, that sometimes arranging a call took time, that it would happen sooner or later, that we were trying our best. But she interrupted me.

"No, perdón, es que sí tuvimos la llamada," we did have the call, she said between snivels. I was confused. They had had the call, but Ana's tears did not sound like tears of joy. I was pacing slowly on the sidewalk next to my car, wondering why she was crying even though she had finally spoken with her daughter. A small crowd was starting to gather by the kiosk in advance of the passing of the fasting medal.

"¡Ah, qué bueno!" I responded, uplifted. That's great.

"Sí, pero..." and she broke into tears again.

What was the but? After a long moment, her breathing slowed, and I could hear Ana calming down.

"Es que sí tuvimos la llamada, pero casi no pudimos hablar," she finally said, her voice tired from fighting through the tears, and I imagined her swollen eyes and blushing face. They had had the call, but they hardly spoke.

"¿Cómo?" I did not understand what she meant.

"Es que nos la pasamos llorando, casi no pudimos hablar," she said again. We cried the whole time, we could hardly speak. And then she wept some more.

A knot closed my throat, and I stopped pacing. Ana couldn't hold her tears back. We cried the whole time, Ana said. The little they were able to speak, Juliana kept asking, "Why did you leave me, mommy? Why won't you come and get me? When will you come get me, mommy?"

They had spent the five minutes allotted for their call listening to each other weep. The phone call we had pushed ORR for weeks to arrange had been five minutes of torment, with Juliana asking Ana why she had left her. I swallowed hard but had no words of comfort this time. An executive order and a federal injunction had not been enough for her and Juliana, and the Inter-American Commission was still reviewing our complaint. Those were the legal tools I had as a lawyer, and they were incapable of returning Ana to her daughter.

More and more people were walking along the sidewalk toward the kiosk, oblivious to Ana's despair as they strolled casually past me. A reporter was setting up her camera on a tripod in the distance, and a squirrel dashed in front of me and climbed up one of the oak trees. The sound of Ana weeping felt so distant from life at the park.

As I reflect on that phone call, it is hard not to think that the time Ana and Juliana spent crying to each other on the phone was another form of torture, yet another re-victimization as a result of the separation. And then having to tell me what had happened, struggling through tears to repeat how Juliana had, in her innocence and ignorance of the cruelty humans are capable of, asked those raw, piercing questions.

When Ana spoke again, she asked me if I had an update on her case. We had contacted an attorney in Denver who had offered to meet with her husband, and who was going to represent her and Juliana in their immigration case. "That attorney should be contacting your husband this week," I said. She thanked me, her voice somewhat more composed, and we said goodbye.

I looked around me and saw more supporters descend from their cars around the park. One of them waved at me, and I waved back instinctively although I did not recognize her in the distance. Unsure what to do, I walked back to my car.

It was all too much to process. Every time we felt we had achieved a small victory for a family, another gut punch would remind us of what each parent was going through. The sense of futility was all too real. Their pain seemed to bleed through every attempt at progress. I forgot about the fast, opened the door to my car, and sat there, as if in a void. I felt tears coming, and I didn't even fight them this time. I wasn't sure if I was crying for Ana, for Juliana, or for myself.

After a few long minutes, I wiped my face. When I thought my eyes didn't seem so red anymore, I took a deep breath, tried to regain my composure, and headed to the kiosk to claim the fasting medal.

A few days later, I walked into the conference room to find Roberto visibly exasperated. He seemed relieved to see me, but resentful that I was late. It was not so much the fact that I was late that bothered him, as the reason why. That morning, the Mexican men's national soccer team had played against Brazil at the 2018 FIFA Soccer World Cup in Russia, and my brother Héctor and I have watched the Mexico games together, especially the elimination games, since 2002, in what has become somewhat of an unspoken tradition. The World Cup takes place once every four years, and it's always a highlight of the sports year for millions of people around the globe, including Héctor and me. This was the elimination game, in Samara, Russia, at 6:00 p.m. local time, and critically, at 9:00 a.m. Texas time, overlapping partially with the first training of pro bono attorneys.

For weeks now, attorneys from all over the country, from law firms big and small, had contacted us asking how they could help. Roberto had spent the past couple of weeks figuring out how to organize them, and what exactly to ask of them, trying to use Maggy's and Patricia's case as a model. The most urgent task was to get the families reunited, but we asked the attorneys to also commit to taking their immigration cases through completion. Since many parents were detained at the Port Isabel Detention Center in South Texas, we decided it made sense for the attorneys to travel down here, meet with the parents at PIDC, and establish the attorney-client relationship as soon as possible. Once that happened, each attorney and their law firm would be responsible for seeing that case through, with our guidance and support.

Roberto had scheduled the meeting with the pro bono attorneys this Monday morning at 10:30 at the TCRP office. I showed up about thirty minutes late, after watching Brazil trounce Mexico yet again. The attorneys were still marveling at the mural in our conference room, a colorful homage to the struggle for human rights in Texas, with portraits of Emma Tenayuca, Dolores Huerta, Dr. Henry P. García, and César Chávez, icons of the workers' rights movement in the twentieth century. Like many visitors who saw the mural for the first time, they had questions about who the people in the portraits were and what the imagery symbolized.

Roberto had had to start the training without me. I had insisted that it would be fine, and that he could start by laying out what was happening, explain the general status of the cases and what we knew about the parents' situations, without getting into any specifics of immigration law. Still, he felt I was letting him down by putting too much responsibility on him and asking him to begin the training of more than a dozen attorneys, including many with more years of experience than me, when he was not himself an attorney but a volunteer who had been hired only recently.

Before coming to TCRP, Roberto had been teaching math to high schoolers as part of Teach for America, his first job after college. He was so nervous to lead the meeting with attorneys that he had asked me if I could skip watching the game altogether, and he was incredulous when I told him I couldn't. Watching that game felt like the only break I had had in weeks and a semblance of a life before Zero Tolerance.

When I walked into the conference room, I saw his relief, and he quickly introduced me to the volunteer attorneys.

"Hi everyone, apologies for being late," I said.

The attorneys had started asking questions of Roberto that he could not answer:

Are all the parents subject to expedited removal?

Do any of them have a deportation date set yet?

Have they all requested a Credible Fear Interview?

When are they scheduled for?

What about their children?

Are their immigration cases consolidated with their parents'?

Do we need to file motions to change venue?

Should we consider filing habeas corpus petitions?

Roberto and I told them what we knew, and what we did not know. Like them, we had more questions than answers. Roberto had prepared a visitation form for each attorney to sign and assigned a parent to each attorney.

"You need to fax this form to PIDC, including your client's name and A-Number," Roberto explained.

In the days leading up to the meeting, Roberto, Laura, and I had discussed which cases should be our priority. There were so many parents at PIDC, over one hundred at this point—many more than volunteer attorneys in our conference room—that we had had to make a decision: Which should be the first ten parents to get legal representation? We started with what we thought made sense: any child with medical issues or a disability, where it seemed like reunification was most urgent, or any parent with a particularly compelling asylum claim, where their risk if returned to their home country seemed greater than others—some parents had showed us gunshot and stabbing scars, for example, from the persecution they fled.

Still, deciding to assign a lawyer to one parent over another felt extremely unfair. We knew so little about these families, only what we had gathered in a few rushed minutes in court, and here we were, making life-altering decisions for the parents to whom we assigned an attorney, and for those to whom we didn't. It was such a consequential responsibility, and we felt the burden. For every parent to whom we assigned a pro bono lawyer, there was another, equally deserving parent to whom we didn't. No, for every parent to whom we assigned a lawyer, there were *three or four* to whom we did not. Roberto tried to have me confirm that this or that family was the right choice as a priority, and I sensed that what he wanted was for me to make the decision. I felt no better positioned to make that call. As I stood above his shoulder by his cubicle, a stack of manila folders organized with dozens of intake forms on his desk, a spreadsheet with names and dates of birth constantly up on the computer screen, and filing cabinets lined with case documents against our office wall, as if standing guard, none of it seemed to truly capture each family's story.

It did not cross our minds at the time that the reason we were feeling the weight of this responsibility, the reason we found ourselves making such significant calls for dozens of parents and children, was that Zero Tolerance existed in the first place. Perhaps we shouldn't have felt the burden so heavy on our shoulders, but we did. We knew that the odds of an immigrant winning their asylum case or otherwise not being deported were more than 2-to-1 for those represented by an attorney versus those who faced the system alone. Whoever we chose, we knew that our actions were sure to put some families on a path closer to asylum, and others further from it.

In a famous moral philosophy thought experiment called the trolley problem, five people lie on railroad tracks tied down, unable to move, and a train is approaching to crush them. The person doing the thought experiment has the ability to pull on a lever and change the track the train is on. Pulling the lever sends the train onto a different track, one on which only one person is awaiting her death, therefore sparing the five but crushing this one person who would have been fine but for the pulling of the lever. The question is what is the morally right thing to do? Should one pull the lever? Is it as simple as "saving" the greatest number of people, a utilitarian approach? College professors play with the number of people on each track to make the thought experiment more or less challenging for students, and sometimes even set it as the same number of people on each track, except those in one group are terminally ill, or others are medical geniuses who may discover the cure to diseases, others are artistic prodigies, such as Beethoven or Michelangelo. Do you still pull the lever if doing so will save twenty people but will kill Michelangelo, and the world will never know the Sistine Chapel or the David?

Except Roberto and I were not engaged in a thought experiment. We had a group of attorneys in suits waiting in the conference room, and we had to provide them a list of names and A-Numbers. They had traveled from afar and were anxiously waiting for their list of assigned clients, eager to start drafting documents and thinking about applicable immigration regulations, not philosophical quandaries. The question in the train hypothetical focuses on the moral responsibility of the person pulling the lever; it does not really engage with what set the train in motion in the first place. "Assume the train is already in motion," the professors will say. For the families on our list, on our railroad tracks, the train had been set in motion by Zero Tolerance.

But there was no way around that. We had hundreds of parents on our list, and twelve attorneys in the conference room.

Roberto handed them their visitation forms, and nobody asked how we had chosen those families. Each of them received a piece of paper, with a name and A-Number, and that was their client, that was their mission, and they zeroed in on it. They had no idea

Roberto and I had had to pull levers to draft that list. Hundreds of other families, from Brownsville to San Diego, still lay on the railroad tracks.

By late July, reports of families separated nationwide surpassed 3,000. As we approached the reunification deadline set by the *Ms. L* court, we saw that process unfold up close.

We first heard reports that there was a lot of movement near the main Catholic church in San Juan, a small town west of Alamo, where the TCRP office is located. Laura walked into my office one afternoon that month, perplexed.

"Apparently some of the families are being reunited and taken to the Basilica, not to the bus station in McAllen.... Does that make any sense to you?" she asked.

It did not. Laura had learned this from one of the pro bono attorneys, who had received a call from his newly assigned client. Confused, all the mother had been able to tell the lawyer was that she and her son were now near a church, *una basilica*. She was not sure exactly where. The lawyer had then called Laura, trying to make sense of this news.

"La Basilica," as it is known in the Rio Grande Valley, is located in the heart of San Juan. Built in 1954, the Basilica of Our Lady of San Juan del Valle is the largest Catholic church in South Texas, dedicated to the Virgin of San Juan. The Virgin of San Juan originated in San Juan de los Lagos, Mexico, after miraculously saving the life of a dying child in the 1620s, one of multiple miracles reported during the early years of the Spanish colonization of Mexico as part of the efforts to spread Catholicism throughout the mestizo and indigenous populations. Today, the Basilica is designated as a national shrine and draws more than a million visitors every year, over 20,000 per weekend on average. Devout Catholics from all over the country and beyond visit the Basilica every week to fulfill a promise or to pray for a miracle. The very first time my parents took Héctor and me to Sunday Mass at the Basilica, I was struck by what I saw: instead of a traditional choir, a Mariachi band sings the hymns, a constant reminder of the close ties between the shrine, its community, and Mexican culture.

"That is odd," I told Laura. "But let's try to find out what's going on."

What I did not know at the time was that next to the Basilica, the diocese operates a hotel with nearly one hundred rooms used typically by pilgrims and other visitors who wish to spend the night near the church. As it turned out, dozens of parents who were detained in South Texas were reunited with their children per the court order and then bused to the Basilica hotel. There, they would get a clean change of clothes, a warm meal, and spend a night or two until their relatives could buy a bus ticket for them so that they could travel from McAllen to their destination elsewhere in the country.

Staff at the hotel initially did not want anybody to have access to the families housed there. They told Laura they had orders to not allow any members of the media, which made some sense—unscrupulous reporters would seek to interview even children for the sake of a viral story—but we were the attorneys representing many of these families. Even so, it would take multiple phone calls and emails for us to be allowed to visit our clients at the Basilica hotel.

Once Laura and I got the okay later that week, we visited the hotel and brought a stack of Change of Address forms with us. When an immigrant is released from detention, the release documents include their destination address, where ICE will mail them important documents. For every family sent to the Basilica, their destination address was listed as: 400 N. Nebraska Ave., San Juan, Texas, 78589, the address of the Basilica hotel.

This meant that this was the only address in ICE's database for the hundreds of families who passed through that hotel. All correspondence, including important notices such as court appointments, would be mailed here. This could be many months later, when the families would be long gone from the Basilica and would never receive such notices. If they missed their court dates, they risked being deported. Once the diocese staff realized this, they became much more open to us coming to the hotel to assist families in filling out the forms so that they could notify ICE and the immigration court of their correct destination address.

When Laura, Alexis, and I arrived at the hotel that Friday in late July, I wasn't sure what to expect. We entered into a large lobby, which was abuzz with people coming and going. The woman at the reception desk called us over right away, surely noticing that we were not immigrant families and asking how she could help us. To the right side, wooden stairs headed up to the second floor, and women and children with backpacks or small duffel bags were constantly climbing up or down. Multiple conversations were happening at once in that lobby. There were a few young people—they may have been high school students—who appeared to be volunteers, pointing the mothers and fathers to their rooms, or to a van in the parking lot to be taken to the bus station.

"Right, right, you're here to help with the address on the paperwork?" the woman at the reception said after we explained who we were. She knew we were coming.

"Yes," I said. "Is there somewhere we could meet with the families?"

We were taken to a small conference room on the second floor. There were vending machines at one end of the room—full of cookies and candy bars that nobody had money to purchase—and one of the volunteers set up a table at the other end. We unpacked our Change of Address forms and the list of families that we knew had been held at PIDC, and settled into our table. Foldable chairs had been arranged for parents to sit along one of the longer walls in this rectangular room. A plain analog clock hung from the wall above the chairs, and a crucifix faced the clock from the opposite wall.

In the midst of all the flux going on at the hotel, there was really no way to ensure that every family came to see us. Some were just arriving, tired, trying to find a shower and change into clean clothes. Some were eating in the cafeteria. Others were already rushing out, trying to hop on a bus that they hoped would finally take them to their relatives in North Carolina or Iowa or Massachusetts. A few children played in the hallway with their mothers, smiling and giggling, a brief reminder that they were, after all and despite all, just children. The air in the hotel was reminiscent of the air I had breathed in the courtroom time and again: a stench of clothes that had been worn too long.

Laura and I decided to make an announcement in the lobby and around the hallways, encouraging families to come to our makeshift office. We were attorneys, had important paperwork and information for them regarding their immigration cases, and could answer any questions they had.

Mothers and fathers started trickling into the room, their children with them. One of the first to enter the room seemed familiar to me, and I thought I had seen her before, but couldn't be sure. She was probably in her early thirties, with short hair and dimples that became noticeable when she smiled to greet us.

"Hola, buenas tardes," I said. Good afternoon.

"Buenas," she replied, with the faintest of smiles. She was carrying the yellow envelope ICE agents had given her when she was released, which included her and her son's paperwork. She pulled out her forms without letting go of her son's hand, and sure enough, her "alien's address" was listed as 400 N. Nebraska.

"Do you remember if you went to criminal court in McAllen?" I asked her in Spanish.

She thought so.

"Well if you did, we are with the same group of attorneys that you spoke to about your son in court, before the judge came in."

"Sí, yo me acuerdo de usted." She nodded as she said she remembered me.

"Ah," I said, somewhat taken aback. I had interviewed her, but did not remember details about the interview or her background. By now the interviews blurred into one another in my mind, and I felt bad that she had become someone whose story had already escaped into the recesses of my mind. I could not recall her name. Her son looked six or seven years old.

"¿Y cómo está? ¿Cómo está su niño?" How are you, how is your little boy, I asked.

Her smile went away, and she looked down at her son playing on the floor.

"Pues... él no está muy bien," she said. Not very well. "He does not want to be apart from me even one minute," she shook her head, and seemed to get lost in her thoughts. "Even when I take a shower, he wants to be inside the bathroom, or I have to leave the bathroom door open. He wants to be able to at least hear me, know that I am there, that I am not leaving...."

I did not have words to respond. While separation anxiety is typical, older children who exhibit this symptom for long periods of time may develop it into full-blown separation anxiety disorder (SAD). It is common for the anxiety to express itself as unrealistic worry that something will happen to the child if the parent or caregiver leaves, even for a short period of time, an unexplained fear of being alone, and even physical symptoms such as headaches, stomachaches, and repeated crying. Experts consider that the most likely causes of separation anxiety disorder include a significant stressful or traumatic event in the child's early life, such as a stay in the hospital, an unstable caregiver situation, or the death of a loved one. There was no doubt in my mind that the weeks-long separations that all of the children in the hotel experienced were such stressful and traumatic events, and I wondered how many of them would go on to develop separation anxiety or other emotional or mental health disorders. Tragically, many of them would likely suffer life-long consequences from the trauma.

"He's going to need some help," she continued. "Probably see a counselor or something."

"Yes, that would probably be good," I said, stating the obvious but unsure of what else to say.

"I'm not doing too well either," she added. "I'm going to need to see someone too."

I pursed my lips and nodded in agreement. Her smile revealed her dimples yet again.

Laura and Alexis explained how important it was for her to change her address to the one where she was really headed, so that she would receive any mail from ICE or the immigration court. She said she understood, and would be sure to put the Change of Address form in the mail. Alexis put a checkmark next to her name on our list of parents we had interviewed in court, and gave her the names and contact information of the pro bono lawyers who were willing to take her case. Those lawyers, in turn, would take care of filing the paperwork to transfer her case from immigration court in South Texas to the court closest to her destination.

She thanked us and walked out of the room, still holding her son's hand with one hand and carrying their yellow envelope in the other. We never saw them again.

CHAPTER 14

I Don't Want Your Parents to Call Me

(2001–2002)

When I arrived at the Penn campus, summer was winding down. Locust Walk, the pedestrian walkway that bisects the university, was lined by elms, honeylocusts, and Japanese zelkovas, all trees I wasn't familiar with, and which were weeks away from turning their leaves. When I learned English, I became intent on discovering the names of trees with which I was familiar in Spanish—encinos (live oaks), nogales (pecan trees), álamos (ashes), huizaches (a thorny acacia shrub), ébanos (ebonies). I always had to look them up, except for mezquite, of course, which conveniently carried over almost directly. Even as an urban campus in West Philadelphia, Penn was full of gorgeous cherries, dogwoods, and cedars whose names I had to look up in reverse, from English into Spanish.

I have long been fascinated by mature trees, especially those that are decades or centuries old. The realization that trees can live much longer than humans and in their silent, static existence can witness so much more than we do in our fast-paced lifetimes has always intrigued me. In Mission, Texas, just west of McAllen, a nine-hundred-year-old Montezuma bald cypress stands firm next to the Rio Grande. Monty, as Missionites have affectionately nicknamed this local celebrity, has been there since before this country was founded, before any border existed, before Columbus crossed the Atlantic, even before the Black Plague. And after all that, it is now threatened by a border wall. I marvel at the intergenerational perspective that a tree like Monty would have if it had consciousness.

The very first college class I attended was a political science lecture on a Thursday afternoon. There must have been three hundred of us in that auditorium, putting in stark perspective my high school graduating class of one hundred and two. The students sitting at the front constantly raised their hands and asked questions, while I sat in silence near the center of the room.

Toward the end of the hour, the professor dimmed the lights and brought out a projector. He said he wanted to share with us a quote that he had reflected on often during his years in academia, an ancient Chinese proverb. When he turned on the machine, large black letters appeared on the white board: "May you live in interesting times." Ours weren't very interesting times, he bemoaned, but he was glad we were interested in studying the science of politics and looked forward to a wonderful semester with us.

The following week, as I headed to class one morning, I came upon a commotion in the lobby of my dorm building. The day before, everyone had filed out of the low-rise in a streaming flow of eagerness, freshmen and returning students heading to class for the first Monday of the semester. But today, no one seemed concerned about getting to class on time. At first I didn't know what was happening. Students and staff I hadn't yet met stood near the TV, and the few whose faces weren't glued to it were hugging one another, weeping, some were sobbing audibly. No one was sitting, backpacks and purses taking their places on the two old couches and some on the floor, as everyone had stopped on their way out, their plans for the day suddenly upended. The entire place radiated confusion, uncertainty, crisis. An older student was pouring cups of water for anyone who wanted one, and most did. Then finally, through the crowd of bodies crammed in the lobby, I caught a glimpse of the TV screen: the Twin Towers were up in smoke in New York City.

Classes were cancelled that day, and for a few days after that, but the next time we convened for the poli sci lecture, the professor apologized profusely for having invoked that Chinese proverb. Interesting times, he said, were not always better times. The auditorium, which was half empty still, fell into a long, uncomfortable silence.

Later that semester, when autumn was feeling more and more like winter, I ran into a trio of friends across from High Rise East, one of the university's largest student dormitories, at the corner of Locust and 39th Streets. Two of them, Agustina and Guillermo, were international students from Mexico and had become part of my new circle of friends. Agus and I, in particular, were becoming close, as we were both in our first semester. I recognized the two of them from a distance, but I had never met the third person walking with them.

I greeted Agus and Memo—the typical shortened version of "Guillermo" in Mexico—and their friend held out his hand to introduce himself. The three high rises located at this intersection create a wind tunnel that often leads to a full-blown gale, and I felt the crisp cold air hit my hand as I held it out too.

"Hi, nice to meet you," I said. "I'm Effrin."

Agus and Memo burst out laughing as if on cue. It wasn't a mocking, bullying kind of laughter, but more out of curiosity at how I had butchered my own name. Their friend was confused.

"Güey, qué pedo, te llamas Efrén," Agus said between chuckles, still recovering from the laugh.

"Yeah, his name is Efrén," Memo translated for their friend, adding that it was funny to hear me say my own name anglicized in this way. Memo continued the explanation in his characteristically academic, dissertation-style manner, sprinkling a mundane conversation with all sorts of arcane, interesting, and wholly unnecessary factoids. Years later, Memo would obtain his PhD in Chinese History with a focus on maritime trade during the eighteenth century, which in a strange way befit him perfectly. Before coming to Penn, he and Agus had attended the American School in Guadalajara, a private school whose curriculum was largely in English, a language they both spoke fluently with less of an accent than me. They came from families of greater means than mine and were here on student visas, and we connected at Mex@Penn, the student organization made up largely of international students from Mexico. I wasn't an international student, as it turned out, but I gravitated toward them, I suppose, for cultural affinity reasons. Mex@Penn members, undergraduate and graduate students alike, knew the lyrics to all the classics by Juan Gabriel, Maná, and José Alfredo Jiménez, were used to machaca con huevo for breakfast on the weekend (at least those from northern Mexico), and watched Mexican soccer league games religiously every weekend. I felt at home.

I blurted something out about how I had said Effrin to accommodate this English-speaking friend, since I assumed he wouldn't be able to pronounce my name, so why even bother, but of course, of course my name was Efrén.

After we parted ways, alone with my thoughts, I kept beating myself up. Why had I done that? How many times had I done it before without realizing, without anyone around to call me out? Unable to pinpoint where Effrin had come from and mystified about when or why I had internalized it, I didn't think back to that first day in math class at Valley View. I did not make the connection to my graduation speech either, and to whether this may have been yet another attempt to show that I belonged. What I did identify that day was the question of my immigrant identity. Was I the same boy who had grown up in Allende, now living in Philadelphia, and my name had merely been lost in translation? Or had I become a different person altogether? Part of me was convinced that I was Efrén; no question about it, I badly wanted to be. But that afternoon would not be the last time that I asked myself these questions, or that I introduced myself as Effrin.

Toward the end of my first year, I walked up the concrete steps into Logan Hall. This was the first time I had reason to enter this imposing olive-colored building, its stone-covered facade, heavy wooden doors, and rust-colored columns and windows making an intimidating impression on me. Although its architecture made it seem much more ancient to my untrained eye, Logan Hall was built in the early 1870s and originally served as the medical school. In the early 1900s, it was repurposed to house the headquarters of the College of Arts and Sciences and administrative offices, which were still there when I walked in. (Three years after I graduated, the building was renamed, not without controversy, Claudia Cohen Hall, after the *New York Post* Page Six gossip column editor whose ex-husband had donated twenty million dollars to the university and chose to honor his ex-wife's memory by naming the building after her.)

I was here to see my academic advisor. As an underclassman, I was only permitted to register for four courses, and after having done well in my classes so far, I wanted to take five the following fall. The online system would not allow me to matriculate for that fifth class—an elective in Spanish literature—unless my advisor lifted the limit, and I was here to make the request.

The information desk inside Logan Hall was of a polished, refined wood, bolstering my suspicion that this entire building must be from an epoch long gone. An expansive staircase and the eerie silence inside made the place seem even larger than it was, palatial I would say, and made me feel so small that I questioned whether I really needed to take that literature class.

With curly salt and pepper hair, round glasses that contrasted with his scrawny, angular face, and wearing suit and tie, my advisor welcomed me in. His office was, like the entrance to Logan Hall, outfitted with shiny wooden furniture—a heavy wooden desk and heavy wooden chairs with comfortable cushions, far from those in Ms. Hernández's office. I sat down and set my backpack on the other chair.

I shared the reason for my visit, and he listened attentively, letting me make my case.

"I see you've done well in your classes so far. What's your rush?" he asked, seeming genuinely curious.

There were so many interesting classes, I explained. I had gotten used to the rhythm of the coursework and didn't think one more class would cause me any trouble. Plus, the class I was hoping to take was in Spanish, and since I was a native Spanish speaker, I didn't see that particular class as too much of an additional burden.

The professor shifted in his seat. Gesticulating uncomfortably, he told me he had seen many students make this mistake before. Before they fully adjusted to the rigorous demands of academic life in college, students wanted to swallow more than they could chew, and their grades suffered. He didn't want that to happen to me too. He advised that I take it slow.

"But that won't happen to me," I insisted. "Especially not with this class." I already knew the language, so I had a leg up over my classmates. I didn't think this was much of a risk, and I was willing to take it, to the extent it was a risk at all.

He smiled condescendingly, like saying I'm telling you, I know better. "The thing is," he added, trying to remain polite. "I've seen this happen many times. And when students' grades start to drop, I get phone calls from angry parents....I don't want your parents to call me."

I sat in silence for a few seconds, looking at him, with nothing to say. I hadn't noticed the artificial scent in the air until that moment. It must have come from one of those plug-in fresheners. He looked back at me, his smile reflecting the satisfaction of accomplishment, as if he thought that what he said had finally cracked a code, had made me understand and desist from my sophomoric request.

I told him I understood, stood up to leave, and thanked him as I threw my backpack over my left shoulder. We shook hands and I walked out of his office. As I exited the building, I tried to imagine who these parents were who called their children's academic advisors.

I felt completely alienated by the professor's comment, distressed by what I perceived to be his disconnect. Or was it my disconnect? I felt like we came from different worlds, so distant and removed that I did not even know how to begin to relate to him. There I'd been speechless in his office, unable to articulate a response. As I walked up Locust Walk, still ruminating over his remark, what bothered me most was not that the professor did not understand the world I came from, but that he assumed that I came from a world like that of the other students he advised, perhaps a world like his. Sure, he knew nothing about me or my life, but that was precisely the problem; he knew nothing about me or my life. How could he advise me about my academic performance or aspirations? When he made that comment, he seemed to truly believe that it might be a possibility, that one day my mother would ring him to ask why he had allowed me to take a course on Cervantes's *Don Quixote*.

To me it was inconceivable. My parents had no idea how many classes I was taking; they did not know that I had struggled mightily in Calculus I during my first semester or that I was undecided between majoring in political science or philosophy. It was a world simply and entirely foreign to them. For the first time since I had arrived at Penn, I felt like I was markedly different from my classmates. Did their parents *really* call?

When I came home for the summer, my mother picked me up at the airport in her light blue Pontiac LeMans. "Blue's Clues," a friend had dubbed it, because its sides had a few dark blue spots of Bondo plaster reminiscent of the cartoon dog. I was still wearing a sweater from the chilly May morning in Philadelphia when I boarded the plane, but it was a hot May afternoon when I exited the airport in McAllen. I removed the extra layer as I got in the car, and ten minutes later we were home.

It wasn't entirely surprising that my father hadn't been the one to pick me up, since I knew he had had surgery a few weeks earlier. His mitral valve needed an upgrade, the surgeon had said. The operation he had had in Monterrey more than thirty years earlier had run its course, and even though my father had been dreading the procedure— he couldn't get it out of his head that he had come to before the surgery was completed back then, and he was afraid the same thing might happen again—the cardiologist had explained that medical technology had come a long way since then. The procedure, although serious, would be much different in 2002, he assured my father. Plus, it was absolutely necessary. My father begrudgingly assented.

When he opened the door to greet me that afternoon, I was taken aback. I had last seen my father over winter break, and I should have expected that he would have lost weight after the surgery, but I couldn't have imagined that it would be so much. If I didn't think of his semblance as emaciated, it was only because I wasn't familiar with the word at the time. A clear oxygen mask covered his face, which he had not shaved in a day or two, and his normally deep complexion had given way to an ashen stubble. I couldn't tell if this loss of color was due to the unshaven face, the loss of weight, or if his skin had simply turned shale since I had last paid attention. A pair of plastic tubes ran down his side and connected to a green oxygen tank that came up to his thigh. He made his best attempt at a smile and a hug, but he struggled dragging that thing, and his mask shifted out of place as we embraced. Even his hug felt weaker, like he was trying to hold me tight, but he simply didn't have the strength. I could feel the sharp bones on his back when I wrapped my arms around him.

I wanted to turn to my mother and ask how come they hadn't told me. But I suppose it is like this with illnesses—for those who are there on a daily basis, things don't look so different so quickly from one day to the next. Maybe things even look better on a certain day, as part of the ups and downs of an illness's slow progression. And every little thing, like that mask, is an attempt at recovery, an improvement over the previous day when there was no assistive oxygen. But for those who are not there to see the day-to-day, the change from healthy to ill feels sudden, unexpected, like a midnight storm in the summer.

He asked how the semester had gone, adjusting the green elastic band that held his mask in place.

"Bien," I said, flatly, not very interested in the question. What I wanted to know was how he was doing. "¿Tú cómo vas, Pa?"

"Bien," he said, not very interested either.

I didn't share my experience at Logan Hall, but I'm sure the last thing on his mind was how many classes I planned to take.

I didn't share the full cost of my first year of college either. Tuition and fees, plus room and board, had topped $44,000, and that didn't include other living expenses. Not that I was hiding it, but it was not something we talked about. The first time I saw my father's IRS forms—el incám, as we called it back then—the year after we moved to McAllen, his annual income had barely surpassed $24,000, and that was a killing coming from Allende. And here I was, at nineteen years old, spending twice as much on my college adventure.

I wasn't taking from my father's income to fund my college expenses, but it still felt somehow wrong that what I was doing cost twice what my father earned in an entire year. I was the prototypical scholarship boy, a role model for other students at Valley View, but it was not lost on me that many students there still went home to unpaved streets, the forgotten colonias of the border.

Many other students from my high school have since gone away for college too, with financial aid packages better than mine, and some streets have been paved now. I haven't heard of the Po'Boys being active in a long time. But with a median individual annual income of under $20,000, South Texas counties still rank among the poorest in the country, and more than one in four residents still live in poverty. Despite the atypical feel-good story, perhaps including my own, border communities continue to exist at the margins.

One afternoon the following year, I strode into the campus's Greenfield Intercultural Center (GIC) and headed straight to the third floor. Founded in 1984, the GIC was a not-so-well-known three-story gem located on Chestnut street, where mostly students of color gathered for cultural talks, free meals, or simply to hang out and vent about their experience at the university. As it turned out, the gem was very well-known among the "minority" affinity student groups, though I had never heard about it at Mex@Penn meetings. How I came to land a work-study job at the GIC I will never know. One day during my first semester, I received a call at my dorm from the late Tiffany Anderson, the center's program director, who said she had received my application and would like to interview me. I didn't remember applying to the GIC and did not know what the job entailed, but since I was desperately trying to find a job, I said sure, I'd come by and interview. And that was that. I worked there all four years I was at Penn.

I was surprised to find someone else already on the GIC's third floor. It was understood that if someone was on the third floor, it was because they needed quiet time to focus, maybe study for an upcoming test. The first floor of the GIC had a large living room where most events took place, a kitchen, and a small meeting room. It was generally busy with people coming or going. The second floor housed most of the Center's offices, and was quieter than the first, but it was still hard to find a quiet place to focus on homework. The third floor was my favorite. There was a small study room toward the north end of the house with a desk and two small windows: one of them facing Chestnut street, the other a church with colorful stained-glass panes and, beyond it, the downtown Philadelphia skyline. Squirrels often peeked their heads up to these windows, dashing and jumping around the tallest red maple branches. The rest of the third floor was mostly used for storage, half-empty cardboard boxes laying around the hallway, so no one was usually up here. Except today.

I did not know the girl who was sitting at the office and was bummed when I realized that I wasn't going to have the quiet I had hoped for. I figured she must be an insider, like me, because the third floor was only open to GIC staff. She seemed disappointed to see me too.

"Hi," she said. "I'm Julia," I heard her say. It would take me weeks and many attempts to get her name right, and I still mess it up sometimes.

We struck up a conversation, and neither of us got to the reading we were planning to do. Julija (pronounced Yuliya) was a sophomore too, from Los Angeles. Later that afternoon she shared that actually she was from Mostar, a small but well-known town in Bosnia and Herzegovina, and yet a little later that she was also sort of from Sardinia, an island off Italy's Mediterranean coast. I had never heard of Mostar, but soon learned about its medieval origins and its world-famous Old Bridge. A marvel of engineering and architecture for its time, the "Stari Most" was originally built in the sixteenth century during the Ottoman Empire, destroyed during the Croat-Bosniak War, and rebuilt in the first decade of the twenty-first century.

In the early 1990s, when Héctor and I were in Allende hoping our father would visit for the weekend, armed conflict had broken out in what was then still Yugoslavia, and Mostar was besieged. Months after we met, Julija shared with me that when the bombing wouldn't stop one night, she curled up in a ball in a corner away from the windows, her hands covering her ears, and prayed in silence: "God, if you exist, please make the bombing stop." She repeated that over and over, but the bombing didn't stop. She must have been seven years old.

When the fighting broke out, Julija's parents sent her and her sister to live with temporary foster families in Sardinia. Their parents came to Italy months later, and the family eventually reunited and made their way to California in the mid-1990s, around the same time that Héctor and I boarded a car and moved to McAllen.

Julija was the first person I met who was my contemporary, to whom I could relate, and who had lived through a war. Under international human rights law, a refugee is a person who has left her country of origin and is unable to return because of persecution due to her race, religion, national origin, political opinion, or membership in a particular social group. The 1951 Refugee Convention and its 1967 Protocol, to which the United States has acceded, provides that governments shall not impose penalties on refugees on account of their unauthorized entry or presence in the country, as long as they promptly present themselves to the authorities. Domestic U.S. law has adopted largely the same definition of refugee since the passage of the Refugee Act of 1980. I did not know any of this or the details of Julija's immigration application, but she and her family met the criteria.

Generally speaking, an asylee or asylum seeker is a person who meets the same definition of refugee, but who is already present in the United States or is attempting to enter. Notably, the immigration statute provides that a person who is physically present in the United States may apply for asylum irrespective of her status and regardless of whether the person entered at a designated port of entry. Even if a person enters "illegally," she may still apply for asylum if she meets the eligibility criteria and submits her application within one year of entering the country.

My first reaction when I learned Julija's story was to minimize my own. She had survived a war, lived with a family of strangers who welcomed her in as a child, learned two languages along the way, traveled across an ocean, and literally taken years to make her way to the United States. I—by contrast and despite the difficulties in the years leading up to it—had ridden in a car for three hours one day and descended in McAllen. I felt silly even thinking of our experiences coming to the United States as similar in any way. Her family had been displaced by war; I thought of mine as just your average immigrants. By "average," I suppose I envisioned something like my particular story.

But over time, I came to see more commonalities than differences between us. Leaving life as you know it at an early age, moving to a country whose culture and language you are not familiar with, and being away from family in the process can create a particular consciousness about being part of a "nation." The bond with fellow countrymen and women is there, but it is not above the common humanity shared with those from other countries. The national identity, the sense of nationhood, is not derived merely from *jus soli*, because you have left the place where you were born. It is not derived from a flag or an anthem or a shared history either. Some might say the sense of nationhood comes from a shared aspiration to certain ideals, ideals of justice, equality, liberation, ideals that transcend any one history or religion. That is, indeed, what many would argue makes "American" nationhood different, a nation based on principles, not on race or creed. Under this version, those principles apply equally to every person, regardless of their race, of where they were born, of whether they are a refugee or an economic immigrant. Adherence to those precepts is what makes the United States the United States. If those principles cease to apply, the nation ceases to exist. Or so the argument goes.

Years after I unexpectedly met Julija at the GIC, I was strolling through the Mayan ruins in Tulúm, Mexico. The ruins themselves are not the most magnificent or historically significant, but their location on a bluff off the beach makes for a spectacular sight. The archaeological site ends at a cliff that drops into white Caribbean sand and crystalline shallow water, a breathtaking blend of nature, history, and heritage. As I traipsed along one of the trails past cordoned-off grassy areas to protect the crumbling structures, I came upon one more explanatory plaque. Imagine it's October 1492, the message began, and you're standing on this same spot. Far off into the distance, you spot three strange vessels slowly approaching. They have large sails and bearded, blond men aboard like you've never seen before. You imagine they are gods. I looked up at the ocean and felt chills up my back, calm turquoise water extending into the horizon as I tried to picture the scene.

Now imagine you're a Spanish explorer on one of those ships, the writing on the plaque continued. You've been traveling for weeks, uncertain about whether you would survive this journey. As you see land ahead of you for the first time in over a month, your excitement turns to worry when you notice people on the beach, barely clothed, running around and flailing their arms, and you wonder if they might be dangerous.

I shuddered at the thought. Maybe because it was the Spaniards who posed the greatest danger. It was the Spaniards and other colonizers who murdered, tortured, and raped a continent, and the peoples who survived have still not recovered from the pillaging. That plaque also highlighted for me that human beings have moved across the earth, trekking over land and sailing across oceans, for millennia. Some do so in search of a better future, looking for gold or as romanticized pioneers, others fleeing wars and famine in a desperate effort to survive, but the impetus to migrate has always been part of us. It's a defining characteristic of our species, and neither border walls nor zero tolerance policies have ever, will ever, contain that most basic human impulse. The difference, though, is that while our history books romanticize the Spanish conquistadors and the pilgrims on the *Mayflower*, our laws demonize those making the trek today. We put past migrants on a pedestal of bravery, perseverance, and the epitome of the human spirit, and put present-day immigrants in cages.

The year after we met, Julija spent a summer in central Mexico and became fluent in Spanish. Drawing from her own experiences surviving a war, she now works to bring restorative justice approaches to public schools in Southern California. She and Agus, who is now a marketing executive in San Francisco, also became close, and when Karla and I got married in 2016, they were both at our wedding.

CHAPTER 15

At the Margins

(July–August, 2018)

Not all families were sent to the Basilica hotel. Soon after the court ordered the reunification of separated families, we learned that Border Patrol was taking some reunited families—those who hadn't been deported, anyway—directly to the McAllen bus station. There they would spend hours, sometimes even stay overnight, waiting for family members to purchase a ticket so that they could board the bus that would, at long last, take them to their destination.

A group of self-motivated and big-hearted volunteers who called themselves the Angry Tías and Abuelas—aunts and grandmas—had been organizing to provide assistance to the families who showed up at the bus station. They would give them a backpack with a sandwich, a cellophane-wrapped apple or two, and a bottle of water, and explain to them how to change buses at the Houston or San Antonio Greyhound stations. With thick, black markers, the Angry Tías would write on the yellow envelopes in big letters, "I DO NOT SPEAK ENGLISH, CAN YOU PLEASE HELP ME FIND MY BUS?" I worried that this might tip people off that these families were vulnerable and could be taken advantage of, but it seemed like the most helpful thing to do at the time.

As soon as we found out, Alexis and Georgina rushed to the bus station, and they quickly realized that some of the mothers and fathers we had interviewed in court were among the families sent there. Unlike those sent to the Basilica hotel, these families were not getting a warm meal, a shower, or a clean change of clothes.

"Some of them don't have anything on them," Georgina said, concerned, when she returned to the office. "I don't even know how they will get any food until they get home."

By this point, the Texas Civil Rights Project had begun receiving donations from around the country to support our work on behalf of separated families. I did not know it at the time, but over the course of that summer we received donations equal to more than twice our annual budget, a flow of donations unprecedented in TCRP's thirty-year history.

Zenén Jaimes Pérez, our director of communications, was in the office when Georgina walked in and explained what she had seen at the bus station.

"We should just give them some cash," he suggested, pouring himself a cup of coffee as we stood in the office kitchen. The day's dirty cups were starting to pile up in the sink.

I hesitated. "I'm not sure we can," I said.

I was thinking of the ethics rule that prohibits Texas lawyers from providing financial assistance to clients. A lawyer shall not provide financial assistance to a client with pending or contemplated litigation or administrative proceedings, reads Rule 1.08 of the Texas Disciplinary Rules of Professional Conduct.

I don't know why I felt constrained by this rule. Laws, rules, and policies are the product of fiction. These precepts are ostensibly designed to regulate behavior and prevent abuse, but they are nothing more than the product of the imagination of men and women—mostly men, mostly white men—who came before us. They certainly have real consequences in the lives of many people, but they are, inherently, fiction. Ethics rules are no different. In this respect, Rule 1.08 was no different from Zero Tolerance. What was my worry, that someone would file a grievance with the State Bar of Texas that I breached my ethical obligations? Or was this simply a lawyerly inclination to "follow the rules"? I don't know what it was, but I felt we could not simply withdraw cash and give it to these families. At the same time, I knew they desperately needed it. Many had absolutely nothing on them, other than the clothes they were wearing, and the yellow envelope ICE had handed to them upon release. Those who were lucky enough to run into some Angry Tías volunteers may have gotten a snack. Some of their bus rides would last for days until they made it to their destination.

"Well, good thing I'm not a lawyer!" Zenén declared.

"I can't tell you to do it," I said. Doing so might still have violated the rule, as I would have been using Zenén as my "agent." I threw my hands up as if saying, don't look at me, and walked to my office as he and Georgina continued discussing in the kitchen.

I sat in my office chair, and before I logged on to check my email, I thought: *what am I doing?* The families' bus rides could be days-long. They needed money to feed themselves along the way, make a phone call, get some water for their son or daughter. Some parents were traveling with two or three children. My desire to spare the families any more suffering or discomfort after everything they had gone through overcame my concerns over the ethics rule. I stood from my chair and walked back to the kitchen where Roberto had joined Zenén and Georgina.

"They need the cash," I said. "We need to get it to them if we can."

Zenén let out his unmistakable, characteristic laugh. He had laughed that same way months earlier when he recalled that, as a college student at Georgetown, he and other progressive students had organized a demonstration at the Washington, DC, home of Jeh Johnson, then-Secretary of Homeland Security, to protest DHS's use of killer drones in the Middle East.

"Ok," he said. "I will go to the ATM and get some cash."

A few weeks later, Zenén submitted a reimbursement request for $750.00 to TCRP. Georgina had managed to hand out $50 to each of the fifteen families she encountered at the bus station.

Late one of those July afternoons, I was ready to leave the office for the day, when the phone rang. I pulled it to my ear and placed my briefcase on the floor as I sat back down. It was Maggy Krell. For weeks, stacks of papers had been piling up on my desk, daily reminders of other cases that had gone unattended for far too long. Since May, Zero Tolerance cases had taken over our docket, every other case seeming much less urgent.

Maggy had good news about her clients, Patricia and her six-year-old son, Alessandro: Patricia had been released after the *Ms. L* order, and she and Alessandro had spoken by phone. He was still at a shelter in San Antonio, about four hours away, and Maggy had spoken with the ORR case manager to try to coordinate his release and reunification with Patricia. I wondered if he received any medical attention he needed at the shelter.

"But the caseworker's telling me that he has to go through the same process as unaccompanied minors," Maggy said, worry in her voice. "Do you know if that's right?"

Alessandro had never been "unaccompanied," of course—he had been traveling with his mother all along, when they crossed the border and when they were apprehended—but ORR took the position that all children in its custody needed to go through the same process in order to be released to a "sponsor." From ORR's preposterous position, it did not matter that the "sponsor" was the very parent from whom Border Patrol agents had separated him. We had insisted to ORR caseworkers again and again, pleading that it was not fair, and in fact was doubly punitive, to require separated parents to provide the same information as other sponsors. After one government agency took their children from them, another was requiring them to provide a host of information they hardly had in order to see their children again: proof of residence, proof of financial support, fingerprints, and a FBI criminal background check. The system that had abducted their children was now setting the conditions by which they would return them to the victimized parents. Some caseworkers even claimed parents had to pass a mandatory "home study" conducted by ORR social workers, which entailed an extensive review of whether the home where Alessandro would live was suitable and appropriate for him. This requirement seemed especially absurd to us: after the government had forcibly taken him from his mother, sent him to a shelter with strangers, and jailed her, now their reunification might depend on whether their housing arrangement met this agency's standards. But our pleas were to no avail. Even with a federal injunction in place, ORR officials repeated that Patricia and Alessandro had to follow this process. It was the protocol, they said again.

Meanwhile, Patricia was desperate to see her son. After Maggy finally secured her release from PIDC, they immediately drove to San Antonio to visit him at the shelter. Then Maggy and Patricia faced a dilemma, which was the reason Maggy had called: should they try to have Alessandro released to Patricia while she was still in San Antonio, where she did not have stable housing but was literally at the doorstep of the shelter? Or should Patricia travel to Maryland, where she and Alessandro were originally headed to stay with relatives, and try to have Alessandro released then, and then have him travel to Maryland with an ORR chaperone? The concern was that if Patricia tried from San Antonio, she may not pass the home study, as she was staying at a hotel with Maggy. Traveling to Maryland and continuing the process once she had more stable housing seemed like the more compliant option, even though it would take longer.

Either option felt unfair, and the limitations of laws and policies at yielding justice were evident yet again. Federal agents and prosecutors had enabled their separation in the name of Zero Tolerance, and now an injunction, public outrage, and a team of lawyers could not reunite them quickly enough. ORR protocols were getting in the way, invoking—to our disbelief—the "best interest of the child." Where was the best interest of the child when Alessandro was taken from Patricia's side in violation of human rights standards? Where was that principle when I interviewed her in court? Their separation was so unjust, and yet it had happened so easily, person after person making it possible every step along the way. Reunification was so just, and yet it was ensnared in bureaucracy, as if the purpose of the government apparatus wasn't justice at all, person after person putting up roadblocks at every turn. Maggy and I went over the pros and cons of each option on the phone, struggling to rationalize our advice to Patricia that prolonging the separation was likely the best thing for her and Alessandro.

But Patricia would have none of that. She insisted that she wasn't leaving Texas without her son, and at the end of the day, it was her case, her son, and her decision. Her strength and determination always amazed me: from the time we met in court and she told me about her last-resort decision to flee Honduras, to now, seeing her perseverance to be with her son at all costs, no matter how precarious the odds were. Her courage was at once both hard to fathom and an inspiration. None of this came out at her Zero Tolerance hearing, not when she was read her charges, not when she stood up and said culpable as she looked shyly at the judge, pleading guilty to a federal crime through an interpreter. None of this came out when she was at PIDC, incarcerated for weeks without any news of Alessandro. But her grit had endured within her all this time, always part of her, and Maggy and I were now seeing glimpses of it in her resolve to be reunited with her son no matter what.

A week later, after Patricia and Maggy had been in San Antonio calling ORR every day and showing up at the shelter to visit Alessandro, ORR finally agreed to release him. It really couldn't be any other way. After leaving Honduras with him, making it past Guatemala and then traveling more than one thousand miles by land across Mexico, never leaving his side, dealing with an obstinate ORR caseworker did not really faze Patricia.

When Maggy sent me a photo of Patricia and Alessandro, finally together, I thought of the day in early June when I first met Patricia at the Bentsen Tower. They had been separated for more than a month, and her face in the picture showed that same combination of youthful hope and mature serenity. I will never know what must have gone through her mind during the days and nights she spent apart from her son, alone with her thoughts and emotions in a cold cell. Despite the frustration she must have felt lying awake at night, staring at the ceiling and the metal bars of her cell, she somehow found her strength again to persist until Alessandro was with her again.

In the black and white picture Maggy sent, Patricia rests her right arm around Alessandro, holding him by his shoulder, close but not too tightly. He, on the other hand, presses his face excitedly against her body. He wants to be as close to her as he can and not

Photo credit: Maggy Krell.

let go. His smile reveals slight dimples, and a name tag is clipped to his shirt, the undeniable sign that he too had been in custody.

Many months later, in the week leading up to their asylum trial, Maggy—in an act that went well beyond the scope of her legal representation—offered to care for Alessandro if Patricia was deported and he was not. Their immigration cases had not been consolidated, so there was a real risk that one of their cases would be granted and the other would not. The relationship between Patricia and Maggy had grown so strong that Patricia was willing to entrust her son to Maggy, should it come to it. After the emotional buildup in the days before their hearing, preparing the legal claims and considering all possible outcomes, and carrying the heavy burden of the last year and half, the immigration judge finally granted asylum to both of them. Patricia and Alessandro's ordeal had come to an end in some ways, but what our government put them through will stay with them their entire lives.

Other reunifications were just as troublous. After Viviana's anonymous donor paid her $13,000 bond in Seattle, she left the prison she had shared with some ninety other mothers, by her own estimation. Meanwhile, her son Sandro was still at a shelter in South Texas, where he had been since May.

Viviana and Sandro had been headed to Houston, where a distant relative lived, and Zero Tolerance took her across the country, while Sandro remained at a shelter near the border. There was no rhyme or reason to ICE's decision to transport Viviana to Washington state, so far away from her son and her intended destination. But as a result of this decision, coordinating her reunification with Sandro became the most challenging piece.

Similar to Patricia, Viviana faced the dilemma of deciding whether she should travel to South Texas, where she would not have a place to stay, and try to have Sandro released to her from there; or head to Houston instead, where she would have a place to stay, and then hope ORR would release her son and send him to Houston with a chaperone. Viviana's pro bono attorneys, from the organization Kids in Need of Defense (KIND), were based in Houston, and that seemed to weigh in favor of her flying to Houston. Laura and I discussed this decision with Viviana and her attorneys, and traveling to Houston seemed to all of us to be the more prudent option.

Facing the pressure of the looming deadline to reunite parents in the *Ms. L* lawsuit, ORR agreed to release Sandro and fly him to Houston. Their own protocols seemed to matter less and less as the deadline neared. The nonprofit organization FWD.us agreed to pay for Viviana's flight from Seattle to Houston, and we were asked to coordinate the reunification. Priscilla Mendoza, one of our summer law student interns based in Houston, offered to pick up Viviana at the airport the night she arrived. Like Alexis, Priscilla was between her first and second year of law school that summer. Originally from El Paso, she was fluent in Spanish, and even though she was assigned to our Houston office, we had asked her to relocate to South Texas for a few weeks to assist with our work in June, during the height of the separations. She had since returned to Houston. Sandro was scheduled to arrive early the following morning, and Priscilla offered to drive Viviana to the airport again and meet him there.

Again, as with most other separated families, coordinating the logistics of the reunification fell on nonprofits and volunteers, while the government agencies and agents who perpetrated the separation—traumatizing mother and child and upending their lives, from Washington to McAllen—carried on with their reliable routines at their jobs. As I reflect on this, as cruel and arbitrary as the process was, I can't envision us at TCRP doing anything differently. The circumstances of our job, those interviews in court, and Zero Tolerance placed us in a unique position to advocate for these families, and if we could do anything to help expedite Viviana's reunification with Sandro, I am sure we would do it all over again.

That Saturday morning, my son Julián was up early, as usual. He would sometimes sleep in a little during the week, but on weekends he was invariably up long before seven. I yawned and rubbed my eyes as I scooped coffee grounds into the coffeemaker when a notification sound pinged my cell phone. I looked around the kitchen but didn't see the phone right away. Before searching for it, I threw in an extra scoop into the coffeemaker, and turned it on.

My phone pinged a message from Priscilla to the office Whats-App group.

"Viviana & Sandro reunited at last ♥," Priscilla's message read.

And she sent a picture: Viviana and Sandro hugging at the airport by a baggage claim sign. Sandro, two months shy of his twelfth birthday, was almost as tall as Viviana. Viviana's backpack got in the way of him reaching to hug her tightly. He wore dark jeans, a long-sleeve navy-blue pullover—surely to keep him warm during his early morning flight—and a long silver rosary with a crucifix around his neck, reminiscent of the crucifix at the Basilica hotel. Their faces were hidden, buried in each other's embrace, but I imagined tears of joy.

A few minutes later Priscilla sent another picture, a selfie of her smiling next to Viviana and Sandro, and I did not need to imagine

Photo credit: Texas Civil Rights Project.

their expressions anymore. Priscilla smiled effusively as she snapped the photo, her face full of joy at having accomplished and witnessed yet another reunification, ending the acute suffering for one more family. But Viviana's and Sandro's faces told another story. Neither of them smiled. They stared at the camera blankly. There were no smiles on their expressionless faces, no joy. There seemed to be no end to the suffering for them.

This was the first time I had seen Sandro's face. He did not look like his mother. His skin was a shade deeper than hers, his face less round. Did he look like his late father? His eyes reflected maturity beyond his years, his childish innocence extinguished. While other children his age around the country worried about entering 6th grade the following month, Sandro had spent nearly two months wondering if he'd ever see his mother again. After having lost his father earlier that year, murdered in a field in the Guatemalan highlands, he must have worried daily if he had lost his mother too. "To cope with unbearable feelings of helplessness, impotence and despair," wrote a trauma expert at the Washington School of Psychiatry that summer, "trauma victims often think that there is something they should have done to prevent this catastrophe. This belief often leads to guilt, panic and shame." Sandro's stoic face stared right back at me.

Viviana's blank eyes looked sleep-deprived—perhaps from the anticipation of seeing Sandro after eight long weeks, perhaps from the nights she spent in a prison. She looked as if she was trying to produce a smile for the picture, and failing. She looked straight at the camera, and I wondered if she had been annoyed at the request to pose for a picture after all she had gone through. In some ways, that morning at the airport was only the beginning of their attempt to stay in this country.

"This story," said Viviana months later at an interview, "this problem that has happened in our lives, will stay with us forever. It can never be erased."

Like Patricia and Viviana, Mario Pérez Domingo had waited for weeks to be with his daughter, Oralia, wondering all the while whether he would ever see her again. After the DNA test results came back positive, HSI simply closed its investigation, and ICE and ORR handled the reunification, providing us little to no information. The day after we received the news of DNA test results, our friendly ORR caseworker confirmed that Oralia was scheduled to fly from El Paso to South Texas to be reunited with her father.

With HSI's investigation now closed, Mario was no longer in the custody of the U.S. Marshals, and even though he had all of our contact information—including Laura's and my personal cell phone numbers—we had not heard from him. The following day, a Friday, Alexis offered to go to the Basilica hotel in the evening. If Mario and Oralia had been reunited, we figured they were likely to pass through there.

"FOUND HIM," Alexis's WhatsApp message read, at nearly 11 p.m. My son Julián had been asleep for a while, but Karla and I were still up. We tried to spend some quiet time on weekend evenings, after Julián was asleep and work tended to slow down. But tonight it didn't, and I opened the message excitedly.

Along with the message, Alexis sent a picture of herself, with Mario and Oralia in the background. Mario grinned eagerly, looking straight at the camera, and Oralia gave a bashful smile as she dug her hand into a small bag of Cheetos. She was in a flowery blouse and pink bow, and Mario in what appeared to be a clean change of clothes, blue jeans and a white T-shirt, which reminded me how distant he was from his indigenous village in Colotenango. I had never seen Mario smile this widely. The joy in Oralia's face was

Photo credit: Verónica Gabriela Cárdenas, Texas Civil Rights Project.

hard to put into words. Their happy faces hid the torment they had gone through in the past month, hundreds of miles apart from each other. I allowed myself to share in their happiness in that moment.

The next day, Georgina escorted Mario and Oralia to the bus station in downtown McAllen. She accompanied them until they boarded the bus that would, finally, after multiple tormenting weeks, take them to their destination.

When the HSI agent told Laura that the DNA test had yielded a match, he said that concluded their investigation. The case was closed. Mario was not convicted of any crime, after the government inexplicably dropped all charges against him for having crossed the border. And yet, he had spent a month apart from Oralia, not only unsure if he would ever see her again, but also facing threats of human trafficking charges and the prospect of spending years in prison. Despite the lack of evidence to justify the separation or support the accusation of human trafficking—and in fact, despite evidence to the contrary, including Oralia's birth certificate and the consular certification of authenticity—the government had incarcerated Mario and sent Oralia to a foster family for a month. Surely, I imagined, someone would be held accountable for this. Someone would lose their job over this.

Nobody did. Nobody ever apologized to Mario. Nobody was even reprimanded as far as we knew. Not the Border Patrol agent who coerced Mario into saying Oralia was not his daughter, not the agents who took Oralia away, much less the architects of Zero Tolerance within the Department of Justice and the scores of agents who carried out the family separations within the Border Patrol, ICE, and other agencies.

To this day, I struggle to come to terms with the lack of accountability for the abduction of children, the separation of Mario and Oralia, and thousands of other families. DHS Secretary Kirstjen Nielsen and Attorney General Jeff Sessions eventually lost their jobs, but that was hardly for their role in the separations. In fact, the apparent reason they were induced to resign was that they did not do *more* to stay loyal to President Trump and further his policies. Testifying under oath before Congress, Secretary Nielsen had even denied that there was a family separation policy at all within DHS. "We do not have a policy of separating families at the border. Period," she had tweeted in mid-June.

But a leaked memorandum showed that she had indeed explicitly approved the separation policy from among several options her subordinates presented to her. Despite the now widely reported evidence, no official has been held accountable for what was one of the cruelest systemic human rights violations in this country in recent memory. Along with the torture of hundreds of Muslim detainees in Guantanamo Bay, the family separation policy was one of the most abhorrent policies the United States Government has pursued in the twenty-first century. It is estimated that the total number of separated families surpassed five thousand—nearly a fifth of them separated in McAllen. Some were reunited that summer, but others were apart for months. The Biden Administration set up a family reunification task force, and that has led to additional reunifications, but dozens of parents who were deported without their children remain unaccounted for and may never be reunited. As these pages go to print, lawsuits seeking monetary compensation for the separated families are making their way through the courts, and only time will tell if those cases will hold any officials accountable. Some countries have set up truth and reconciliation commissions after civil wars or other human rights atrocities to attempt to achieve meaningful healing and accountability. To date, there have been no serious proposals for a similar process in the United States.

Why is that? Why hasn't there been a more forceful call for accountability? It is as if the notions of due process, justice, equality before the law, all fall apart at the border. At the margins of society, the precepts that we hold so dear in the rest of our country seem to fade away.

In his seminal book *Imagined Communities*, Benedict Anderson examined the rise and spread of nationalism worldwide, showing how nationalism binds together large groups of people in ways that religion, race, or even a shared history alone do not. In the United States, that "imagined community" is not bound together by a single religion, race, or nationality. Children in American schools are taught that what makes an American an American is adherence to laws and the ideals of justice, respect for the Constitution and its institutions, and a commitment to abide by principles such as freedom, the rule of law, and due process. That is what defines American nationhood and, we are told, what sets it apart from other nations cohering around religion or ethnicity.

But that imagined community falls apart at the margins, where laws do not apply the same way. The geographical border becomes a legal border, and those at the margins of the country end up at the margins of its laws as well. In 1976, in the case of *United States vs. Martinez-Fuerte*, the Supreme Court ruled that Border Patrol agents may stop and question drivers at permanent immigration checkpoints—immigrants and U.S. citizens alike—even if they do not have the "probable cause" required to justify an arrest in the rest of the country. Even the protection in one's home is diluted. Unlike in the interior of the country, within twenty-five miles of the border DHS agents may enter private land without a warrant or probable cause "for the purpose of patrolling the border to prevent the illegal entry of aliens into the United States." It's almost as if those first twenty-five miles from the border are not even part of the United States, as the statute contemplates preventing the "entry" into the country that far in. Entire cities lie within that swath—the Bentsen Tower, with its federal courthouse inside, is less than ten miles from the Rio Grande River.

At the edges of the country, the validity of these and so many other principles withers away, and with them the line dividing what is permissible from what is not. What was once unthinkable becomes the norm. Even empathy and compassion begin to erode. At the margins, it becomes easier to justify taking a two-year-old from her father. Even after hearing children weep in that viral audio, some people tried to justify the policy in the name of so-called American values. Well—some insist, claiming to be defending the rule of law—the parents broke the law; they should have thought of their children before they brought them here illegally. If these were white, U.S.-citizen children being taken from their parents in the interior of the country, those same individuals would be clamoring for due process and the best interest of the child.

But not at the border. Not when the parents and the children were brown.

CHAPTER 16

Órale mijito

(2006)

Four months before my father died, I thought he would live another thirty years. After all, my grandparents had lived to ninety-two and ninety-four, so I expected my father to live at least as long. I must have thought he had the longevity genes. When he attended my college graduation in May 2005, he had recovered from his second mitral valve surgery and had fully regained his color. The pacemaker, installed in a subsequent operation, had also lifted his stamina and spirits. I'd like to think that seeing one of his children graduate from college for the first time also helped.

That May before he died, he had tried to go see the doctor, but every attempt had been thwarted because he was needed at work. More than once he had called the bus yard in the morning to say he'd be out sick, and his boss would ask could he come in just today, and go to the doctor tomorrow? So he did. Until one day, his feet were so swollen that he struggled to fit his shoes on. He could no longer walk without pain. My mother later told me between sobs that his testicles were so swollen from the fluid retention that they seemed deformed, and he struggled even to get dressed as a result.

"Me daba tanta lástima con él," she said, unable to hold back tears in a deep melancholy that still gets her every time she remembers. When he could no longer drive to work because of the inflammation, he called his boss again and apologized profusely; he would not be able to drive the bus that morning, but hoped to be back in a day or two, as soon as the doctor gave him the right medication. Could he come in just today, his boss insisted. But this time he couldn't. He had been working at Valley View for more than thirteen years.

Ever since I was kept back a year in middle school, I have felt a perpetual need to catch up. This is why I felt I didn't have the luxury of doing anything other than go straight from college to law school. That month, when my father pleaded with his boss, I was finishing up my first year of law school.

I was not as impressed by the trees in New Haven as I had been in West Philly, or maybe I had become used to them. But the buildings on the Yale campus were even more majestic than Logan Hall had ever been. The Gothic structures with their ghoulish gargoyles, the dining halls with their ornate wooden interiors, the imposing library and gymnasium—which on the outside looked like anything but—and especially the law school, all seemed antediluvian. I became disenchanted when I learned that the law school building had only been constructed around 1930, and legend has it that acid was poured on the exterior walls to make them seem older than they really are, which also took away from their allure. But when I walked into the law library for the first time, I was mesmerized again by its arched windowpanes, a dozen chandeliers hanging from the dizzyingly high ceiling, and a thousand books lining the stacks of the massive main reading room, silent and solemn like the finest basilicas of the Renaissance.

That summer, my mother wondered aloud if my father would ever visit Allende again. He was undergoing dialysis twice a week now, and he was often weak afterward. I had returned from an internship at a nongovernmental organization (NGO) in Chiapas and was preparing to head back to school, unaware that my father would only be around a few more weeks. In particular, I was preparing for "on-campus interviewing," the annual affair in which law firms and other aspiring employers come to the Yale campus to interview coveted law students for summer internships. I still had the one black suit I had snatched at a JCPenney sale in Philadelphia, and I found a few ties in different colors at Burlington Coat Factory in McAllen, which I was able to mix up so that it wouldn't be too noticeable that I was wearing the same suit on consecutive days. When I saw the other students going from charcoal-gray on Monday to navy-blue on Tuesday to striped with a pocket square on Wednesday, I thought each time that I should have bought one of those instead of my boring plain black one.

In early September, before the interviews, the school offered mock interview prep. Local attorneys and other professionals volunteered to come to campus one evening and hear our answers, mainly so that we would have a practice run, maybe get any nerves out. I'm sure none of you need it, one of the volunteers said.

The practice sessions were held in the wing of the law school where clinical courses were taught, a series of smaller classrooms for seminar-style instruction. The smaller class sizes were more conducive to the approach of the clinics, which are practice-based courses in which students file lawsuits and represent typically indigent clients under a professor's supervision. When it was my turn, my mock interviewer sat straight up and greeted me with more seriousness and formality than I had expected for a practice session. He wore a dark brown suit, the purpose of which I could not determine. Was it for his regular day job, or had he put it on specifically for this occasion? It must have been six in the evening; even though daylight savings hadn't ended, it was already dark out, and the clinical class-rooms felt smaller than in the mornings, when natural light flooded through the windows.

"Tell me, why do you want to work with us," my interviewer asked, fully in character after hardly any pleasantries.

I hadn't given it much thought, really. "Well," I started, "my family lives in Texas, and I'd be very interested in being at one of your Texas offices, maybe Houston or San Antonio." I had signed up for interviews only with law firms that had offices in that state. Lacking any kind of savvy to appreciate the difference between a job interview and meaningful personal connections, and perhaps thinking that offering a personal touch would improve my chances, I added that my father had fallen ill recently, and I hoped to be near my family so that I could provide any support they needed and saw this job as an opportunity to return to Texas. I felt proud of my comprehensive answer.

"Let me tell you what I'm hearing," my interviewer said, coming off character. "I'm hearing you say that once your father dies, you'll no longer be interested in working for us. That you may leave the firm the minute he dies. And I'm not sure that's how you want to lead in your answer. I know it may sound harsh," he said as he unclasped his hands and opened them palm up, "but I'm telling you, that's what I'm hearing."

He said it so casually that it shook me. I tried to keep a straight face and seem appreciative of the feedback, but I swallowed and felt my stomach tighten instinctively. I hadn't given much thought to what might happen if my father died, much less that he might die soon. To hear the pretend interviewer say it with such matter-of-fact certainty, like a mathematical equation, if A then B, pushed me to imagine the possibility. But I couldn't, either because I was unable or unwilling to consider the scenario. I felt so far away from McAllen that I had this feeling of safety, comfort almost, at the thought that even though I couldn't see my family every day, they were always back home, the way I had left them. I had a hard time imagining them not being there the way I had last seen them. In retrospect, my father's deteriorating condition must have been an evident truth to my interviewer; to me it wasn't evident or true. This guy has no idea, I thought.

But his comment did make me change my answer. A few weeks later, when the first real interviewer asked why I wanted to work at his law firm, rather than telling the truth, I sat up straight and answered that I was very interested in becoming a litigator and was fascinated by contract disputes.

Later that September, I was on the phone with my sister Silvia, pacing aimlessly in the law school courtyard. Students walked to and from class, and somebody ate a late lunch salad on the picnic table. Fall hadn't fully set in yet, and the yard was still an abundant, pleasant greenery full of life. Silvia had visited my father at the long-term care facility where he had been transferred that day. He had been going back and forth between Rio Grande Regional Hospital and Lifecare for a while now, depending on whether his condition improved or deteriorated. I wondered if the constant transfers did more harm.

"¿Y tú cómo lo ves?" I asked Silvia how he was doing.

"Pues no sé, manito." Her voice faded, like she had something else to say but couldn't, or wouldn't.

I broke the silence and asked if she thought I should come home. I had classes and interviews that week, but I told her I could miss classes a few days and try to reschedule a couple of the interviews. I had received the financial aid deposit for the semester, so I had the money in my account to pay for the flight. I really could come home, I told Silvia, if she thought I should.

She hesitated, as if wanting to leave the decision up to me, which it ultimately was. "If you can," she finally said, "I would say you should try."

One day and two Southwest flights later, I was back in McAllen. When I came to see my father at Lifecare that same afternoon, he was in his wheelchair on the patio. The enclosed outdoor courtyard at the center of the facility felt sterile, as the few patients who were out here sat in silence, like my father. Others slowly moped around with their walkers and the assistance of a nurse or a relative, who would offer an occasional word of encouragement. Other than that, the place felt so subdued that I wondered if people had been asked not to make any noise. Unusual for this time of year, there was hardly any wind, so the few short plants and bushes were motionless in the dry, inert dirt.

My father drooped in his chair, his head looking down at the concrete floor. He smiled when he saw me, but he was not really surprised that I was back while the semester was underway. He seemed to have lost that connection with what was happening outside of what had become his new world.

"Do you know where we are?" I asked him after a while, trying to strike up conversation. You would look up and see the sky and a few clouds from this courtyard, maybe a few white-winged doves making their way south, but no real point of reference to identify a location.

He shook his head and kept looking down. He seemed uninterested.

I tried to explain that we were off Ridge Road, close to the gas station on Jackson Road, the route he had driven every morning to work for years. He nodded softly in agreement, but I wasn't sure if he really knew or was simply going along.

A few days later, he was back at the hospital. My mother was with him when I walked into his room. Héctor, who worked at a retail store nearby while he was also in college, would visit him even during his lunch breaks, but he wasn't here now. Like every hospital room I've ever been in, the place was uncomfortably cold, the machines connected to my father's arm and chest beeping and whirring with their never-ending cadence. The white bedsheets had to be changed often, as he was starting to develop sores on his back and legs from being bedridden. He had been drifting in and out of consciousness throughout the day.

"The doctors say they've stabilized him," my mother said, addressing nobody in particular.

I touched my father's forearm, and he opened his eyes, slightly startled. He turned his body slightly to his right, and the side of his left thigh exposed a developing sore.

"Le arde ahí, pero si le soplas tantito le ayuda," my mother said. The sores burned his skin, and blowing softly on them comforted him.

"¿Quieres que te sople en la pierna, Pa?" I asked, and he gave a half nod, his eyes closed again.

I looked around for a chair to pull up close to him. The only one was on the other side of the bed, so I walked around and it took me a minute to pull it through the narrow space between his bed and the wall. I set up close to the sore on his leg.

"Órale mijito," he said, urging me to get to it. It wasn't an ask out of impatience, but more of a plea to assuage his pain. C'mon son, will you, he seemed to say.

I brought my face close to his leg and blew softly on the new sore. He did not say anything, and I wasn't sure if I was helping. But I kept at it awhile, swiveling my head back and forth to cover the sore entirely, keeping my lips close to one another so that the air from my mouth was cool on his raw skin. I took a deep breath and did it again, exhaling until I emptied my lungs on his inflamed pink flesh. He still didn't say anything. Then he fell asleep.

That was the last day I saw my father alive. Those were the last words he ever said to me. It's remarkable how two seemingly mundane words take on an entirely new meaning when they become the last two words your father ever said to you. "Mijito" is a contraction of "mi hijito" and means my little son. "Órale" is an informal, versatile Mexicanism that can mean "wow," it can mean "come on" as in "hurry up" or as a motivating push, it can mean "okay," and it can also mean "fine, good to know." My father probably meant it in the sense of "c'mon, hurry up and help me out here." But over time, as I hear those words in my head, they have turned into a recurring term of encouragement that I return to in times of adversity. Whenever I stand up in court to address a jury or argue a difficult motion, I hear those words, my father urging me to persevere. I'd like to think that, even in that moment of pain and discomfort, he wanted to encourage and uplift me, knowing the end was near, knowing that I'd have to go on without him.

The days that followed are a foggy blur in my mind. I remember in broad strokes the ordeal to obtain authorization to transport my father's body to Mexico, the viewing at Allende's lone funeral home, and the emotive burial at the town's oldest cemetery, but many details and the order in which things happened are jumbled in a mix of vague recollections and outright gaps. The effects of trauma on the brain and its ability to orderly store memories are no small thing. And yet, despite these effects being widely known, scientifically proven, and documented, U.S. laws still require asylum seekers to recount their deepest traumas in a concise, cohesive, and chronological manner—often within hours of being detained and in perilous conditions at a border station—in order to even be considered for relief. The lack of compassion is effectively built into the system.

The following month, back in New Haven, Marilyn Drees invited me for a cup of coffee at the local Così. She was in charge of student life at the law school and had one of those smiles that seemed to never go away. I had been considering dropping out for the semester, as I was having a hard time focusing in class since I'd been back.

We walked into the coffee shop and looked for a quiet space. The place was busy at this time of the afternoon, so we retreated to the second floor and found a secluded table near a nook by the corner. I told Marylin that I had been pondering whether to drop out, but that now I was leaning toward sticking it out. I had dropped one class, and that made the days somewhat more manageable.

"Besides," I said, taking a quick sip from my scalding porcelain cup. "That's what my father would have wanted."

She smiled and nodded in what I interpreted as support.

After a few seconds, she leaned forward slightly and asked, almost in a whisper, "Have you thought about what *you* want?"

It was such a basic, yet eye-opening perspective that I simply hadn't considered. For weeks since my father died, I had been thinking that dropping out was what my mother and my siblings wanted, so that I could be by their side more often. Now that I was considering staying enrolled, I thought that was what my father would have wanted. But it had never crossed my mind to stop and consider what *I* wanted; or rather, I had jumbled together what I wanted with what I thought my loved ones wanted.

I had not felt this stupefied in years, since that one afternoon in writing class my freshmen year in college. After we had read Virginia Woolf's *A Room of One's Own*, the professor led a discussion about the choice some women made, and still make, between having children and pursuing a professional career. At some point I proudly raised my hand and commented that, well, for most women it would surely be more important to have children than to have a professional career. The professor looked at me with kind bewilderment and asked: "But have you considered that most men don't have to make that choice at all?" I had been left speechless at my own juvenile arrogance and cluelessness, and I felt the same way that day sitting in front of Marilyn. I didn't say anything in response, pondering her query silently.

Like my college advisor, Marilyn knew very little about my life or my father, but her question forced me to consider this newfound perspective carefully. In that moment, I had a hard time distinguishing whatever it was that I wanted from what I thought others wanted or would have wanted. I took another taste of my black brew, still thinking about it. She asked how old my father had been and expressed even more sympathy when she heard "sixty-three."

When I think of the sacrifices immigrant parents make so that their children may aspire to a better life, I think of my own mother and father. Was I successful because I attended Yale Law School after having grown up in poverty in Mexico? Was my immigrant father successful because his son achieved that, even though he never attained economic stability or enjoyed a day of retirement, going literally from driving a school bus one day to the hospital the next? I will never know if that fit his definition of success. I never did ask him. Is the "success" of a child of immigrants also the success of the immigrant parents? Who gets to define that success? From the immigrant parents I have represented, to my own, I see families endure varying levels of adversity. Some sacrifice it all and literally lose their life in the process. Some immigrants perish while attempting to cross the barren Arizona desert; others while they plead for medical care in a Border Patrol station cell. Some die slowly, after decades of toiling away in the baking sun in the fields of South Texas; others go quickly, suffocating painfully after inhaling liquid nitrogen at a poultry plant. Did they give their life, or did we as a country take it from them? Do immigrants give their life to this country, or does this country squeeze the life out of immigrants? Is that the price we expect people to pay for being here?

I wasn't thinking about this the morning of my law school graduation. In his keynote speech, Professor Kenji Yoshino encouraged us to look not for a job, but for a career; to look not for a career, but for a vocation; to look not for a vocation, but for a calling. We listened earnestly from our neatly arranged seats in the courtyard, our cap and gown attire adorned with the purple velvet hoods characteristic of the juris doctorate regalia. The magnolia in the far corner had lost its spring blooms, but the towering eastern white pine near the center stood tall, firm as always.

My mother watched from somewhere near the back, along with my siblings Héctor, Leoba, and Tania, who had managed to make the trip. When the ceremony concluded, we tossed our caps into the air, and stood up to fetch them as we sought out our families in the dispersing crowd. Students and their relatives swarmed in every direction, and I looked around for mine. After a while, I found my mother at the foot of the stairs in the hallway leading away from the courtyard and into the main building, right outside room 124. Inside that room, on Monday afternoons, I had often scratched my head in the Equality, Citizenship and Sovereignty course, frustrated that the theoretical discussion of these topics hardly concerned itself with the realities people faced on the ground.

When I saw my mother, I rushed up to her and instinctively put my arms around her. Then, unexpectedly, we both started weeping. I was surprised at how uncontrollably I bawled. She didn't say anything, and I didn't say anything. We hugged without words, tears streaming down our faces as other students and parents walked

around us exiting and entering the building. I felt my mother trem-
ble and heard her sob as we both stood there for what felt like a long
time, as long as it took. I was trembling too. I hadn't thought of this
moment in advance, what I might say to my mother or how I might
react once graduation day came. It was also unlike me to be so overcome by emotions, so they caught me unprepared.

I've thought many times about that effusive clasp with my
mother that morning in May. I haven't cried with such abandon ever
since, and perhaps never in my life have I been so overcome by such
an uncontrollable mixture of emotions. I lost sense of time while we
embosomed, and I don't exaggerate when I say that I went briefly
into a type of trance. We didn't say—then or since—why we were
weeping, but I knew, and I think she did too, that we were both
thinking the same thing. On one level, it was that my father was
not there to see me graduate. But it was also the inescapable thought
that this was what it had taken for me, for us, to get here: my father
sacrificing his very life along the way. Was it happiness or sorrow, I
cannot say. It was a type of instant nostalgia, a present-day grief that
evoked foregone joy that will never be again, that perhaps never
was, all encapsulated in that fleeting moment.

While certainly each of my siblings has in his or her own way
manifested a narrative of progress and success, for me that day was
also a type of closure. Not just closure of my schooling, but closure
of my immigrant father's journey, partially expressed through my
own, into this single day of achievement. And I discovered that I no
longer needed to hold the strongest emotions closely bound inside
me. I was finally able to liberate them, and myself.

*   *   *

As with every December since I obtained my green card, I found
myself driving back to McAllen after having spent a few days with

my relatives in Mexico for the holidays. There were only a few days left in 2019, and with Julián and our two-month-old daughter, Inés, in their car seats, Karla and I were pleased to find only a few dozen cars in line at the Reynosa-Hidalgo International Bridge. This time of year, and especially in the evenings, it was not unusual to encounter hundreds of vehicles making their way back to the U.S. and to spend hours in line to cross the border.

As we slowly made our way north over the bridge, some fifty yards to our left, on the Mexico-bound lanes, I could make out a few dark silhouettes of people sitting close together on the bridge. Those lanes are also used for pedestrian traffic, and those shadows were likely families trying to "present" at the port of entry to apply for asylum. But instead of processing them, immigration agents would now stop them right at the bridge's halfway point, where the technical boundary between the two countries lies, above an imaginary line at the middle of the river.

A few days earlier, on our way into Mexico, we had driven past a group of no less than twenty sitting on that part of the bridge, waiting. They had been holding babies in their arms. Some would wait weeks, depending on the charity of passersby to subsist, only to be turned away eventually. Others, especially those with young children, would try a few times, and after being rejected repeatedly, would try to swim across and turn themselves in to a Border Patrol agent, if they made it. Many were victimized by smugglers on the Mexican side. It was denial of asylum by attrition. This practice of stopping asylum seekers in the middle of the bridge, known as "metering," was challenged in litigation, but thousands had been turned back in this way.

How lucky we were, sitting in our air-conditioned car, our passports in hand to show the official at the window. Those families and mine had so much in common, and yet were worlds apart. Their children, like mine, were the children of immigrants. But theirs was a dire situation, ours a privileged one. They had left everything behind; we were simply coming back home. Like my parents years earlier, they were merely trying to do what was best for their children, and only they knew the desperate circumstances that drove them to this point.

As we reached the inspection booth, I rolled down my window and stopped the car. The officer took a quick peek inside and asked the same question I've heard so many times.

"U.S. citizen?"

Author's Note

The stories I have shared here are based on my recollection. When possible, I have cross-referenced my memory against documents, court filings, and correspondence to confirm factual details as much as possible. Memories can be highly subjective and are often incomplete and imperfect, especially when they arise from chaotic, traumatic moments, so others may remember things differently than I do; that is the nature of memory. To aid in the telling of the narrative, I sometimes relied on literary devices such as compression of time but always remained faithful to the events.

Many names, especially those of children, have been anonymized or replaced with pseudonyms to protect the identity and privacy of those involved, unless their identity was previously in the public domain or they provided their informed consent.

Regarding specific cases narrated in the book, Viviana and Sandro were reunited, and their cases remain pending in immigration court, along with their asylum application. Patricia and Alessandro's asylum applications were granted, and they now live together on the East Coast. Mario and Oralia were reunited, and their immigration cases remain pending. Arturo was reunited with his daughter Miriam in California. Leonel was reunited with his son Daniel, and their removal proceedings are still pending. Dagoberto and his son Jorge were reunited in California; an immigration judge ordered Dagoberto deported from the United States, and his appeal remains pending. María was released and reunited with her children, and their immigration cases remain pending. Antonio was deported without his son, who remained in the United States. At the time of writing, I had not been able to locate Antonio again. Juliana was reunited with her family in Colorado. Cindy and Jimena were also reunited.

The Inter-American Commission on Human Rights granted our petition for emergency precautionary measures and requested the United States to stop separating families and reunite our five petitioners—the first human rights ruling of its kind in the Americas—but the Trump Administration refused to comply with the request.

Some of the content of Chapter 5 was published previously in the *New York Times* in a different format.

Excerpt from the poem "Owl," by José Antonio Rodríguez, is reprinted with the author's permission.

How to Help

As these pages go to print, the situation for immigrants and asylum seekers at the border continues to be dire. If you would like to support organizations on the ground working on behalf of immigrants and their families, I hope you will consider the following:

Texas Civil Rights Project (TCRP), www.txcivilrights.org

The TCRP is Texas lawyers and advocates for Texas communities, boldly serving the movement for equality and justice in and out of the courts. TCRP envisions a Texas where all communities thrive with dignity and justice, and without fear. TCRP believes that legal advocacy and litigation are critical tools to protect and advance the civil rights of everyone in Texas, particularly the State's most vulnerable populations, and to effect positive and lasting change to law and policy. TCRP believes that by serving the rising social justice movement in Texas with excellent legal representation and bold strategies, we can respond to the needs of the communities we serve.

Texas RioGrande Legal Aid (TRLA), www.trla.org

Founded in 1970 to represent Texas farmworkers, TRLA has grown into the nation's second-largest legal aid provider and the largest in

Texas. TRLA provides free civil legal services to residents in sixty-eight Southwest Texas counties, and represents migrant and seasonal farmworkers throughout Texas and in six other states. TRLA also operates public defender programs that serve multiple Texas counties, representing low-income and indigent people accused of felonies, misdemeanors, and juvenile crimes.

La Unión del Pueblo Entero (LUPE), www.lupenet.org

LUPE builds stronger, healthier communities where colonia residents use the power of civic engagement for social change. From fighting deportations, to providing social services and English classes, to organizing for streetlights and drainage, LUPE responds to the needs of the community, and takes action that creates a chance for a better life. LUPE's strength derives from its more than 8,000 members throughout the Rio Grande Valley.

South Texas Pro Bono Asylum Representation Project (ProBAR), www.americanbar.org/probar

ProBAR empowers immigrants through high-quality legal education, representation, and connections to services. ProBAR serves immigrants in the Rio Grande Valley border region with a particular focus on the legal needs of adults and unaccompanied children in federal custody.

Angry Tías and Abuelas of the RGV, www.angrytiasandabuelas.com

The Angry Tías and Abuelas' mission is to provide basic necessities for health and safety and support for human dignity and justice to individuals and families seeking asylum at our borders and as they embark on their journeys to designated destinations in the United States.

Las Americas Immigrant Advocacy Center, www.las-americas.org

Las Americas is a nonprofit organization based in El Paso, Texas, providing free and low-cost legal services to immigrants and refugees in West Texas and New Mexico. Las Americas provides legal representation through both attorneys and accredited representatives through the Department of Justice.

Florence Immigrant & Refugee Rights Project, www.firrp.org

The Florence Project is a nonprofit legal service organization providing free legal and social services to adults and unaccompanied children in immigration custody in Arizona. The Florence Project strives to address this inequity both locally and nationally through direct service, partnerships with the community, and advocacy and outreach efforts.

Al Otro Lado, www.alotrolado.org

Al Otro Lado provides holistic legal and humanitarian support to indigent refugees, deportees, and other migrants in the United States and Tijuana, Mexico, through a multidisciplinary, client-centered, harm reduction–based practice. Al Otro Lado provides direct, free, legal services on both sides of the U.S.-Mexico border and beyond. They engage in zealous individual representation, medical-legal partnerships, and impact litigation to protect the rights of immigrants and asylum seekers.

Justice in Motion, www.justiceinmotion.org

To make justice across borders a reality, Justice in Motion formed a Defender Network of human rights lawyers and nonprofit organizations throughout Mexico, Guatemala, El Salvador, Honduras, and Nicaragua. Defenders partner with U.S. lawyers on concrete legal cases for migrants, as well as advocacy and community education projects across the region. Justice in Motion works to defend the rights of thousands of migrants from across the region each year—from parents separated from their children at the U.S. border, to migrant workers exploited by U.S. employers, to children seeking safety from harm.

Acknowledgments

This book would not have happened without the support, mentorship, and inspiration of José Antonio Rodríguez. Your guidance and clarity of thought helped make this book something it never would have been without it. I have said it before, but I can't say it enough: Gracias. I am forever indebted.

Thank you to my family, and especially my wife, Karla, without whose love and patience I wouldn't have managed to write this book at a time when our little family grew from three to four. Te amo. Thank you to my mother and my father for the sacrifices they made, each in their own way, so that my siblings and I could aspire to a better life.

My literary agents, Amy and Peter Bernstein: thank you for supporting the idea of this book and pushing me to refine it and make it the best possible version of itself. Thank you to my editor, Lauren Marino, for believing in this project from the beginning and for your thoughtful and clarifying vision.

Thank you also to all my colleagues at the Texas Civil Rights Project, without whose steadfast support our work on behalf of our clients would not have been possible. Thank you to all the attorneys who volunteered and took on one or more cases pro bono, those named here as well as those unnamed. Know that your work made an immense difference for the families you represented. Thank you to TCRP's partners, allies, and supporters in the immigrant justice field, for your work on behalf of immigrants that summer and since. I want to thank Professor Jim Silk, a mentor and a friend, for his continued guidance throughout the years and for his eager and resourceful fact-checking assistance. Thank you to Valerie De Cruz, also a mentor and a friend, for being the first person to ask whether I would turn these stories into a book.

Thank you to Adrián de la Garza, a dear friend, for his meticulous reading of a draft of this manuscript.

And above all, thank you to our immigrant clients. You continue to be an inspiration of resilience, bravery, and perseverance despite the unimaginable suffering our government has inflicted upon you.